ADAPTIVE KNOWING

ADAPTIVE KNOWING

EPISTEMOLOGY FROM A REALISTIC STANDPOINT

by

JAMES K. FEIBLEMAN

Tulane University

MARTINUS NIJHOFF / THE HAGUE / 1976

PRINTED IN THE NETHERLANDS

TABLE OF CONTENTS

A SYSTEM OF PHILOSOPHY

The present volume is Part Four in a seventeen-volume system of philosophy which is nearing completion. Each of the volumes can be read independently but together they constitute a comprehensive effort. The volumes without final dates are the ones as yet unpublished, those with dates indicate when they were first published.

J.K.F.

PREFACE

The acquisition of knowledge is not a single unrelated occasion but rather an adaptive process in which past acquisitions modify present and future ones.

In Part I of this essay in epistemology it is argued that coping with knowledge is not a passive affair but dynamic and active, involving its continuance into the stages of assimilation and deployment.

In Part II a number of specific issues are raised and discussed in order to explore the dimensions and the depths of the workings of adaptive knowing.

ACKNOWLEDGMENTS

"Activity as A Source of Knowledge" first appeared in *Tulane Studies in Philosophy*, XII, 1963; "Knowing, Doing and Being" in *Ratio*, VI, 1964; "On Beliefs and Believing" in *Tulane Studies*, XV, 1966; "Absent Objects" in *Tulane Studies*, XVII, 1968; "The Reality Game" in *Tulane Studies*, XVIII, 1969; "Adaptive Responses and The Ecosystem" in *Tulane Studies*, XVIII, 1969; "The Mind-Body Problem" in the *Philosophical Journal*, VII, 1970; and "The Knowledge of The Known" in the *International Logic Review*, I, 1970.

PART I

COPING WITH KNOWLEDGE

CHAPTER I

THE PROBLEM OF KNOWLEDGE

I. THE CHOSEN APPROACH

You are about to read a study of epistemology, one which has been made from a realistic standpoint. It is not the first of such interpretations, and it will not be the last. The special thesis that distinguishes this realistic epistemology from the others is called 'adaptive knowing', because it describes the various moves made by the individual in his efforts to cope with knowledge. It assumes that there is a feedback from knowledge which conditions further learning. It assumes also that the cognitive process is a stage process, and that the stages are those involving the acquisition, the assimilation, and the deployment of knowledge.

Perhaps it would not be possible to write an epistemology which did not represent an approach from some standpoint, and indeed that very fact tells us something. It tells us that to state anything in epistemology is to make a metaphysical presupposition. The most empirical investigation possible would have to assume the principles of empiricism, and empiricism itself includes generous portions of what there is, an entire apparatus of quality-containing objects and organ-sensitive subjects, with one-way receptors acting as consciousness. The entire apparatus upon which theories of knowledge are constructed amounts to a tall assumption, and worst of all: one that cannot itself be validated by any epistemological investigation. For epistemology is not self-validating.

II. EPISTEMOLOGY AND METAPHYSICS

Findlay is not quite correct when he asserted at the outset of his study of Meinong that "realism in English-speaking countries has in general contented itself with exposing the fallacies of idealistic arguments."[1] Philosophers anyway tend to be right in what they affirm and wrong in what they deny. The attempt to construct a realistic epistemology was undertaken in Great Britain by Thomas Reid, John Laird, G. Dawes Hicks, the early G. E. Moore and the early Bertrand Russell, and in the United States by C. S. Peirce, E. G. Spaulding, R. B. Perry, E. B. Holt, W. P. Montague, F. J. E. Woodbridge and D. C. Williams.

With the exception of Peirce all of these philosophers were inclined to subordinate metaphysics to epistemology. That such an arrangement has been assumed without examination, and that other alternative arrangements are possible and might even be preferable, is at least worthy of investigation. There are, as a matter of fact, three views which can be taken of the relation of epistemology to metaphysics: that they are separate but equal, or that one is subordinate to the other.

To make them separate but equal puts off forever the prospect of a coherent and complete system of philosophy. It would place on a dubious parity the world that we know and the method by which we know that world. Given the size of the world and the infinitesimal part we play in it, that would not seem to be a credible position. Relating the two principal portions of the system would have been rendered all but impossible.

To make metaphysics subordinate to epistemology would mean adopting some form of subjective philosophy, and nothing short of solipsism would do the job logically. But to suppose that the world is my idea of it means not only that it is not yours but also that I am the mightiest of creators, a contention which can be supported only by those who are pathologically crippled, more specifically by the catatonic schizophrenics.

That leaves the third alternative, namely, that epistemology is part of metaphysics, that I as well as my knowledge of the world is some part of the world. That seems more defensible, not only for its self-evident modesty but also for its ostensive truth. My grasp of the knowledge of the world is certainly not a grasp of the world in any operative sense, and proves to be as tenuous as my grasp of my own existence, which I know to be a very temporary affair.

In the following pages, after some introductory chapters intended to convey a sense of the whole picture, I shall try to show what a realistic epistemology which assumes its own subordination to metaphysics

---

[1] *Meinong's Theory of Objects and Values* (Oxford, 1963, Clarendon Press), p. 2.

looks like, relying on the method of sampling. For while it is true that the territory of knowledge theory is a vast one, it belongs after metaphysics as an integral part of a system of philosophy.

It is inevitable that such a realistic epistemology would present metaphysics in a different way. Metaphysics is approached ordinarily as though it were an abstract structure, similar in many respects to a system of mathematics. In a realistic epistemology, however, the metaphysics is seen as it appears to a knower.

An epistemologist, such as Rudolph Carnap, who operated without a background metaphysics, assumed that his epistemology *was* his metaphysics; but this assumption left it hanging if not in mid-air then on mid-ground and without any surrounding connections. He did not show its place in the nature of things, for he would have been limiting himself to a seemingly inexplicable knowledge relationship which existed all by itself as a phenomenon. The fallacy of reduction, whereby anger for instance can be shown to be only a physical state of the body, does not help. What is rudimentary does not necessarily mean what is metaphysically fundamental, even though it did to Carnap. The fallacy of reduction is shown in its most absurd form where Carnap has insisted that cultural relations can be reduced to statements about other minds, as though material artifacts: violins, libraries and office buildings could be reduced to elements of other minds, since they are assuredly elements of cultures and themselves have cultural relations. The subjective error of attributing to minds whatever can be known obviously leads to the kind of solipsism which Carnap rejected while inadvertently doing everything he could to lay himself open to the charge.

Epistemology is metaphysics developed phenomenologically, and has the task of providing evidence for metaphysics. In a system of philosophy which includes them both there is no such things as a proof. As Peirce once remarked, all proofs of metaphysics are moonshine. This can be demonstrated, somewhat along the following lines. In a system so wide that nothing is excluded (and metaphysics always makes this all-presumptive claim), where could the proof be found? Obviously either inside the system or outside it. But not inside, according to Gödel; and not outside, for nothing *is* outside. Nevertheless, short of proof there can be a kind of crucial usefulness, and so we cannot afford to confine ourselves to the indubitable. Metaphysics has a necessary position to occupy and a necessary task to perform, and one way to approach it (though not the way adopted here) is to infer it from an epistemology by the method of assumptions.

Epistemology in practice shows, for instance, how a metaphysics is held. In metaphysics the system of philosophy is presented as it is and not as the knowledge of it was acquired; the epistemology itself is derived. The whole aim in epistemology is to discover a method for obtaining reliable knowledge. The problem is to account for the acquisition of knowledge before making any statement about the condition of being, and then and only then to show how the knowledge of being itself was derived.

Many of the difficulties which have confronted investigators who have tried to solve the problems of epistemology without going outside of it is that the field itself is not a wholly independent one. The human individual and what he knows are immersed together in the background of a material world which contains very much more than both and which sets conditions for them not readily evident when either is being examined in isolation. Staunch advocates of knowledge theory are quick to insist that metaphysics is dependent upon epistemology. And so it is but in quite a different way. For knowledge is conditioned by how we know yet only in the sense of being limited and selected by it. Despite this qualification, what is, is, independently of how we know what it is; that is a necessary initial assumption. Without such an assumption we put the burden on the knower of performing an impossibly double perceptual function: that of creating the perceived object while simultaneously perceiving it.

The primacy of metaphysics shows itself in the details of procedure. It would be possible to write an entire system of metaphysics without once concerning oneself with epistemology, but writers on epistemology inevitably find themselves proposing a metaphysics. In explaining *how* it is that we know, they do not seem able to avoid referring to *what* it is that we know. Meinong did, certainly, and so have many others.

An investigator who approaches metaphysics through the cautious step by step accumulation provided by methods of epistemology feels himself on safe ground. He thinks that he has demonstrated every stage on the way and therefore that his findings have more going for them than they would have from a metaphysics presented as a completed system, as though it were a finished building from which the scaffolding had been removed. A bricklayer or a worker in structural steel might have a distorted view of the whole edifice; the architect has a somewhat broader conception. Now the metaphysician is an architect whose city plan has already been executed; all that remains is to describe it in detail.

Epistemology when employed as a starting-point tends towards subjectivity and this is unavoidable. For such an approach presents material objects in relation to the knower, not in relation to each other; and the same can be said for abstract objects *mutatis mutandis*. The theory of material objects and of abstract entities according to which each is in relation to others of its own kind, has an epistemology, too, a realistic epistemology; and that is the one I will try to develop in the following pages. It is best to look for metaphysics in the relations which all things have necessarily, and for epistemology in the relations which some things have accidentally, that is the fundamental difference between them; and it is one which discloses metaphysics as obviously prior, and epistemology if not as derived then at least as secondary.

III. PHILOSOPHY AND SCIENCE

What we are confronted with as a matter of brute fact, what we are called on to explain if we can, is not the spectacle of the world as it is represented in the mind of man but rather one of the entire man, the whole organism, situated in the world. The evidence of geology is unmistakable. Life on the earth is not over a billion years old, and human life far less than two million; whereas the earth itself has been here for some three and a half billion years. The steps in the emergence of man from the earth have been traced. It is man who has had to adapt in order to survive, not the earth. The subjectivists and idealists continually insist upon the importance of man to himself, a fact which none can deny. But that is no reason to confuse importance with existence. While no one who has practiced any introspection at all can doubt that there is an inner world, no one who has taken any part in practical affairs can doubt either that there is an outer world and moreover one which is larger and more inclusive than the inner world. It is the outer world we shall have to account for first, and then if we like we can try to fit the inner world into it. We can do this best if we consider it as though we were looking at that aspect of the outer world in which it is inward-bound.

The theory of knowledge has become a jungle of introspection in which there are no reliable and well-marked paths. The mind has proved a good place to hide. The philosopher, frightened by the incursion into his ancient territory of scientists who do better there than he has done, is only too willing to take refuge in consciousness and to feel as he stumbles about there that he is making progress and advancing knowledge. C. I. Lewis has served as a particularly useful fellow in this regard. How else could one interpret his statements, often made in the same paragraph, that qualia are "purely subjective" and that they are universals?[2] That he has only updated Kant is not always noticed, and Kant after all was the one who insisted that certain knowledge of things as they are is forever impossible.

From LaMettrie's *l'Homme machine* published in 1747 to Woolrich's *Mechanical Man* in 1968[3] marked the passage of some 220 years, but it meant more than that, for the kind of viewpoint presented in both books has met considerable resistance even though the evidence has become increasingly strong in its favor. LaMettrie's thesis was that the diversity in the order of phenomena are to be located somewhere in the complex organization of matter. Woolrich insists that man is a complex kind of machine. Both have argued that life could be *explained* on the basis of physical and chemical phenomena, but they have been attacked for having proclaimed that life could be *reduced* to physics and chemistry, which they did not say. That the most perceptive materialists have insisted that explanation is not reduction has been noticed by few if any. Given the 'integrative' or empirical levels in nature, we can see now that the explanation of any material entity always lies one analytical level lower than the entity to be explained. The organism has emergent qualitative properties at its own level, consciousness, for instance, and such properties undoubtedly do exist. But if we wish to find consciousness among the analytic levels, we must move one analytical level lower, and look there for the mechanism. Consciousness then can be seen as an analytical element of the brain stem reticular formation.

The logical positivists have pointed out that philosophy cannot compete with science in the search for empirically-founded truths, and since there are no supernatural truths the business of philosophy must be exclusively concerned with the clarification of meanings in science. So A. J. Ayer, for instance.[4] But this argument is a *non-sequitur*. There most assuredly is other business for philosophy: there is for instance the business of organizing all of knowledge in a system which must include not only common experience but also the findings of the ex-

[2] C. I. Lewis, *Mind and The World-Order* (New York, 1929, Scribner), pp. 121–124. On p. 60 there is a warning not "to confuse such qualia with universal concepts." Critical realism, Lewis here wrote, "confuses the logical universal with given qualia of sense." How mixed up can one get?

[3] Dean E. Woolridge, *Mechanical Man* (New York, 1968, McGraw-Hill).

[4] A. J. Ayer, *Language, Truth and Logic*, 2nd ed. (New York, 1946, Dover).

perimental sciences, the fine arts, and even philosophy itself. This task no special science undertakes and yet it must be undertaken. It is the task *sui generis* of philosophy.

The entire import of the logical positivists' position, which Ayer has set forth so ably, is that a statement to be meaningful must be either an empirical statement made in one of the experimental sciences or a decision to use language in a certain tautological way, as for instance in logic and mathematics, the former a matter of verifiability and the latter a matter of adequate definition. Led in this respect by Carnap, though adhered to by the other positivists, is the assertion that the business of philosophy is the analysis of the *language* of science. He should have said the *findings* of science. Once again, meaning is substituted for reference, whereas it exists only to serve reference.

Metaphysics by this school is held to be literally non-sense. The charge would be a serious one for metaphysics had not Ayer left us two ways out. He does not seem to have been aware of the first way, though he did contrive the second way himself without recognizing the connection. The first way is to consider metaphysical statements empirically verifiable, with material human culture as the relevant empirical field. Put the other way round, culture is concrete philosophy. The second way is conceded in the admission that there are methods of testing systematic orders of hypotheses in which the confirmation of any part tends to confirm the whole,[5] the whole in this case being culture and the systematic orders of hypotheses being metaphysical systems (for that indeed is what they are). Like Wittgenstein, Ayer manages to say a good deal about what cannot be said, and he would not like it to be considered non-sense anymore than he would like it to be called nonsense.

There is no point in philosophical speculation about propositions which lend themselves to scientific investigation, this much can be conceded to the logical positivists. The whole domain of the acquisition of reliable knowledge calls upon observation and experiment. The extreme simplicity of classical proposals in knowledge theory ought to be enough to make us suspect their adequacy. Moreover, the proliferation of rival theories of mind seems to have settled nothing. Given the experiments of the psychologists and neurophysiologists, is there any need, then, for epistemology? I have already noted in it, very much curtailed, the evidence for metaphysics. The evaluation of the evidence is a very difficult task indeed.

[5] *Ibid.*, p. 100.

One of the strongest arguments against the exclusivity of the scientific explanation is the bare fact of consciousness. Nothing in human experience has proved more elusive. The neurophysiologists, as we shall see, have a theory of how it operates, but that still does not explain what it is. Will it ever be possible to investigate the nature of consciousness by the scientific method? Certainly no one can demonstrate just now that it cannot. Meanwhile there are coordinating tasks awaiting the investigator who faces the bewildering new data which flow in a never-ending stream from the experimental sciences.

Philosophical systems, as distinct from scientific knowledge, consist in just those ideas which are necessary in order to put all scientific knowledge together. Not a single one of the sciences is engaged in this enterprise. But looked at from the widest point of view the whole problem is more complex still, for in addition to scientific knowledge there is, as we have noted, knowledge from other sources which cannot be omitted, such as artistic knowledge and knowledge from common experience. These have to be included along with scientific knowledge if there is to be a system of ideas more general than any other. Now epistemology alone cannot accomplish this task but is a necessary adjunct to metaphysics which can.

Full concreteness, understood as the actual exemplification of the infinite richness of nature, means that all abstractions will have to be justified on the basis of particular examples, and these, I insist, do not come from the experimental sciences alone. Art considered as a method of discovery also has much to tell us about the composition of the natural world, which it studies in quite another way. Art, mathematics, philosophy, each discipline will have to have its own empiricism.

IV. NAIVE REALISM

The fallacy of simplicity which I have been levelling against the subjective idealists is not theirs alone. It is to be found also among the naive realists. By the term 'realism' I mean of course the existence of an external world apart from all human perceptions of it. That is epistemological realism. Metaphysical realism requires also a second story consisting of logical universals and affective qualities and values. The epistemological realist may assume that there are one or two such domains independent of his experience of them. The naive realist assumes that there is only one domain: the material world. The more sophisticated metaphysical realist assumes two; not only the material domain but also a logical domain of universals and values.

A contrast with two classical philosophies may make this position a little clearer. Plato worked with a strong separate domain of Ideas and a weak domain of matter. Aristotle worked with a strong domain of matter and a weak imbedded domain of Ideas. I work with two equally real, though different, domains. Without conceding that there is a shred of difference with respect to their reality, they may be looked at as one structure consisting in a two-storied world, for they are related and interwoven.

To the naive realist the Platonist appears to be saying that there are real things that do not exist. It is always fallaciously assumed that inherent in the broad Platonic position is the assumption that the Ideas or intelligible things, which have their being separately from the material or sensible things, do not also exist in the latter. There is no warrant for this assumption and there is indeed some evidence against it. The evidence against it is contained in the analysis of abstraction. If we learn about the Ideas from observing sensible things, if for example we learn about circularity from observing what round things have in common, they must have been there first. It would be impossible to extract from a material the knowledge of what was not in it. Thus we come to the theory that Ideas (or universals or what we would now prefer to regard as classes whose membership is undecidably large and possibly infinite) exist both in things and apart from things; that is to say, they exist as well as (in Meinong's term) subsist.

The naive realist cannot explain the encounters with abstractions when they occur. Euclidean geometry may have first been discovered by observing the properties of the earth's surface, as is said to have happened when the flooding of the Nile River made a fresh survey of the land an urgent practical necessity. After many generations the geometry has long been established. That the three angles of a triangle are equal to two right angles is a fact as stubborn as a stone.

Not all abstract things of course, not hippogriffs and leprechauns. It is the business of experimental science to say just which abstract things. When abstractions have been around long enough and have been the subject of routine belief, they do not appear to be abstract any longer but take on the properties of concrete things. This is the case with Euclidean geometry, Aristotelian substance and Cartesian mind and matter.

The point I am trying to make is that for the kind of epistemology which is to be examined in this book abstract things are just as real, just as genuine, just as irrefrangible and resistent, as concrete things.

We have to reckon as much with the law of gravitation as we do with material bodies which attract each other in the prescribed way.

I do not like the distinction between objects of thought and objects of sense, for obviously we can think about material objects as well as about abstract objects, and in fact we do think about both. The observer prefers to take his reading from the objects themselves since the realist takes his stand on the objects and not on the subject, on *what* is experienced rather than on *who* is experiencing. To take a stand on the subject is empirically unjustified: no subject does it. When he does he is unfaithful to what actually happens. For the observer does not observe his observations any more than he observer himself observing. Neither one is what he observes. He observes the object, just so. All else is a kind of philosophical construction and not an analysis of what actually takes place.

Nothing empirical can ever be absolutely demonstrated. However desirable from the point of view of belief, absolute proof belongs exclusively to the province of logic and mathematics. But in the empirical domain we do have evidence and it can be weighed. The evaluation of the data is precisely the point at which all procedure usually falters and often even fails. However, what we call epistemology is of this character. It is not a fully grown-up topic like metaphysics or ethics, and the Greeks did well to give it slight attention. The modern emphasis on methodology has, however, brought it into the foreground, and it does have a legitimate place. Epistemology, as we have already noted, is the evidence for metaphysics.

In traditional epistemology the unstated principle was observed that the investigation of the knowledge process was to be conducted on the basis of ordinary, unaided experience alone, common experience. This is an unwarranted approach to the problem, and, judging by the degree of disagreement which has prevailed (and which still does) among its investigators, between the idealists like Collingwood and the realists like Moore and Whitehead, for instance, it must be pronounced an unsuccessful one. Common experience did not guide the investigators to a common agreement about the nature of knowledge and the method of its acquisition.

But why limit the investigation in this fashion? Surely it would be reasonable to accept help wherever it can be found. Some help can be found in the sciences of psychology and neurophysiology, some can be found in physical optics. No single individual has any great fund of experience, and we learn most of what we know from the experience of others. The emphasis of classic epistemology on individual experience is therefore to some extent misleading. We learn most from specialized experience, we learn to see by watching what the painter's canvases tell us he saw, and we learn from photographic plates what the astronomer has arranged for us to see. Experience is a collective effort, involving not only the trained observations of specialists but also the assistance of complex instruments. We are no longer confined to the simple experience which was the result of the unaided senses.

That, however, has not been the accepted view in philosophical circles. The Continental rationalists, Descartes, Spinoza and Leibniz, relied on reasoning primarily, the British empiricists, Locke, Berkeley and Hume, relied on sense experience primarily, and moreover on one sense in particular, the sense of sight. Much thought and many publications were devoted in the first half of the twentieth century to the sense-datum theory. Then the topic was dropped, as though philosophers were not concerned with genuine problems but only with "thinking too curiously upon the event." Sense-data do not exist by themselves, as we now know, and this remains true whether one hold them to be contributed by the subject or inherent in the object. Realistic epistemology relies upon the entire man not only with all of his faculties but also – and this is to introduce a new note into the study of epistemology – with such instruments as he can construct in their aid.

V. REALISM WITH INSTRUMENTS

The epistemologists have thus far ignored the challenge to traditional studies of ordinary experience presented by the new discoveries of continuous worlds, the world of the very small and the world of the very large, the microcosm and the macrocosm, which are adjacent to and continuous with the world of ordinary experience, the mesocosm. The physical scientists have been operating for some time now in terms of a new principle of empiricism. The old principle of empiricism meant the validation of knowledge by means of the senses. The new principle of empiricism includes the old principle but more specifically calls for the validation of knowledge by means of instruments. I need cite only a few examples. The microscope extends perceptions into the microcosm, the telescope extends them into the macrocosm. For the mesocosm we have the colorimeter in place of the human eye, the vibrating membrane in place of the human ear, and the weighing scale in place of the muscle sense. These and other instruments have enabled us to extend considerably the knowledge gained through the senses.

The central problem of epistemology may now be restated somewhat as follows. *How can we forge a new common sense based on the instrumentally-gained knowledge of the wide-ranging two-story external world with its three connected segments, as outlined above?*

The task of epistemology, which is to discover a method for obtaining reliable knowledge, is certainly related to the problem of what there is. And there is more on both sides of the area disclosed by ordinary experience than we had formerly supposed. The new scientifically discovered worlds of the microcosm and the macrocosm are not 'owned' by science, they are not in themselves scientific except in so far as it is the scientists who have disclosed their existence to us. They are extensions of the world of common experience with which in the future we shall have to be prepared to reckon. The result of all this is that we must remember that we have added instruments to our equipment and no longer count on the senses alone; we must conceive of a different view of experience, one which is extraordinary as well as ordinary but both of which are empirical.

We shall have to abandon that criterion of experience according to which the senses remain in continuous contact with the object and so in a way substitute for it. This was true certainly of idealism, and even of some brands of naive realism. Mach's "sensations," Avenarius' "pure experience" and Reid's "common sense" are all left behind by the knowledge gained by means of experiments conducted with instruments. We are not alone with our unaided sense organs, instead we have discovered extensions for them which probe much deeper and farther than they ever could. For it is to instrumental extensions of his senses that the scientist looks, and not merely to his own ordinary experience.

The new scientific methods of investigation of course bring new problems with them. I will mention only one. Psychology and neurophysiology these days come very close together. The only difference so far as experiments are concerned is whether or not there is any interference with the experimental animal. The psychologist allows himself to use the technique of conditioning so long as there is no physical interference, while the neurophysiologist implants electrodes in the brain and windows in the stomach. But the conditions sometimes imposed by the psychologist come very close to interference: confinement, food deprivation, and the like.

What are we to do with the problem presented by the two sorts of knowledge, empirical knowledge and logical knowledge? That there is an essential difference between them is shown by the kinds of resistance to change they exhibited. The knowledge gained through sense experience is corrigible; further and more refined sense experience compels us to review and revise the earlier knowledge. Logical knowledge is gained on *a priori* grounds, not by means of sense experience but by means of calculation. Guided by the law of contradiction and by the rule of unlimited substitution as well as by the law of identity, knowledge is gained through deductive operations. Each kind of inquiry has its appropriate extension. Empirical researches are aided by means of instruments, logical researches are aided by means of mathematics. The ideal of logical formulation is tautology.

The two processes though quite different have one thing in common. Resistance is encountered in both cases, clear evidence of the presence of something real. One is the order of material existence and the other the order of logical existence. Both are entirely independent of our methods of acquiring knowledge of them, and consequently also of us. We learned about the elements of the logical order from the material order, and we can apply the elements of the logical order back to the material order; and yet they are not the same. The ideal of knowledge would be instrumentally derived empirical material mathematically formulated.

Epistemology properly speaking ought to begin operating on the speculative level only when it is ready to combine the findings of all the scientists in whatever specialty so long as they are concerned with the relation between the organism and the environment. It is one thing to discover a system of philosophy and quite another to show it in action. Both tasks are necessary, but the former must precede the latter since 'knowing' is only a form of 'being' (if the metaphysics in question is the kind which includes epistemology as a special case). The preferred method of analysis with ordinary disclosures, then, ventures through levels of analysis not evident on the surface but supported by the certification of experience, only to return to common experience enriched and deepened and able to extract more meaning from future encounters.

The possession of knowledge by an individual is simply an aspect of the world as reflected in a portion of itself. Both are of course partial, pitifully small in fact, and as such atypical in themselves. What is typical is the process of reflection as a sample of the kind of interaction that takes place. The mind receives information, reorganizes it, and then makes deductions from it relative to the actions required, all against a background of assumptions of a metaphysical nature. It begins the process of receiving and acting on knowledge by assuming what the world is like.

What can we understand about the world from the fact that it gives rise to such a wide variety of interpretations on the part of the intelligence it has itself developed? At the very least we can understand this much: that it has depths which render all our feeble efforts at interpretation finally inadequate. All that we can hope to gain, I suppose, is a temporary and partial kind of enlightenment; but in the degree of darkness that always prevails in the human condition, even that is very well worth having.

VI. ADAPTIVE KNOWING

The modern study of the theory of knowledge assumes it to be a more or less static affair. There have been notable exceptions of course, from Hegel to Dewey. But both men have taken the effect of knowledge on the subject of knowledge to be more important than the knowledge itself: understandably, I suppose, for in the last analysis the human individual tends to see things in his own terms and as though everything were under his own control. Now it makes perfectly good sense to take this view: for what are we, after all, if not human, and what would we investigate were this not the case? And yet the situation turns out to be somewhat less simple than such an assumption would indicate. Man, as it turns out, is not entirely his own creation nor the master of his own fate; indeed the facts are quite different. We know neither why we are here nor what the end results of what we are doing means.

To see man in anything like the proper perspective, therefore, it is necessary to step as far as possible out of the charmed circle of the egocentric predicament in order to look at man in his immediate environment, as thought both were available for our study. Admittedly, this is an impossible goal. As critics are never tired of pointing out, we ourselves are human individuals and it is monotonously true that anything we do must have been done by us. That is so, and I readily admit it; but was it worth saying? That we cannot achieve complete detachment for our observations is no argument that we should not struggle toward such detachment. Even a little would be helpful in aiding us to comprehend the enormity of the problem, chiefly by enabling us to understand the measure of the human involvement with, and utter dependence upon, the immediate environment.

By 'adaptive knowing', then, I mean the extent to which man learns as much as he can about the contents of his environment but also makes those adjustments in his knowledge which are made necessary by his alterations of that environment and by the effects such alterations have on him. Given the facts of biological evolution, that organic changes in species are infinitesimal and that such infinitesimal changes are continuous over millions of years, discreteness, as exemplified in organic types such as *Ramapithecus*, *Australopithecus*, and the *Homo erectus* which preceded *Homo sapiens*, it follows that what is significant is the continuity. It is our ignorance of the intermediate stages which allows us to emphasize the types that we have discovered. But the sheer fact is that man is unstable and given to change, a fact which is made even more important when we realize that in recent times the human environment has altered sharply in shifting to an artificial background, and that there must now take place such adaptive changes as the new background calls for. Primitive man altered his immediate environment very little, but civilized man, literally 'the man of the cities', with his immense new technology, has made changes in almost everything around him. In so doing he has arranged for changes to occur in himself of which he remains largely unaware.

I mean to call upon new developments in biology in order to show this, and also on equally startling new developments in modern physics. However, this is not a popular introduction to scientific progress and so I shall not be that specific. It is an epistemology, and therefore I plan to show only its effects on that field. For the purpose of epistemology (though perhaps for that purpose only) I see the problem as one of endeavoring to understand man as an animal we observe while he is in the midst of grappling with knowledge. He gains it, he learns what it means, and he uses it, and in using it he makes adjustments in it which enable him to learn still more.

At every stage in the long historical development of such processes there must be a pause and a summing up. I take it that the present treatise represents one such effort. This will mean that there is much talk about how knowledge is obtained and a little also about what it is that we acquire knowledge of, in short about the constitution of the world to be known. We are part of it, but we are that special part of it that knows about it, and if not about all of it then about as much of it as we can manage.

In the remainder of Part I of this book I intend to round out the general picture of knowledge theory. In Part II I intend to raise sample issues and to discuss them somewhat in depth, if for no other purpose than in order to show how complex the problem of knowledge actually is.

When we talk about epistemology we are, as I see it, referring to three separate though related areas. We are talking about the human subject in his relation to knowledge, we are talking about the world to be known – nature is perhaps a better term. And, finally, we are talking about the system of ideas at which the subject arrives in his efforts to understand nature. For to understand it means to have some conception of the whole of it in all of its immensity and complexity. Knowledge-seeking in its smallest moments may be a matter of refining the details so as to know what kind of thing it includes. There exist small issues, as small as can profitably be studied. But there exist the larger issues also, and these include the third area: a system of ideas which I have noted is more general than any other, one which is both consistent and complete. Epistemology ends in the service of metaphysics, to which it must deliver up its final result, and no less so because it must be continuously revised. Epistemology as a methodological undertaking must therefore always be with us.

The most urgent social need of the present moment is the necessity for man to adapt to the changes he has made in his immediate environment. He has made in effect a new world and now he must learn how to live in it, and this he most assuredly has not done. His efforts to do so are in desperate need of organizing and planning, for now they are approached in only the most hit-or-miss fashion. Adaptive knowing, viewed in this context, is tantamount to a method of species survival.

CHAPTER II

THE ACQUISITION OF KNOWLEDGE

I. BEFORE PERCEPTION

I start with the assumption that 'being' is more fundamental than 'knowing'. I might argue for instance that 'Water is wet' implies that there is water, wetness and connectedness, for if not then water could not be wet. And I would proceed to add that not only is 'being' more fundamental than 'knowing' but that 'doing' is, too. For there would have to be the experience of the wetness of water before anyone could say that 'Water is *known* to be wet'.

In this and the next two chapters I propose to discuss the principal epistemological concerns. Each of the three chapters will be devoted to one of the following: *feeling, knowing* and *doing*. It might be strange to find the category of 'feeling' substituting here for 'being', but I would contend that 'feeling' in itself is, or in its functioning discloses, the most primitive kind of 'being'.

I propose in this chapter, then, to begin by examining perception, in the sense in which epistemology is concerned with it. Yet perception if I am correct is not an absolute isolate. It has an elaborate set of preconditions, and it has an equally elaborate set of consequences. It depends upon the former in much the same way as the latter depends upon it. Since we shall be concerned in this chapter primarily with perception, I will sketch out rather than elaborate the preconditions, and then devote most of this study to their consequences.

In the examination of the process of perception we must not forget that the study of epistemology is one which presupposes a human individual and a world into which he is born and in which he lives and dies. We look for the most rudimentary and presuppositionless beginnings of the primitive process of the acquisition of knowledge, but the early stages must not be allowed to blind us to the fact that the human individual is an animal engaged in a continuous process of interchange with its material environment. He must obtain from that environment the substances which he needs in order to maintain himself. There are three primary needs: food for the stomach, water for the tissues, and sex for the gonads, and three secondary: activity for the muscles, information for the brain and security for the skin. Only one of these concerns knowledge; information is an organ-specific need of the brain.[1] Only the last of these, a need of the brain, has the endorsement of the idealists, although all are necessary if the organism is to survive. The primary needs look to the immediate survival of the individual, the secondary needs look to longer-range, or ultimate, survival. The "purposive activity" of Blanchard, Pepper and others can be fractioned therefore into a number of need-reductions, only one of which is knowledge.

Man has been gifted with a brain which enables him to ask the ultimate philosophical questions but not with one sharp enough to find the answers. That is one of the accidents of biological evolution. The brain is the mechanism of the mind. That is to say, the mind is one organizational level higher than the brain and thus is productive of qualities which cannot be reduced to the brain. Consciousness is the most obvious of these qualities. Needless to add, we can influence the qualities by manipulating the mechanism of the brain, as for instance by chemical means. Against the charge that studies of the brain from the outside tell us nothing about the condition of the mind from the inside, there is the hard evidence that by means of drugs and other manipulative techniques we are able to control and to a large extent determine the states of consciousness.

It is a fact which is rarely discussed by the practicing epistemologist that for an individual to know the world in order to act in it in such a manner as to extract from it those material things which are essential to the reduction of his organ-specific needs, that world must exist and have those material things among its components, and he must learn how to adapt to it. Only the spokesmen for a world of matter as that world is described in the current experimental sciences can inform the individual in search of his need-reductions that it contains the physical chemical, biological, psychological and cultural things that he needs. It is a world of matter truly, but not the one described by the older materialists, only the one investigated by the new scientists. That is the world in which the individual acquires, assimilates, and deploys his knowledge, to the end of reducing his needs.

[1] James K. Feibleman, *Mankind Behaving* (Springfield, Ill., 1963, Charles C. Thomas).

Against this background we can now turn to the more germane topic of perception. We must not forget that perception takes place in the subject, who is an human individual, in the presence of a material object. The first element of experience is a sensation or bare impression, usually of some property of a material object, a color, say, an odor or a sound. It can occur of course without an external object, as for instance in the case of a twinge of pain; but we are concerned with impressions which are occasioned by objects. We are interested in the subject only to the extent to which he is an observer; he is one of two variables, specifically the one whose interactions we describe as perception. At some very low level there is an interaction; for instance given two material objects, a perceiver and a material thing perceived, light is deflected from each to the other and has a definite though minimal effect upon the perceiver, producing a reaction in him. We can neglect as minimal in this connection the effect of light falling on the material object and concentrate on the effect of the light on the subject. In him it produces a sensation, and sensation depends upon wave lengths of light, their duration, rhythm, pitch, timbre and amplitude. Signalling by means of sensory nerve impulses has been followed no farther than the cerebral cortex.

But we should begin much farther up the line; more specifically, at the level at which there is a human subject and a material object, with the object kept within range of his sense organs. Perception is the name of the first response of the subject to the influence of the object. What are the conditions which makes this effect possible?

First the object itself. Analytically, it is qualitatively infinite. Particle physics has taught us in the last few decades that the material particular is inexhaustible. There is first of all the level of the particles themselves, of the atomic constituents: electron, proton, neutron; and there may be levels below that. Our knowledge of the material object must perforce always be incomplete. The incompleteness, I might add parenthetically, belongs to our knowledge of the object, not to the object; the "incomplete object" of Meinong does not exist. There is true perception even though it is only partial.

The 'object' I have been talking about is something material in the field of nature. Nature is structured, although at a glance the seams do not show. There is an ascending series of increasingly complex organizations from the physical through the chemical and the biological to the social or cultural. Structures at each of the levels include myriads of structures from lower levels plus one emergent quality; mere force at the physical, valence at the chemical, life at the biological, and ethos at the cultural. That is to say, the 'object' is a physical object (e.g. a stone), a chemical object (a compound, salt), a biological object (a dog), a psychological object (another human individual), or a cultural object (a computer). All in a sense are material, and it has been the mistake of the critics of materialism to suppose that only the physical is material or that the terms are synonymous. Cultures, for instance, consist in human individuals, who surely have their material side, plus artifacts, which are the material objects which have been altered through human agency for human uses. There is no danger that such an analysis calls for, or even permits, the reduction of the higher to the lower levels. The emergent qualities and the degree of complexity of organization stand in the way.

The empirical levels of organization referred to above are natural and, except for the last and highest, owe nothing to human agency. The independence as well as the objectivity of the world to be known is something that most modern thinkers find it hard to grasp because they have been under the spell of subjectivity for so long that they are largely unaware of its pervasive influence. Piaget, for instance, though he saw enough to move from psychology to biology in his efforts to understand the process of knowledge, still fell into the way of thinking of organization as always having been organized by some human subject.[2]

There is a partial special explanation of perception for each of the empirical levels. I will choose the lowest, that of the physical level. According to this account, perception (in this case sight) begins at the primitive point where radiant energy (in this case light) flows from two uniform structure-free patches of identical size and shape to the eye of the observer, who is able to distinguish between them.[3] Next to that is the physiological account in terms of retinal rods and cones, etc. Rival theories of color still compete for acceptance.

There are difficulties, of course. For instance we are very far from understanding the subtlety and extent to which the subject's role in a particular culture influences the character of his perceptions. The epistemological tradition from Locke to Hume is predicated on the existence of a kind of absolute and universal sense experience, as though it would make no difference to perception whether the subject

---

[2] Jean Piaget, *Biology and Knowledge* (Chicago, 1971, University Press), p. 362.
[3] E. U. Condon and Hugh Odishaw, eds., *Handbook of Physics* (New York, 1958, McGraw-Hill), Ch. 4, Sec. 1–2.

was a native of the Kalahari Desert or a citizen of Chicago. But the fact is that we should recognize the broadly cultural rather than the narrowly individual nature of sense experience in speaking of the subject. On the other hand, it is obvious that the capacity of the object to serve as a stimulus for an act of perception is only one of its many functions, and a surface function at that. Every material object is a busy center of activity, one sliver of which is its impact upon a single observer. The surface function is called appearance, and it rests on many more fundamental levels.

One inflexible law prevails. The material object is always more complex than the perception of it. The subject sees only the appearance, but, as we have noted, the empirical levels of complexity as well as the component parts which exist on the same level provide that the appearance must be partial and moreover changing. This is one manifestation of what we shall name hereafter the 'perspective predicament', which guarantees that the appearances correspond, if they correspond at all, only to part of the reality (as with Kant) and that the reality while not unperceivable is perceivable only one part at a time (unlike Kant).

If the material object is complex, so is the subject. The subject does not function in perception at the lower empirical levels but only at the psychological and cultural levels. The human body, however, is not only a psychological and cultural subject but also a biological, chemical and physical subject. The fundamental type of bond is between the body and its immediately environing external world. The subject has the task of receiving stimuli as it becomes aware of them. In rare instances it may influence them and even cause them, but not usually.

Most of current epistemology rests on the assumption that the direction of perception is from inside the subject outward; so Brentano for all his realism, for instance. Yet the evidence points to the fact that this account is incomplete. From the outside inward, and only afterwards from the inside outward, is the more accurate description. Intentions have to be triggered, and so they are. Stimuli which trigger perceptions in the subject may come for example from the external world of tropistic objects positively, or from the internal world of organ-deprivation negatively.

II. THE PROCESS OF PERCEPTION

In undertaking the long process of examining knowledge I begin of course with its acquisition. Later I shall talk in more detail about its nature. The acquisition of knowledge takes off from the elementary process of perception. I say 'perception' rather than 'sensation' because a sensation does not become knowledge if no one attends to it.

Perception is the most primitive kind of experience. Experience itself takes place in terms of a subject, an object and a relation between them. According to the account furnished by idealism, experience is determined by the subject as the source. I shall deal with that theory in a later section of this chapter. Here I am undertaking the realist view, according to which experience must be said to begin with the object which, through the process of sense experience on the part of the subject, gets reflected to that subject. As observer the subject is at the mercy of the object when he is put in the perspective from which it can be observed, for he can observe it only as it appears to him.

Perception, then, is the awareness of an object. It arises from preferred sensations. The outer compulsion governs in every case, but previous experiences help the subject to take some sensations more seriously than others. The perspective he occupies, as a result of peculiarities in his particular organism and even greater peculiarities in his particular experiences, helps him in his selection of sensations.

In the description of mental processes I must rule out introspection, for if I do not it will be misleading. For example, in perception there is a certain process, but it is a process of which the subject *qua* perceiver remains unaware. To be aware that he is *per*ceiving is to be *con*ceiving, which is a much higher stage. I say, then, that the subject is perceiving, which means in most cases that he perceives an object. He certainly does not perceive his own process of perception.

Perception, which is the reception of sense impressions, is an immediate act, instantaneous and qualitatively indivisible. Kant raised the question of the smallest unit of sensation,[4] but that answer must be left to the laboratory investigations of the experimental psychologists. It is possible, however, to distinguish the parts which go to make up this seamless whole. These are: discrimination and identification.

In discrimination the observer perceives the separation of an object from its surroundings. He sees it, in other words, as an organization of some sort and not as part of some continuous background. This is what the psychologists have called the 'figure-ground' phenomenon.

In identification the observer perceives through its form and its properties (qualities and relations) the class of which it is a member. No

---

[4] Immanuel Kant, *Critique of Pure Reason*, B 210.

one perceives colored patches merely, except perhaps a newly born child. How the transition is made from the indiscriminate to the discriminate will have to be a chapter in genetic epistemology. Meanwhile it is safe to say that perception is the recognition of familiar elements in a new assembly. No memory, then no experience. The observer will have memories of a given range of sensed qualities and perceived relations; it is the degree of novelty in experience which is the unexpected combination.

Many epistemological realists who agree about the objectivity and independence of relations still deny that status to qualities and values. There is some evidence which could be read as the dependence of color on the perceiver; the evidence from optics, for instance, or from the experience of color-blind individuals, and the like. But the bulk of the evidence runs the other way. For instance no one really supposes that a green book ceases to be green when there is no one in the room to observe it. Even Berkeley did not deny that, although he produced a lame theological explanation for it. Again, that force is a quality is often forgotten or overlooked, but more on this later. The exercise of force is something that is felt by the body on which it is exerted whether that be a human body or no. That animals feel pain and in a minimal way that even plants feel something akin to it, can hardly be denied.

The simplest and most primitive perception is based on a single perception, a glance so to speak; but this is not characteristic of the process. When we refer to perception we should remember that it is a part of the behavior of the moving animal who is engaged in a course of action when he perceives. Thus for an object to be perceived means for the observer to move round it and so to acquire the conception of the stereoscopic object, a solid with many faces. Thus it may be that perception is not a complete process but only a stage on the way, and that what we are really talking about is an incomplete conception. That in fact may be what perception is.

A perception is an organized pattern of sensations, a conception is an organized pattern of perceptions. In perception itself there are elements of sensation and of conception, though the former are vivid and the latter are dim. Together they make up a whole, which when it happens, happens simply as a whole and not as a whole containing parts.

We do not perceive merely in the abstract or general, we perceive particular things, particular qualities and particular relations and forms. To say that an observer sees a bird is to say that he recognizes the form, in other words that he recognizes in the object itself that it is a member of a general class. If it is a redbird, say, then he recognizes from the form that it is a bird, and more particular still from the color that it is the kind of bird called a redbird, a still more special class. He sees not only qualities and forms but also relations. The redbird is on a lower branch, on a tree smaller than its neighbor, etc.

Perception, then, has passive and active phases. Discrimination is passive, identification is active. Perception is deliberate in that the objects the subject perceives are independent of his perceptions of them. It is both genuine and at the same time partial. It discloses the impressions made by the object (which are always somewhat less than the whole object) on the perspective of the subject functioning as observer (always somewhat less than the whole observer).

The observer *senses* qualities and *perceives* relations, and he does both by means of his sense organs and at the same time. Thus he sees that the wall is brown but in the same saccadic eye movements he sees also that it is a wall. Could the observer 'see' anything that he could not recognize and even name? If a man rushed in with a horror-stricken face and someone said to him, 'What did you see that frightened you so?' and if it were an object he had never seen before, let us suppose an animal he had never known about before, he would answer, 'I don't know exactly what I saw, but it was an animal with a head like a lion, arms like those of an ape and a body like a giraffe'. If he had not been able to identify the genus, had not recognized the similarity of parts with those of the parts of the species with which he was already familiar, it is doubtful indeed whether he could have said anything, or have even perceived what he had perceived.

Where does all this leave us? When an observer perceives an object – say a basketball – he perceives also that it is a round object. But just what is the status of the 'round' that he perceives? He calls it a circle, but is it an individual circle? Not when he recognizes its affinity with other circular things. It is a universal circle? If we admit that he perceives the form without recognizing it as a form, then he is perceiving that it is an individual, yet it is questionable whether the latter alternative is possible; for if he is perceiving it as a form then the chances are that he is perceiving it as a universal, and this is more likely. However startling a thesis it may be, the fact is that we do directly perceive relations.

The thesis is not one generally accepted, to say the least. And yet it is not entirely unknown. It is to be found for example in Peirce. His name for relations was "thirdness," and thirdness, he insisted, 'is directly perceived."[5] It is perceived in the "perceptual judgment," and according to him it is that part of the mind over which the observer exercises no control. Such perceptions are both genuine and involuntary.

The circularity of the basketball involves a specific set of relations, and I submit that the observer directly perceives relations, that they are in fact ingredients of the material world though not in themselves material. They are paramaterial. The observer perceives the *similarity* of two pennies held close together, he perceives that the pencil is *above* the book. He is able to observe them because he recognizes them when they recur, as they do in a way in which the material objects of which they are parts do not. Relations, like qualities, recur. They are not similarities, for similarity involves the identity of parts whereas what I am talking about is the identity of wholes. That one form can have many appearances is a logical and material fact to which we have yet to accommodate ourselves. When relations and qualities recur, they are the *same* relations and qualities; they are identical, and identity is not a relation.

Relations, universals, classes with an undecidably large and possibly infinite membership – these are synonyms, and for the present I intend to use the term 'classes' and the term 'universals' interchangably. It is important to the analysis of perception that classes enter into the nature of the individual material object in so far as that individual is a member of a class. Material objects of course share in many classes in addition to the class to which each belongs as a whole. It is a member of that class but it is also in part a member of every class to which its relations and qualities belong. And just as classes are not exhausted by their members, so the members are not exhausted by their classes. In virtue of their own intensive nature as active-reactive individuals with their own peculiar properties, they extend beyond classes. But thus far (and so far as our limited knowledge goes) it has not happened that a material object has existed which was not the member of any class.

Experiencing, then, and in particular perceiving, is a process of sampling a class by encountering one or more of its members. In the case of material objects, most of the members of the class are absent either in space or time or both, and the few that are present must be regarded as generally representative. They make possible the representation of absent objects, which is what the class does. Relations and

[5] Charles S. Peirce, *Collected Papers*, C. Hartshorne and Paul Weiss, eds., 5.209–5.212.

qualities are experienced as concrete and in the present; but, being themselves classes, free us from the limitations of the concrete and the present. The sensations of similar experiences in the past are added by classes to the sensations in the present, endowing them with tremendous affective power.

The degree of rationality involved in perception, the fact that it can take place only in terms of universals, has been read as an argument for idealism, as for instance by Blanchard.[6] He assumed of course that universals are mental constructs. In the face of the evidence there is no good reason to agree with him. The realist position is equally supported if we remember that the universals are already there as relations in the perceived object, though the idealist's advantage is that this fact has been neglected by those realists whose business it has been to analyze perception.

The idealists have been fond of pointing out the presence in all perceptions of universals. Well and good, provided only that it is understood they were not products of the human mind (the idealists assert that they were); for once we have established the fact that forms, qualities and relations inhere in things, we have as much as admitted that universals are there, we have only exchanged names.

A little reflection will bring out the additional fact that relations are not merely mental and that the strongest argument can be made for the relation of similarity. When the observer notes that certain things are similar, two blue dishes or two round balls, for instance, just where is the similarity? It is in our minds of course, for that is what we mean when we say that we *recognize* the similarity; but it cannot be *only* in our minds, for in that case what would have compelled the recognition? If two things are similar it is not the observer who makes them similar for their similarity can be measured; on the contrary, it is the inherent similarity which compels his recognition. In his absence from them he does not behave like a man who held himself responsible for their similarity, indeed he counts on it to remain as one of their properties. When he measures a shelf or a container to hold them, he assumes that they are the same in size, thickness, etc.

This still leaves us with a problem, however. For if we admit that the similarity is in the objects, it is fair to ask, just where in the objects? Not in either one alone, certainly, and in the pair only if they are close enough together to be caught up in a single act of observation. No

[6] Brand Blanchard, *The Nature of Thought, passim.*

matter how widely they are separated we will continue to suppose that their similarity still exists, and exists irrefrangibly so long as they are not altered.

Similarities recur, differences perish. The brown basketball once destroyed will never be found again. But its brownness and its roundness will. They will recur in other things, even in other similar basketballs. The basketball was unique, its properties were not. There is nothing in brownness and roundness that cannot be found in things other than basketballs. I have a jug and an ash tray, both of which are brown and round. What has to be explained, then, is the recurrence of qualities and relations which survive the perishing of the material things in which they occur. But since what is in need of explanation is a type of being which can provide for recurrence rather than a type of experience by means of which that being is recognized, this is a problem for metaphysics rather than for epistemology.

There have been a number of epistemological attempts to account for such properties. One of the more prominent of these was the positing of sense data by many English philosophers at the turn of the century. It had a surprising strength considering the difficulties it raised. Intervening variables of this nature double the problems, for instead of having to explain the relation of the perceiver to the object perceived, it was necessary to explain the relation of the perceiver to the sense data and then of the sense data to the object perceived. Nevertheless, the theory had many adherents in both the United States and England, A. O. Lovejoy, for instance, D. Drake, C. A. Strong, C. D. Broad and H. H. Price.

The doctrine of immediate perception, which is here supported, dispenses with the existence of sense data. The first investigator to set up sense data as unknowable and then to seek out their location was influenced no doubt by Hume. But the theory that there are free-floating sense impressions – detached from the object and awaiting reassignment while forbidden to the subject – presents a pretty dilemma and moreover one which seems to have been artificially cooked. This is to create a problem where none existed before. For the fact is that we never do experience sense data as such; we have experiences and we interpret them as disclosing sense data, but this is entirely different. The lost sense data, detached from the object, forbidden the subject, and floating freely in between, had found themselves earlier in Kant's relativism where they were unhappy indeed. Eventually, forbidden or not, they float back into the subject, for where else are they to go? They were never detached from it in the first place, only from the object.

Realism in epistemology has to face the problem of errors in perception. No doubt they do exist, but only as the children of single impressions. If the traveler who is dying of thirst in the desert sees the mirage of an oasis which does not in fact exist, subsequent perceptions will correct his previous impressions. But even so he had not been in error, that is the point. He really had seen an oasis. The configurations produced by radiating heat waves from the sand really had looked like that. It just happened that he had read them wrong, and that was an error in conception, not in perception. Some landscapes really do look alike.

I said that the observer sees things as they really are, but I must modify this a little. I must add that he sees things as they really *were*, since it takes time for light to travel from the object to the eye; and then I must reformulate the statement with a further qualification: he sees things as they really were from the given perspective which he for the moment occupies. To analyze perception by taking as the *analysand* the single sense impression is of course to set up a situation on a basis which is sure to lead to a false abstraction. For the fact is that perception is a continuous and ongoing process in which the object of perception changes in many ways. Also the observer may alter his position and so perceive different aspects of the object. It is this sequence of perceptions in which there is both permanence and change – permanence in that it is the same object and the same observer, and change in that the positions of both the observer and the object observed are altered – which must be described when we undertake to analyze the process of perception.

The examination of perception borders on that of conception, and we have just reached that frontier. The coordination of sense impressions, though strictly speaking still within the classification of perception, lies along that border, though we may follow it just one step farther before crossing it.

The perceptions of the observer are shaped and determined by the perspectives he chooses for his observations of objects and by the way he deals with the resistance he encounters in those objects. Their independence of his observations is something which he cannot ever conclude in any final way, since the proof is not absolute, but there is strong evidence. The strongest evidence perhaps lies in the resistance which objects present to his perceptions. No matter how he might like to see them, he must see them as they compel him to. Then, again, there is the fact of novelty. Objects present him with surprises, which they most assuredly would not do if they were entirely his own creatures. Further evidence may be adduced from the fact that the observations I am talking about are those made by means of the unaided senses. Common sense currently means what we can agree upon on these terms.

On the basis of the coordinated senses the observer by means of continuous impressions made at different times is able to produce the evidence necessary to him to support the construction of an independent solid object. The stereoscopic object is not perceived as such but nevertheless is constructed of perceptions.

Another piece of evidence, and a comparatively new one, is the continuity of the observations made with the unaided senses and the observations made with the senses aided by instruments. This last class falls into two divisions, on the basis of size. You may remember that we agreed to call the world disclosed by the unaided senses the mesocosmos, the world disclosed by the microscope the microcosmos, and the world disclosed by the optical telescope and other instruments the macrocosmos. The important point for our present purposes is that these two latter worlds, the world of the very small and the world of the very large, are adjacent to the mesocosmos, the world of average sized objects to which we are accustomed, and continuous with it.

This phenomenon should I think change a great deal of our thinking about perception. It would certainly lead us to believe that the world is a larger place and a more intensively complex place than we had formerly supposed, and it would lead us to believe also that such a world must perforce be independent of our perceptions of it, perceptions which however veridical are not only feeble but partial.

III. THE THEORY OF PERSPECTIVES

The fact that man always finds himself in the middle between two extremes seems at first glance to be a little suspicious. It does seem as though he is a creature appropriate to the mesocosm, with the macrocosm and the microcosm ranged on either side. There are precedents, of course. Consider the medieval synthesis, in which man stood half way between God and matter, with the angels next to him on the God side and the animals next to him on the other. Now we should prefer to say that he stands half way in physical size between the galaxy and the electron.

When we come to the question of duration of existence the same comparison is continued. Events at the microcosmic level happen more quickly and at the macrocosmic level happen more slowly than they do at the mesocosmic level. But there is in the human view a sort of fallacy of the permanent present: as things are, man tends to believe, so they have always been and so they will always be. There was always a traffic problem, a Russian threat, a declining Europe, supermarkets and television. These seem like commonplaces of his immediate environment, and yet none of them existed half a century ago. Even the solar system has been in existence no more than five billion years, a long time in human life, certainly, but not sufficiently long to be considered eternal.

This sort of provincial view does not excuse the philosopher whose field of interest is epistemology. Even in a world in which nothing at all ever happened, he would have to account for how there happened to be such a world. It does not seem legitimate to make philosophical generalities out of the accidental positioning of the observer. He has no preeminent location but instead occupies a temporary perspective, as indeed every entity and every process does, that is to say, every material thing and every trace of energy.

To make the charge that the perspective predicament is a distortion of which all philosophers are guilty is only to carry the disability one degree further. The critic of epistemological schemes is himself guilty of occupying a perspective predicament which is no less so for being one once removed. There is an infinite regress of criticisms involved here, and so the position had better be abandoned. The perspective predicament is inevitable, and yet we might still learn something from it.

The observer occupies a perspective from which he views the objects perceived. The perspective belongs, however, not to him but to the objects. Each single and quasi-isolated act of perception is only a glimpse of the object. For every material object carries about with it an indefinitely large number of perspectives, any of which may (or may not) be occupied at any given time by an observer. A perspective may be occupied by an observer but is never owned by him. What properly belongs to him is his own peculiar set of conditions and limitations. A man may look at an open book and see print and meaning. A blind man and a dog would see no such thing. Yet both print and meaning are there in the book in all three instances. If the book is moved, all of the properties of the book move with it, and what I have just declared to be true of the three observers remains true. And all remains equally true when one observer is exchanged for another, and even for that matter when there is no observer.

The special theory of relativity in physics is a theory about physical perspectives. Given two similar, regularly running clocks in uniform relative motion, it will be found that one will work steadily at a slower rate than the other. That is to say, each will run slower from the other's point of view. What is involved is the frame of reference; once that is fixed, everything else can be read off from it. "Relativity" is a misnomer, for it has led uninstructed persons to believe that what Einstein meant is that all is relative and nothing is fixed. Fixture relies upon frame of reference; given the frame and all is fixed. The theory of relativity would probably have better been called the theory of relationality.

The world is subjective only in virtue of the subject's selection of it. The subject's view of the object, made possible by the perspective which he can occupy, is subjective only in terms of his own limitations: he cannot see all round it or within it, say, and so widen his perspective; but that is not the fault of the object, which has as many perspectives as it has sides and insides. The material object is perceived in aspects or slices (perspectives). If the observer does not think about one side of the penny but about the whole penny, it is because his ordinary experience over a period has enabled him to put together a picture of the whole penny as though it could be viewed in the round in all of its aspects. This however, is an abstraction which *in toto* is never experienced.

The observer occupies one perspective at a time, and this is all that can be claimed on a strict reading of the process of perception. That he can only occupy one perspective at a time is what I have called above the 'perspective predicament'. This he seeks to overcome by organizing in thought the products of a series of perceptions. Perspectives fall on the side of the object. They disclose universal properties of the material object which itself is not universal. Action puts perspectives together in a way which allows for their organization by thought.

I have pointed out that the observer selects his perspective; after that he must perforce observe what it opens up to him, for he is powerless to see it other than as it presents itself. What is called 'experience' is something which happens to the subject as a result of his exposure to an object. He may have chosen the direction in which his senses are turned, but what he finds there he must take as he finds it. Perception is the response made by the subject when he finds himself confronted by a material object. Theorists tend to neglect the extent of the compulsion involved. It is what is forced upon the subject, as Peirce has pointed out in so many places. The subject may read his experience in a distorted way, but read it he must as it forces itself upon him and compels him to reckon with it in his perceptions. What he encounters in this way is to some extent a matter of chance. Chance, so to speak, presents him with a choice of determinisms.

There is in his immediately surrounding environment a plethora of objects, each with a set of perspectives any of which he may occupy. The final lesson of perception is that he himself is a tiny sensitivity-reactivity absorbed within the world containing many energy levels to which he reacts, first passively through observation with its reception of sense impressions, and afterwards actively. He does not start out with an awareness of himself in the world, but rather with an awareness of the world, in the center of which there is himself.

Thus he reaches to, though does not begin with, an egocentric predicament. The philosophy deduced from the egocentric predicament makes way for the philosophy inferred from the cosmocentric situation, by reinforcing the ego as a typical focus: standpointlessness, if you will, but merged with the universal standpoint; represented by any ego, but now conceived in itself as a center. The cosmological principle states that any entity can serve as an ego, and so saves the egocentric predicament from being an egocentric illusion by turning it into an egocentric perspective. This is the perspective predicament, always occupied on the vague assumption that a perspective taken up anywhere would be the same for any observer who was in the same condition and at the same stage of development. If objects always and everywhere exhibit the same dependence on the subject so far as awareness is concerned, this is equivalent to their independence, and calls for the assumption that behind them there lies an isotropic perspective.

The perspective predicament is solved by the individual through a single comprehensive assumption. He assumes from the evidence of his successive and overlapping occupation of perspectives that they yield up to him the view of a seamless world. At least he has no empirical evidence of any seams, all of his evidence points to an unbroken continuity of existences presented to him as appearances. There is not only a world which is independent of his perceptions of it but also a world which is united behind its appearances. This is an assumption which the idealists had made in the first place. They lacked only the self-corrective feature which correspondence could supply to the realist who held the same conclusive view. And so it comes to this: both the realist and the idealist entertain the belief in a seamless world, but the realist holds it to be open-ended while for the idealist it is closed.

IV. MODES OF THE ACQUISITION OF KNOWLEDGE

In this chapter we have been examining perception, and in the next we shall examine conception. It might be strategically wise here, then, to look a little at the process whereby we get from the one to the other. The classic three capacities of the human individual, which are for thought, feeling and action, will be our guides in this undertaking. We begin then by examining each of them, with the prior assumption that in the process a number of perceptions has already taken place. The more sophisticated approach will be reserved for discussion in the next chapter. Here then the order will be reversed, and action will come first, followed by feeling and finally thought.

Action, for our present purposes, if for them only, consists in making explorations among the world of perceptions. A single perception can never be more than flat, almost one dimensional in fact, but the observer is never content to leave it at that. At the very least he turns his head a little and thus gains another though similar perspective. At best he is apt to move around the perceived object and to confirm his suspicions, accumulated from experiences in previous similar encounters, that the object is multi-dimensional. The result of these primitive explorations is apt to be his conception of a stereoscopic object, with the accompanying suspicions that he still does not know all about it.

From such rude beginnings the observer is apt to be tempted to venture farther into the foreground of his environment which he has reason to believe extends backward away from him. By means of his penetrations he there encounters other objects which are similarly related to him and spatially related to each other, thus disclosing to him a large world of material objects temptingly promising to disclose to him relations among themselves having nothing to do with him directly but possessing nevertheless available knowledge. The original perceptions revealed one sort of world, but repeated explorations reveal still another, for the world of material objects is full of surprises and novelties which in their turn widen his expectations, which is another way of saying increase his experience. In this way activity assists him in gaining the knowledge of a world of material objects which from his original position he could never have even suspected to exist.

Intuition, the second in the order of man's three capacities, is a matter of feeling. Just as perceptions were hooked up together by reason of their similarities, so different sets of similar perceptions are seen to have something in common. The individual sees in a leap of feeling that the different perceptions can be generalized to gain a new insight into the nature of the perceived world. I am not trying to describe here anything so advanced as intuitions in the fine arts or the pure sciences but only the intuitions of common experience which take place in the untutored individual as he is confronted by the world around him. Induction is the sophisticated logical description of what occurs in intuition, but only after the facts disclose it to have been a leap upward in generality, omitting many steps on the struts of a structure that must always have existed. But this is not the way it happens; it happens as a surge of feeling of rightness or fitness, moving bravely into the dark to find there a foothold of security of belief that had hitherto only been suspected to exist.

Intuition is a halfway stage between feeling and reasoning. The reasoning itself is a process which occurs in plain view of the reasoning subject and is explicable by him to others through graphs. Thought is deductive and its steps can be anticipated in advance since they follow well-worn paths. What I mean, of course, is deduction as this takes place in the most ordinary way in observers who are for the most part uninstructed in anything so fancy as logic. The observer is now well on the way to the utilization of all of his mental powers in the acquisition of knowledge. That there is such a thing as deductive discovery is a thesis which need not be labored here. The discovery of knowledge through the utilization of previous knowledge has occurred often, even though it is not the commonest path to new knowledge. The use of Mendeleev's periodic table of the elements to discover new elements by interpolation is a well known historic occurrence and so is the discovery of the planet Neptune. The same can be said for discoveries in mathematics, such as the discovery of the non-Euclidean geometries.

The combination of all of the human capacities for action, feeling and reasoning guided by reasoning but employing equally both of the other two, happens most frequently in the exercise of the scientific method in the physical sciences. I know of no corresponding enterprise in philosophy which attempts to engage all three of the human capacities. In all events, the scientific method is a method of the greatest sophistication, and therefore does not properly belong to the elementary kind of phenomenology we are now discussing. It merely illustrates the power of the combination of capacities which separately aid the individual. I can-

not refrain from noting, however, that while Stace for example was argu-
ing that there is no warrant to go beyond common sense to the extent of
believing in physical objects whose properties we cannot even imagine,[7]
the physicists, chemists and biologists were charting some of those properties as a result of the instrumental and mathematical verifications of
their own hypothetical imaginings.

Most of the discussion in this section concerns the naive individual
as he discovers the environing world for himself, and therefore phenomenology would be a better term for it. I mean of course the kind of
objective phenomenology employed by Peirce in what he called "the
phaneron"[8] rather than the subjective variety which Heidegger has
made popular among contemporary philosophers. What are the responses of perception when the observer's sensory organs first encounter the elements of the phaneron? That is the question which I have
endeavored to answer in this section.

V. QUALITIES, VALUES AND FORCES

In all the discussions of knowledge, its acquisition, assimilation and
deployment, it is always the knowledge of relations that is meant. The
reason is that this kind of knowledge can be gained, displayed and utilized in language, either in the ordinary language of colloquial discourse or in the artificial languages which have been devised for logic
and mathematics. But there is another kind of knowledge which must
be treated – and indeed is – in other ways. I mean the knowledge of
qualities, values, and forces.

Although qualities and values are generically related, are in fact the
same kind of thing, values being in most respects only a species of high
quality, they are usually dealt with in very different ways, and so we
shall have to discuss them separately. Let us look first at qualities, and
then at values. Forces have not been recognized as qualities at all, and
so we shall look at them last.

Qualities are as common as relations, and yet there have been no
studies on the logic of qualities. Material objects are as replete with qualities as they are with relations. Moreover, qualities are more primitive,
in the sense of being simpler. Elsewhere I have sought to define quality

---

[7] W. T. Stace, ,,The Refutations of Realism," in H. Feigl and Wilfrid Sellars, *Readings in
Philosophical Analysis* (New York, 1949, Appleton-Century-Crofts), pp. 364–72.

[8] Peirce, *op. cit.*, 1.284–86.

as that which is ultimately simple.[9] The so-called sense qualities, held by realists to be properties of material objects, can be sensed and that is how we are made aware of their existence, but surely they do not depend upon being sensed in order to possess being. Odors are conveyed through the air by tiny particles emanating from material objects, and nobody has yet had the temerity to attribute odors to noses.

Speaking generally it is fair to hypothesize that every organization of materials into some sort of stable entity or process gives rise to qualities. What we call the secondary qualities are no doubt those which emerge at the level of gross objects, the material objects whose qualities impinge on us through our unaided sense experience. But what about the material entities and processes at other organizational levels? Do not qualities akin to our sense qualities emerge also from organizations of electrons? Do they not emerge from galaxies? In both the latter instances they are unavailable to our sense experience, yet everything we do know inspires us to guess at their existence.

Ever since Leucippus and Democritus, it has been supposed in most philosophical circles that secondary qualities are subjective, in the sense that they are contributed by the subject to the material object of knowledge. Many arguments have been advanced in support of this thesis, but evidently no one ever questioned the double subjectivity involved in the mental function when the observer projects the secondary qualities onto objects and at the same time perceives them there. This would seem on the face of it to be impossible, yet it has been the going theory for many thousands of years. Like astrology, which is even older, it still has supporters.

I suppose the thesis that secondary qualities are subjective continues to have supporters because the opposite thesis also presents difficulties. There is no way to locate sense qualities except to perceive them, and so it seems legitimate to argue that their existence depends as much upon the human subjects as it does upon the material objects in which they are perceived. There is some evidence in favor of this contention. There is some evidence from the physical science of optics and there is some evidence from color-blindness. In the former case, how are the qualities reassembled in the brain after having entered the eye as wavelengths of light?

The clue to the problem is to be found in a proposition which I have advanced already in another connection, namely, that analytical prop-

---

[9] *Foundations of Empiricism* (The Hague, 1962, Martinus Nijhoff), p. 78.

erties carry with them the qualities which emerge at that level. It is the color of a material object which is conveyed by the light waves to the eye and which later appears at the visual center of the brain as the same color. The color of a surface is a function of the character of the light waves which strike it and become deflected. Change the light waves and of course you change the color. The light waves are changed when for sunlight the observer substitutes fluorescent light.[10] Then what had formerly been seen as blue becomes purple. It really was blue, though, and now it really is purple. The observer by changing the light has placed himself in a different perspective and produced different conditions. No surface is ever irrevocably any one color. It is possible to believe that and still to believe that color is not subjective. Given the conditions, in this case the kind of light and the kind of surface, then the color of the surface is fixed.

There seems to be an exception in the case of color-blind people, and so now we must argue against the second defense of subjectivity, namely, that the subject, not the object is the possessor of the color, as the existence of color-blind people demonstrates when they see for instance a red surface as green. Color blindness does not represent a difference of opinion but a defect, usually congenital. The prevailing light by which most colors are seen is sunlight, and most persons agree about colors under those circumstances. But they agree also about color under other circumstances, under fluorescent light in the example above. A reduction in the number of discriminable shades does not indicate anything except a defective vision, and under the influence of such distortion differences do appear. But color for the normal vision is still objective, and so *mutatis mutandis* for the other sense qualities. I should conclude by adding that even the color-blind person sees something, a quality, 'out there'.

I submit that when an observer notes that the leaves of a tree have turned from green to red, he knows something about that tree and can from this knowledge gain further knowledge of the seasons. A dark sky is the sign of a storm, a blush the sign of a thought, etc. Qualities, as Peirce was at such pains to argue, are signs. But I mean something more. I mean that qualities indicate something about themselves and do not merely point to other objects, although they do that as well. Qualities in themselves are capable of having certain direct effects without semiotic reference. This is more noticeable in the plastic arts

---

[10] D. M. Armstrong, *A Material Theory of The Mind* (London, 1968, Routledge and Kegan Paul), p. 283f.

when colors are set in relation to each other, but it is true equally of single colors. Sensitive people respond to single colors alone. I myself find yellow exciting and cheering, while others have the same experience with certain shades of red. My wife is very fond of a certain shade of deep blue. The odor of a good perfume may carry with it all sorts of references, but it can be enjoyed for its own sake apart from everything else. That this is a kind of knowledge is a statement that violates the old definition of the term, but there is no reason to confine knowledge to what can be recorded or communicated. When the observer is made aware through direct exposure to qualities, he knows something new about the world, namely, that they are ingredients in it. Enjoyment produces its own kind of knowledge.

So of course does pain. It is an old truism that he has not fully experienced what life is like who has had no pain. It is one of the great lessons of experience, and even though most of us (though not everyone, not masochists for example) would willingly forego such an experience, this is not to say that we learn nothing from it. Once again I am speaking not merely of pain as a sign of something else but of pain as it is in itself, as a world ingredient: the knowledge that there is pain may be necessary to complete the world picture. It has an important bearing on ethics, too, and so can hardly be counted out of knowledge.

What I have been claiming for qualities is true also of values. Qualities exist at the physical level, values at the cultural. Values have their qualitative aspect, only they have it at a higher level and 'higher' here means more pervasive as well as more prevalent. If we define value as what is needed, then not everything has color – certainly many gasses do not – but everything has value. Value in the sense employed here means chiefly the good and the beautiful. The good is the affective aspect of the bond between wholes, while the beautiful is the affective aspect of the bond between parts. And everything in material existence is either a part or a whole (or both: a whole to its part and a part of some whole).

To feel the impact of values is to have added to knowledge, knowledge which is no less knowledge for being qualitative. No one is the same ever again after having felt the overpowering effect of a great work of art, of *Hamlet*, say, or *The Iliad*. The new condition can fairly be described as one of increased knowledge even though the form of that knowledge is qualitative. The knowledge of qualities and values suffers from not being able to be put into words. I cannot describe what I know as the result of having been exposed to certain qualities and values, and so I cannot describe or demonstrate it here, but every one who has lived in the world and been greatly aware of what was happening to him will know what I mean. That is what enables us to describe, and require for that matter, the educational importance of exposure to great works of art.

And now we come to the last of our three kinds of quality: force. Force has always been classified, correctly, as a part of physics, specifically as that which produces a change of motion. But there is another side to it which is more relevant to our present purposes, a qualitative side. We have always thought of qualities as passive, and so many of them are. Color for instance is a passive quality, though I would argue for the so-called 'passive' qualities that they have a certain minimal impact. But there are other qualities which have a more vigorous force, and I will name some of them. Force as a physical property exerts the quality of pressure, and there is a quality of force also at every one of the empirical levels of organization higher than the physical. The qualities of force at the chemical level are many and varied, from those our senses are unable to detect, such as valence bonds, to those they can, such as odors. The quality of force at the biological level of organization most commonly encountered is life. The quality of force at the cultural level of organization is a pervasive affair and goes by the name of the ethos.

Traditionally force has not been treated as a quality in philosophy, and yet it indubitably is. Force is felt by the organ of the skin, and, if it is powerful enough, by the muscles. Quality, like value, is static and acts through attraction; one is drawn toward the qualities. Force is by contrast dynamic and acts through exertion, either that of positive action or of resistance. We get to know force when resistance is offered to our bodies, when we try to move a heavy piece of furniture, for example. We recognize the same kind of quality by analogy when it extends beyond our senses, when for instance jet engines move a large airplane at high speeds or when large dynamos power the lights of a city. Consider the established fact that all material bodies in the universe are in a constant state of forceful interaction, and you see the prevalence of the phenomenon. All that is necessary then is to remember its qualitative nature.

Forces are prevalent affairs in the material world. The quality of force exists at the leading edge of all encounters between material objects, yet its qualitative nature has not been recognized. This may be due to the fact that it can be measured and all measurement is in terms of relations. But only the measurement is relational, that which is being measured assuredly is not. The same is true of matter, and the qualitative nature of matter is exhibited (and has been well recognized) in what have been known since Locke as the "secondary qualities," which he mistakenly thought to be contributed by the perceiver and hence subjective. Matter is static substance, energy dynamic substance, while substance itself may be defined as the irrational ground of individual reaction. The quality of force which is dynamic is thereby generically similar to the static qualities of matter which we have always thought of when we have thought of quality as such.

As regards knowledge, force has one great advantage over quality; it can be known through language. Since, as I have noted, forces can be measured, we can know about forces in the language of mathematics. We have special units for it. But when we do so we abstract from its qualitative aspect. Force impinges on feeling, at least forces which are not too great to do so; and when we feel a force we are cognizing it on the qualitative side.

VI. AGAINST IDEALISM

It may be nothing more than a remarkable coincidence, but most of the theories which find general acceptance are those which are flattering to man. That the world is only his idea of it has much in common with the religious idea that he is immortal and that he is next to God who is chiefly concerned with his welfare. But do such beliefs rest on grounds any more secure than wishful thinking? Is there any evidence for them?

I am not an idealist if by that term is meant one who supposes that ideas are products of the mind or that knowledge is created rather than discovered. There is a place for idealism in a realist theory of knowledge even though it is a subordinate position which all-out idealists would indignantly reject. I shall first criticize idealism for what I consider its faults and then I shall try to argue for the legitimacy of its claims if they are sufficiently reduced.

Among the arguments against subjective idealism may be included the following: (1) that knowledge increases; (2) that action remains unaccounted for; (3) that errors exist; (4) that the evidence of biological evolution is against it; (5) that appearances are not all of reality yet they are all we experience; (6) that there are differences between experiences which idealism cannot account for; (7) that 'being' and 'being aware' are not one and the same thing; and (8) that the idealist's method of introspection is inadequate. Let us look at these in somewhat more detail.

(1) That knowledge increases would seem to be an argument against idealism because the knowledge is knowledge of an external world and we use our experience of it to learn from it what the world is like when we are not experiencing it. The brute fact is that much happens to us that we had not expected and which compels us to change our beliefs. Belief is at the mercy not of our will but of our experience: what we see we can hardly doubt, especially when it is reinforced by what we hear and smell. Again, what we experience is clearly a part of what we do not experience and moreover continuous with it. Could what we experience really be created by us while the rest of existence is not? This would leave the continuity unexplained – more than unexplained: inexplicable. Experience is after all only a kind of sampling of what there is.

If there is one thing to be learned from experience, it is that the *content* of experience is to be distinguished from the *act* of experience. We do not experience our experiences but the world about us, and we learn to mark those experiences which have an internal source, such as sensations of pain, as interferences.

The idealist (with the possible exception of Royce) relies exclusively on coherence without correspondence, and on meaning without reference. How would a perfectly coherent body of knowledge ever increase if no further knowledge was to be obtained on the outside? Into a closed mental world nothing enters. Clearly the increase in knowledge depends upon correspondence, upon an external world which can yield up its information to swell the size of the coherent body of ideas. This could not be the case if "being known" were able to "alter the mode of being of the object," as Bosanquet said it does.[11]

(2) Knowledge comes from action as well as from perception. Hume insisted that it was the "subverter of scepticism," and indeed there is strong evidence that our perceptions are not themselves creative but only report to us what exists in our neighborhood. Every move I make is evidence against the notion that the world is my idea of it.

(3) If indeed I did create the world through my perceptions or thoughts, how does it happen that errors exist in my thinking? Experience corrects errors, but how did I make them in the first place, and how does it come about they are susceptible to such correction?

---

11 Bernard Bosanquet, *The Essentials of Logic* (London, 1895, Macmillan), p. 8ff.

Errors are possible only if we first suppose that there is an external world which is independent of us and not amenable to our thoughts.

Those who hold an idealist theory of knowledge have failed to distinguish between the subjective holding of a belief and the objective certification of it. Both subjective error and objective truth are held subjectively, but for the truth alone there is an objective correlate. There is in fact an unfortunate correspondence between idealism and mental illness. An equation exists between solipsism and catatonic schizophrenia. The egoistic preoccupation of the neurotic and psychotic makes of them confirmed idealists. That is why therapy exists to help them return to the reality which they must face up to and which exists apart from them and their beliefs.

(4) Those who advocate idealism have not taken a good look at the history of the human species, and so they confuse an episode in anthropology with a condition of the cosmos. Certainly there is much information to show that the material world was here before we were. The evidence of geology, paleontology, and of much of prehistory points in that direction. Both the human brain and all human behavior arose genetically as the result of continual human adaptation to a changing environment. The long history of the interactions between the human species and its environment has had many powerful effects on the species but until comparatively recent times the species has had little effect upon the environment. Now that the species is changing the environment, this cannot help but accelerate changes in the species.

(5) Epistemology, as the relation between observer and observed, knower and known, makes much of sense experience. Indeed idealism considers experience to be creative. But if that were so, then all there is must consist in appearances. Now it is very well known that there is a reality beneath the appearances which experience cannot report. Kant held this reality to be inherently unknowable, but science has contributed to our knowledge of it, for instance by exploring the subatomic world; and so it is not unknowable though not experienced directly. In no case can phenomenological methods when strictly adhered to probe beneath the surface, for the constitution of material objects is complex and extends far below it.

(6) There are differences in experiences which idealism cannot account for. Idealism rests on the single sense experience, and it claims that the subject of the experience is responsible for the object experienced. But the subject observes A at one time and B at another, and it never occurs to him that there is a relation between A and B

which does not depend upon anyone's observation. This oversight was one of the errors of the British empiricists, Locke, Berkeley and Hume.

(7) 'Being' and 'being aware' are not one and the same thing, although the idealists would persuade us that it is. There must be a core of being to which awareness can be attached, and which furnishes the continuity between one act of awareness and another. Awareness of the external world depends upon consciousness, not upon being. Consciousness is only one part of being, for the unconscious, as we now know, exists.

(8) The method of introspection, which is the principal one available to the idealists, can tell us nothing about the essential nature of the knowledge process. It can tell us about the contents of consciousness and that is nearly all. It can tell us nothing about the physiological mechanism, nothing about what consciousness is in itself. It can tell us nothing about the external world and nothing about the different stimuli which together sustain consciousness. It can tell us nothing about the nature of perception and conception, nothing about truth. Introspection can recognize that we are conscious, and it can take us to the next level of self-consciousness, and what is valuable. Introspection does have its legitimate sphere, but also its severe limits, and in the end it is not as effective as other methods.

The most popular form of idealism in recent decades has been the one that stems from the philosophy of Husserl, and so I must reserve a couple of pages here to examine it.

His method of inner observation he called "transcendental phenomenology," and the first step "transcendental phenomenological reduction," by which he meant limiting the field of observation to the inside while "bracketing" or deliberately neglecting all external elements. Husserl credited to the intentional performances of the subjective ego the ultimate elements of experience. Perceiving, remembering, reflecting, these are the ways in which the ego is able to act on its contents. In a second step, called "eidetic reduction," the universal characteristics of the individual contents which in the first step were isolated for examination are displayed. This analysis was intended to show how it is that we can be conscious of something.

A number of criticisms must occur immediately to any philosopher who was not already persuaded of the truth of Husserl's position. I will mention only a few.

In the first place, "bracketing" seems a polite locution for the refusal to consider where the results of observations came from. The influence of the outer world, which is fairly continuous, will not go away simply because Husserl leaves it out of his considerations. It is as though the mind, once having acquired its contents, proceeds to deal with them in isolation, like a man in society who prefers to forget that the money which earns him his position was criminally acquired. In the second place, once acquired the ego can act on its contents as though it had always possessed them, surely a claim which is open to serious challenge.

We might indeed name Husserl's theory *the myth of the ungrateful mind* because it is reluctant to admit that it owes to the outer world any debt for its contents. Perceiving, remembering and reflecting depend upon a great many things, most if not all of which rely upon the outer world disclosed by experience. We can be conscious of something because we believe that what we are conscious of really exists, and by 'really exists' we mean exists outside and independently of us. The ego takes its contents to its bosom, so to speak, and then insists that such contents had never been anywhere else and that they have no other connections.

All of the recent evidence, some of which I have recited in another place, points to the fact that the dependence of consciousness upon the external world is continuous and total: if there is no input of sensory experience, then there is no consciousness, either. When we think about our particular experiences or about the abstractions we have made from them, it is without neglecting altogether their points of origin and without supposing that we own them in any absolute way which makes our own connections with them indissoluble.

Finally, one last point. Husserl seems unwilling to recognize what the cognitions are for, and this despite his emphasis on the *intentional* consciousness. They issue, presumably, in action, but action takes place in the outer world.

One of the arch idealists of late nineteenth century philosophy was of course F. H. Bradley. I have saved the discussion of his epistemology for last because a positive kernel of truth can be saved from it for a broadly-based realism.

For Bradley "appearance" and "reality" are a pair of epistemological categories which tend to be mutually exclusive. Appearances are in most instances illusory, and rarely correspond to reality. This use of the terms must be recognized to be different from their use in metaphysics. In the realistic theory of metaphysics 'reality' is a non-discriminating term: everything is real and moreover equally real. Reality for the metaphysical realist can be defined as 'equality of being'. There is thus nothing to remark about the distinction between the reality of anything and the reality of anything else. All things are equally real, including appearances, which are real appearances.

This kind of epistemology confines knowing to meaning. When meaning becomes the whole – the whole of the universe that is, the 'Absolute' – then reference is ruled out. There is indeed outside of the whole of the universe nothing to be referred to, and that universe is already inside the meaning of 'Absolute'.

Among the arguments in defense of a reduced subjective idealism may be included the following: (1) it considers the way in which knowledge is held; (2) it considers the consistency of the system of knowledge; and (3) finally it considers the fact, which must be recognized, that every knower is a subject of knowledge.

(1) Ever since the work of Kant, one of the topics of epistemology has been the limits of knowledge. He thought that the limits of knowledge are part of our knowledge, but are they? Serious problems have arisen since Kant to show that if our knowledge is limited, we are very far from approaching those limits. The evidence for this statement is the comparison between the simplicity of our knowledge and the complexity of the brain. Presumably the limits of knowledge are those marked by the complexity of the brain, and there is no item of knowledge at the present time which is composed of nine billion parts. That there must be limits can be asserted on *a priori* grounds; for instance that we can never know all there is to know about the brain itself. That is at the intensive end; at the extensive end is the evidence which consists in the fact that we have not yet reached with our sounding equipment, with telescopes of various sorts, the limits of the cosmic universe, and we have not yet even settled the question of whether such limits exist. Perhaps there are none. Meanwhile we must provide in our theory that knowledge can be greatly expanded without encountering the limits imposed on it by the brain.

(2) The consistency of the system of knowledge is what Bradley endeavored to account for in his notion of a "finite center"[12] or what Weinberg called "a solipsism without a subject"[13] in a word, with a consistent system containing all of the experience we can remember, but cut off, so to speak, as a complete set of impressions and ideas. Such a solipsism is temporary only, and subject to renewal through a loss of falsity and a gain of truth.

[12] F. H. Bradley, *Appearance and Reality*, 9th ed., p. 200.
[13] Julius R. Weinberg, *Examination of Logical Positivism* (London, 1936, Kegan Paul, Trench Trubner), p. 68.

(3) That every knower is a subject of knowledge will have to be recognized and given its due.

The valid side of idealism, in short, is how it treats of knowledge after it has been acquired, as sufficient in itself and without thought of further acquisition. I shall have more to say about this later when I come to examine the contents of knowledge. Meanwhile it is illustrative to use the language of idealism to describe the subjective end of the functioning of perspectives. The perspective predicament may now be seen as the holding of knowledge from the point of view of idealism, namely, as though it were sufficient and complete. That is a necessary occupational prejudice and even a useful one. For there may be occasions when one way of looking at the world is not affected by the consideration that there are other ways of looking at the world. The perspective predicament has an advantage in a gain in intensity at the cost of the sacrifice of extensity, and this advantage is one we must assimilate if we are to look at the world in any integrated way. I do not mean to be wholly disparaging when I say that as an entire theory of knowledge idealism will simply not do, and in the next chapter I shall undertake to say why.

Idealism is no longer the fashion in philosophy, which is not to say that it is not still around. There is a good reason for attacking the theory of knowledge of the idealists: as a comprehensive and sufficient theory it is false. But there is a positive gain to be had from it. Philosophers are often partly right in what they assert and partly wrong in what they deny. I see no harm in identifying the end-product of realism, which is a complete and consistent (idealists prefer the term 'coherent') system of knowledge, with the retention schemata, that organized body of beliefs which the individual holds, to some extent at least without his knowing that he does so. This is the kernel of truth in idealism.

CHAPTER III

THE ASSIMILATION OF KNOWLEDGE

I. CONSCIOUSNESS

Those who, like Husserl, talk about consciousness usually mean not consciousness but its contents. Consciousness may be here defined as the qualitative correlate of controlled perception. Consciousness itself is a quality; it is ultimately simple and it is unanalyzable. That which has no parts cannot be analyzed into them.

All of the mental life is tinged with quality, and since all qualities are indescribable, the quality of the mental life is indescribable also. To the extent to which qualities enter into experience (and it is not total) this simple syllogism has a conclusion which is inescapable and very discouraging. Not all of the mental life is qualitative, however. There are frameworks for it, and to the extent to which they exist we may retain our hope of describing something of the mental life.

There is no description of consciousness beyond what the neurophysiologists have said of it, namely, that it is the state of alertness or wakefulness of the organism. Mental states are qualitative emergences of states of the central nervous system but surely cannot be reduced to them. Consciousness is a function of the reticular activating system discovered by Magoun and his colleagues,[1] the mass of neurons near the top of the brainstem. Let me hastily add that this information implies no reduction of the mind to the brain. The mind is dependent upon the brain but the brain is not the mind. The mind is the end result of the way in which the brain works. The laws of the empirical levels are involved here, and the higher cannot be reduced to the lower however strong its dependence upon the lower. The existence of emergent qualities warns us away from any such interpretation as that. Besides, organizations are always one level higher than their elements

---

[1] H. W. Magoun, *The Waking Brain* (Springfield, Ill., 1958, Charles C. Thomas), Cf. also W. Grey Walter, *The Living Brain* (London, 1957, Duckworth), p. 2.

of analysis. The fallacy of reduction is often committed by materialists when they need not, as is the case with the epistemology of R. W. Sellars. D. M. Armstrong somehow fails to define either matter or mind, but I fear that his version of matter is the old and outmoded one employed by philosophers from Democritus to Feuerbach, and not the matter with its properties which has been disclosed by the new physics in the last fifty years.

Consciousness is a quality and qualities always depend upon structures one integrative level lower, more specifically upon the high frequency of nerve impulses; but consciousness cannot be reduced to them. The brain is an electric machine which runs on 25 watts[2] and makes consciousness possible. Consciousness as such is non-reflective. It is consciousness of an object which is before it, not consciousness of itself. It continually receives signals from the outer world or from the body, both of which of course are external to it. When a subject is conscious of his own state of consciousness, that is what is called self-consciousness. But self-consciousness is the consciousness of the consciousness of objects, never the consciousness of itself alone.

The first step in consciousness comes from the force of the object which impinges itself on the subject. Peirce was at great pains to argue that the knowing subject is helpless in the hands of the data. The evidence of novelties and surprises would seem to indicate that consciousness does not determine its object but rather the reverse. What Brentano and Chisholm after him call the "intentional consciousness" is in effect a second stage; it might be another name for attention, which is often deliberate. But that does not alter the nature of the first stage, which is not. In the first stage of knowing there are no deliberately chosen targets. So long as an individual's eyes are open he is powerless not to see what lies before them. Once faced in a given direction he is compelled visually by what lies in that direction. Chisholm himself seems to have recognized the inadequacy of the intentional consciousness in a later work in which he appeals to animal faith and to the role of a synthetic *a priori*.[3]

Consciousness is free to choose its objects but only within certain limits. The limits are determined by the state of the organism. Thus it happens that with some regularity of repetition pressures in bladder

---

[2] W. Grey Walter, *op. cit.*, p. 75.

[3] For the "intentional consciousness" see Chisholm's "Intentionality and The Theory of Signs" in *Philosophical Studies*, III 1952, pp. 56–63. The later work is *Perceiving* (Ithaca, N. Y., 1957, Cornell University Press).

or rectum preempt conscious attention under appropriate circumstances and there are many other such organic preemptions.

Consciousness is only one kind of nervous response, a response at the highest level of the central nervous system, but there are other kinds of nervous responses, many of them organic. The organism responds to many stimuli in a way which does not affect consciousness. An individual may die from inhaling carbon monoxide gas without ever feeling or knowing what is happening to him. Some types of carcinoma give no pain signals until the very end. It is possible to fall in love without recognizing it for some little time. And, above all, the unconscious processes of thought take place in such a way that the individual is not rendered aware of them until a conclusion has been reached.

Consciousness is the state of the subject when that subject is turned toward an object. The object may be a material object out in the world, or an internal object, such as an image which we say is 'in the mind', but without an object there is no consciousness. In the uncharted alembic of consciousness, fragments of physical and social events take on a strange arrangement, but they are still fragments from an external world.

As a state of alertness or wakefulness, consciousness is hopelessly dependent upon the external world. Monotony of input, as the neuro-physiologists have ascertained experimentally, causes the subject to lose consciousness, as may happen with a driver of a car alone on a long straight road at night. There must be a continually varied input if the subject is to maintain consciousness. Thus consciousness is a dependent function, and the arguments of the function are the material objects in the external world considered as variables.

Consciousness is the internal end of perception. It is dependent on the tensions between the brain and the external world, involving communication across the brain when operating as thought. As a function it makes a connection between the brain and the world by means of the central nervous system, and can be considered in isolation only with the understanding of its dependencies. Introspection is the awareness of the subject that he can now operate by means of signs by finding relations between them.

I have reserved discussion of the 'self' until after the discussion of consciousness because what we mean by the 'self' these days, at least in philosophy and psychology, is that which is conscious or aware. Since Hume it has been clear that there is no special location for the self and no special composition has been discovered for it. No doubt those reactions which we attribute to the self take place somewhere in the central nervous system or the cortex, but just what this means or how it functions is not understood. All that we can say with safety is that there is a consciousness and that there is something which is conscious. To ascribe it to the human spirit is no help unless what is meant by spirit becomes better known. If it means what I understand by it, namely, the dominant inner quality of a material thing, then we are no wiser. But consciousness is a fact and the fact is about a function, and there must be something which functions in this way.

The most familiar common understanding is that the self is a synonym for the knower. Perhaps; certainly knowing is part of the work of the self, but that is not the whole story because the self is not only that which knows but also that which senses and therefore cannot be identified with the knower but instead is considered to be the knower in one of its functions. The self as well as knowing is what experiences pleasure and pain and is able to receive the slightest trace of sensation. Until we achieve a greater insight we shall have to consider the self as a center of all experiences, including consciousness.

That the self is a center implies that it is the center of something, and so it is. The 'something' in question is the rest of the organism. In so far as the human individual is a moving sensing vibrant being it has an organization, and the organization is centered on the self. The unity of the organization with the self at its center is always a tenuous affair. For as the psychologists have learned, everyone is at least two people, though they tend to merge in most cases. However, leading 'a double life' is not all that uncommon, and in pathological cases there may be two distinct personalities involved in the same person, with one almost unknown to the other.

II. THE MIND

It is necessary to begin a discussion of the mind by distinguishing between the mind and its contents, just as we had to do for consciousness and its contents in the previous section. The mental state is one of being aware of an object, regardless of whether that object is internal, as is the case with an image, or external as with a chair. The contents of a mental state is what Meinong called the *vorstellung*, what stands before it. The mind is made possible by the brain, and the brain is matter in a highly complex state. It is possible of course to have a brain without a mind, as happens with a patient in a coma, but it is not possible to have a mind without a brain. Since the brain is a material object, I shall have to describe the mind as *para-material* in some as yet unspecified way.

The only secure domain of the mind so far as reliable knowledge is concerned is what can be abstracted from the world of matter and energy in space and time, the material world. The material and the physical, it may be parenthetically remarked, are often confused. Matter is the substance of all actual organizations, and the physical is the lowest level of organization. As we have noted in the previous chapter, others are, in ascending order, the chemical, the biological, the psychological and the cultural. The physical, then, describes only the lowest of the material levels. Energy is of course only the dynamic state of matter.

Material objects at all levels constitute the working field for the acquisition of knowledge by the mind. 'Knowledge' is after all only a representation of the environment. It is highly selected and only approximate. It is based on experience (including the knowledge from other sources, such as from books and from other individuals) and it is corrected continually. I mean by 'material objects' of course not only those material objects which exist now but also those which have existed and those which will exist. This is the sum of the inventory, the pool, from which knowledge is abstracted. It must be extended, though in a somewhat more nebulous way, to what may exist as well as what could or will exist. Note that we have added to our conception of the actual world to include possible worlds. The two together just about sum it up, though of course that leaves us with many problems and puzzlements.

The individual has a way of dealing with those possible objects which are not present, with absent objects. The status of absent objects as part of what the mind knows is a topic which has been much neglected, and I plan to deal with it at length later on in this book. There is another class of possible objects which extend both over present and absent objects. We may for want of a better name call them 'impossible objects'. Meinong discussed them at length, and gave as examples "golden mountains" and "round squares." What is allegedly involved is of course a contradiction, but I wonder whether that can be charged to any material thing. Somewhwere as yet undiscovered there may be a mountain made of gold. It is not inherently contradictory. A round square of course is. While certainly Meinong's "golden mountain" and "round square" do not exist, gold and mountains, round things and square things do. It is doubtful whether Meinong would ever have thought of their unusual combination if they had not. We must have a special category, though, for what could not exist apart from what could or does, and our resident domain for it is the mind though it is not purely mental.

Mental objects are not all of a kind but all do offer some variety of existence. It is not easy to form an image of a round square, if indeed it is possible to do so at all; but it is possible, and as a matter of fact quite easy, to form an image of a golden mountain. The mental state is a private state although thoughts can be communicated, and the contents of thoughts are not private. The feelings are private, though we know by inference and analogy that something like them occurs in other individuals.

What is called 'the mind', then, is not a single function but a loose collection of functions to which we have given a common name. What is meant by the mind is that sense impressions are received, retained in the unconscious, and combined in thought. They are stored as beliefs and revived as memories. They are even projected onto the world, from which they came as raw impressions, by means of the will and by impulses to actions. 'The mind' is only a description of the way in which we examine a segment of the world in abstraction from the experience by means of which we obtained the knowledge of it. We have the capacity for thinking about what we have learned and so of learning more about it.

When I say that the individual copes with knowledge, what I mean is how his brain copes with information, how it matches the input. The object of coping with knowledge is the survival of the individual, immediate survival first and then ultimate survival. Immediate survival is more importunate, ultimate survival more important. With respect to knowledge, the human organism is a self-regulating mechanism based on the workings of subordinate systems. The reception, organization and application of knowledge is one such system, but there are others, such as the temperature of the body, the regulation of the rate of blood flow, etc. Some of these systems are autonomic, some are not; the knowledge system is not.

'Mind' may be defined here as 'conduct toward knowledge in a living organism', more specifically, as the way in which man copes with knowledge. This includes its acquisition (consciousness or alertness), its storage (memory), its manipulation (thought) and its use in the initiation and direction of action (decision or will). In perception we receive knowledge, in memory we retain it, in behavior we employ it. It operates only in the presence of an immediate environment of sufficient variety to provide the necessary novelty required by alertness. Mind, in other words, is the general name for that process by which the human animal moves from sensations to universals, from the barest of experiences to the possession of general knowledge, and from thence to the employment of force. Thus every mental function consists in dealing in some way with knowledge. It is not possible to think of the mind apart from it.

I have already defined substance as 'the irrational ground of individual reaction', matter as 'static substance', and energy as 'dynamic substance'. Mind, then, is energy at the psychological level of organization. The distinction between mind and matter should now be clear. Every material organization exists at some energy level.

There is nothing in the mind that was not first in the external world except the capacity to acquire, assimilate and deploy knowledge, and to devise error, a capacity, in other words, for dealing with truth and for inventing falsehood. I would include in this capacity the ability to organize truths by combining and separating them. Also I am speaking of course of content. Capacity for apprehending truth is mental. Thought is mental, and there are mental states, such as belief and doubt. What is in the mind in the way of truth is of course both partial and general. What it lacks through partiality it makes up somewhat by being general.

By definition the mind is incapable of comprehending the powers which it has as a whole. For if it comprehends them then it extends beyond the whole, and if it extends beyond the whole then the 'whole' was not a whole. Thus the mind is incapable of apprehending itself as a whole. We rarely attend to our mental states but, on the contrary, it is the mental states by means of which we attend. Even thoughts, which command our exclusive attention and concentration, are not entirely mental. We think about something, after all, and what we think about can be traced to one of the two stories of the two-story external world: the ground level of individual material objects and the upper story of logical objects (the entities of logic and mathematics for instance).

When I say, then, that there is nothing in the mind that was not first in the external world except the capacity to acquire, assimilate and deploy knowledge, and to devise error, I am entirely aware of the large inventory of nature that this implies. The external world we refer to so often in knowledge theory *is* nature, and nature contains more than any of our limited schemes. It is not only the case that men are ingredients of nature but also that they emerged from the background of nature as themselves natural objects, albeit of a special sort. Thus everything that enters the mind of man is natural. Man himself could almost be defined as the animal that invents falsehoods. Accepting truths is something he does in common with other animals. The difficulty contained in the subjective view entertained by the idealists is probably due to the fact that we have attributed to our powers of invention much that was due instead to our powers of discovery.

The mind of the individual is subject to two sets of influences. One comes from his genetic history and the consequent adjustments of the biological organism, the other is epigenetic and comes from the immediate environment of culture, one is internal, the other is external. Both are organized by the mind. Sanity depends upon the ability of the mind to make a single synthesis out of its various influences.

The structure of the organism is generally credited to its genetic origins, and no doubt there is something to the claim. But the point is that the organism is whatever it is regardless of how it got to be what it is. In any cross section of time we have the spectacle of a mind receiving stimuli from the material culture as well as from within the organism. Those from within are apt to be chiefly organ-specific, whether it is thirst from dry tissues or pain from a sprained ankle. In both connections the mind functions passively, as a mere receptor of stimuli. Only after that is there either an instantaneous or a delayed response.

The current attempts of the structuralists to bring language and the brain together by attributing to the brain an inherent grammar rests on nothing stronger than the recognition that the members of *Homo sapiens* employ languages in most if not all of their operations. The dissection of the brain is known to be a very primitive kind of analysis at the present time, and though no doubt progress will be made in this direction it will be a very long time before the presence of syntactical structures are discovered in the neurons, if indeed they ever are. Anyway, it is a serious mistake to confuse methods of communications with systems of ideas. Complex mathematical systems were discovered, not invented, and they were not discovered for the sole purpose of communicating them. Logic is no more a part of the brain than the material world is a part of our senses, though the brain is instrumental in discovering logic and our senses are instrumental in discovering the material world.

III. THE IMAGE

What is before consciousness is either a material object or an image, in either case a centrally aroused portion of some previous perceptual experience. The image is either a memory trace or a product of the imagination. The memory trace conveys what remains of the perception of an object in the past. The products of the imagination combine images in unfamiliar ways. Images in general may be described as reflections, and reflected being is that part of the phenomenon which shows itself privately. Immediate perception does occur, but only some of what is perceived is retained. The image is the remembered percept; it is by definition partial, since not all of the perception is remembered.

The material world is the origin of all images, and this remains true even when the images are of things which do not exist. Let us suppose that I imagine a cow with a single horn in the middle of her forehead; we will call her a 'unicow'. No one has ever seen a unicow among material objects, and there is good reason to doubt whether a unicow exists. But I can *imagine* a unicow; that is to say, I can have in my mind the image of a unicow, can have at the center of my consciousness the image of a unicow which I proceed to contemplate. The unicow did not come from the external world, but the parts of the unicow did: a cow and the horn of a rhinoceros. The mind in imagining a unicow has simply put some parts of experience together so that they can be experienced in a way in which they were never experienced separately. That is in fact what the imagination always does. Even when it invents parts they must have come from sense experience.

The epistemological doctrine of realism is after all only a recognition of the remembered facts. If I look at a mountain and then shut my eyes, I can see an image of the mountain. Surely the image represents the impression, more or less accurate, made on me by the mountain. Now, it seems to me that the idealist would have to assert that the image came first and that the mountain itself was nothing more than a projection of the image, which is patently a false description of what actually happens. Eidetic images occur chiefly in childhood.

This description is no less true because invention works the other way round from perception. I first imagine a chair of a certain unique shape, and only then do I set about to fashion one out of wood intended to resemble it as closely as possible. Most epistemological sequences, of course, do not involve inventions, and even after they do the realistic account remains faithful. Moreover, the chair in the imagination, which exists nowhere else until one is made of wood, has as its elements parts which had already been perceived and known.

There are in general two kinds of mental objects: those which exist and those which persist. Both have objective counterparts which are the sources of their representation in the mind. The first kind is the image of a particular and the second kind is the image of a universal. The image of a particular abstracts to its peculiar features – the face of a friend, say. The image of a universal abstracts to its general features: what is common among many similar material objects, the number of elements in an organization or the pieces in two jigsaw puzzles. They go in different directions but have in common that they do not exactly represent any one material object.

There are other differences. For instance the image of the face of a friend cannot be communicated to other individuals except as a picture which is never more than approximate, but the number of pieces of a jigsaw puzzle can be represented by abstract signs and communicated precisely, by the number 215, say.

We ordinarily think of perceptions as well defined experiences and of mental images as vague and imprecise. In the main this is true, but it is not so true as we have supposed. The perceptions of most individuals are only vague impressions and remembered badly: that is why errors are so common and why they spread so very far. It is difficult for the average individual to recall with any precision what he has seen or heard, and his recollections can be very misleading. Only those individuals who have trained themselves to perceive, experimental scientists, for example, or painters, can both perceive with any exactitude and recall with any faithfulness. The vagueness of the image is the rule rather than the exception.

I might here add a footnote to point out that images can be under the control of the will, as for instance when one decides to think about an absent person. In some forms of art, the novel or the play, it is as though the will of the reader had been handed over to the author, for the reader has just that succession of mental images which had been largely determined for him. Art involves a logic of its own, and we had next therefore better have a look at one which is similar.

IV. DREAM LOGIC

In everyone's life there is a kind of image sequence which is not entirely uncontrolled and yet does not seem to be subject to the will. I am referring of course to dreams. There is some kind of unconscious control of dreaming, for it presents a high degree of organization, and yet the dreamer knows that he did not deliberately organize it. Dreaming is a part of common experience, no doubt of that; and yet the difficulties in analyzing the process remain.

Experience may be the richer for dreaming, and even if nothing more results it is still true that all subsequent experiences are rendered more intense by it. Dreams, like art, intensify life by lending to it the depth provided by the spectacle, and the experience, of alternative possibilities.

We know something of the logic which governs our ordinary thinking, but dream logic is unfamiliar to us. I propose here then to suggest tentatively what some of its axioms may be. An axiom-set could be considered a proposal. I am not of course thinking in any absolute terms even though such a proposal is a call to absoluteness. The axioms then will not be the absolute presuppositions without which dreams could not occur but only those most likely to occur. I have no grounds for asserting that the set is comprehensive, only that each of the axioms is independent and the set consistent.

The axiom set for dream logic runs somewhat as follows.

1. All acts are inherently complete.
2. The subject is always passive.
3. What could have happened does happen.
4. Reality is determined by value.
5. Proximity implies relatedness.
6. The environment is a threat.
7. Only intense extremes prevail.
8. Logical contradictions suggest material compatibility.

It must be remembered that dream logic is a part of concrete logic. The dreams must be regarded therefore as action theorems, that is to say, actions which follow logically from events functioning as theorems: event axioms. The axioms listed above purport to be such a set. To be a logical set the axioms must possess as a set both consistency and comprehensiveness. The axioms are consistent if all the properties they set forth are found in dreams. A consistent system can always be obtained for dreams simply by negating the modalities of waking life. For instance what is possible in waking life becomes impossible in dreams, and conversely; and similarly what is unnecessary in waking life in dreams becomes necessary. They are comprehensive if only the properties they set forth are found in dreams. The structure of any dream ought to be deducible from the axioms. It should be all that is needed to explicate the dream, if all the interpretations fall within it. Thus no absolute proof is available for dream logic any more than it is for any variety of concrete logic. Such evidence as there is must be regarded as supportive only. Of course it should be remembered that more than one interpretation of a given dream may be acceptable. Dreams, like the waking life to which they are related, are complex and not necessarily exhausted by any single interpretation.

Let us now take a closer look at each of the axioms.

(1) Dreams are usually well-integrated affairs, like well-made dramas. They have no loose ends but all proceed in an orderly fashion. Just what that fashion is may sometimes be hard to discover, but that there is an over-all motive seems clear. Every dream has a plot, and actions conform to it pretty well. This is as true of the long dream as it is of the short one; there is a sense of shape and an emotional tone that is unmistakable. Hence the meaning of a dream is inherent in it, as much so as it is in any deliberate composition.

(2) The dreamer is a spectator at the dream. He has had no part in its occurrence, it is simply something that happens to him, as much as external experiences do. He is helpless to affect the turn of events which it portrays, and can only watch even when, as so often happens, it appears that he is to be a victim; and he is a victim more often than he is a victor. On the other hand, the subject is always present; he is aware as he dreams that what is transpiring is happening to him. He is involved completely even though he is powerless. This feeling of involvement without control adds to the terror which is usually present. The dreamer is the prisoner of his dream. It is as though he had been tied to an unwelcome sequence of events and at the same time was unable to avoid its undesirable consequences. For most dreams, though certainly not all, are undesirable to the dreamer and therefore furnish additional evidence of the passive role he plays in them.

(3) The relation of the reality portrayed in dreams to that of the waking life is a complex one. The elements of the dream – all of them – are taken from the world as disclosed to ordinary experience but they are reassembled in ways which permit them to convey new meanings, meanings that in other, more familiar, assemblies they did not have. There is some correlation between the dreams of an imaginative person and those of an unimaginative one. Dreams are works of the

imagination but how this work is accomplished remains thus far unknown. It is tied to the question of dream control. Not that of the dreamer through his conscious mind, nor even of the dreamer through his unconscious mind. As we have noted, probably there is no control except that the free-floating recombinations of visual images answer to the one requirement of organization which is forced on the dream by the singleness of attention of the dreamer: it must have unity to be dreamed at all.

What is true of art therefore is true of dreams; they are compositions made up of the elements of the material world but significantly selected and reassembled. They are never all of the selections which could be made but only some which are made. Each dream is a consistent set of contrary-to-fact conditionals having its own axiomatic events and theorematic consequences. The dreamer remembers what could have happened, or perhaps his memory needs refreshing and he imagines what might have happened. The dream itself reveals a possible world, as possible as the actual world must have been in order to become actual but this time with another kind of actuality. It is and at the same time it is not quite the reality to which it offers an alternative but possessed of some of the potential meanings reality had but did not display.

(4) For the dream does make its own claims to reality and seems in its own nature to be justifying that claim. The conviction that what the dreamer is witnessing or participating in is actually happening is very strong. Only, for the purposes of dreaming the basis of reality has been subtly shifted. It no longer hangs on the insistence of fact but has moved to a condition in which it is grounded on value. A dream does not represent its meaning, it *is* its meaning. It is shot through with qualities which together add up to some sort of value. Its substance so to speak is value and not fact. That other daytime reality in which most of us spend two-thirds of our life is a composition in which fact dominates values; such values as we are able to achieve must be reached through as well as over and around the basic facts. Goals are made up of values, but the steps taken to reach them may be much more pedestrian. In ordinary waking experience, qualities enter the picture only at the frontier of encounters. But dreams provide a different picture. These values dominate facts: indeed values *are* the facts. And this makes for a reality which has that odd combination for the dreamer, which is found in every dream, of familiarity and strangeness. It usually seems to the dreamer of the scene he is witnessing that he has been there before but then it was nothing like this!

(5) The essence of dream logic is the juxtaposition of places and times. Two rooms years apart in time and miles apart in space may yet have a common door through which a person in the dream may pass quite easily and naturally. Differences of this sort are not erased, they simply do not exist. There can be an intimate connection between any two remembered occasions even though there may be other changes as well. For instance someone who was present on neither occasion may now be present at both. All events become contemporaries, all places neighborhoods. This puts at the disposal of the dream anything that may be in the experience of the dreamer.

Dreams run reversals; anything which can be expressed in logic is permitted by dreams. In dreams what belongs together occurs together. A little girl whose father was a novelist dreamed that the editor of her father's books tried to kill her. Clearly this is symbolizing a threat as well as running it backwards. Because of jealousy she wished to kill the editor in order (as she thought) to stop her father from publishing books. In the dream $(p \supset q) \supset (q \supset p)$. Dreams play with episodes as though they were logical expressions easily manipulated.

(6) The dream is usually a menace. Dreams do not only solve problems, just as often they create them. The nightmare is a frequent and familiar experience, though no less terrifying to the dreamer for all that. Dreams of terror due to predicaments, such as falling off a cliff or of being chased by a monster, are common. Dreams of losing limbs or of missing planes, of being in a burning building or of being in a closed space which is growing closer, are quite familiar. Happy dreams accompanied by delight, do occur but they are relatively rare. The more typical is the agonizing feeling resulting from a danger of some sort, a danger which seems immanent and mortal. The environment which contains the threat may consist in a physical predicament such as I have been describing, but as often it may be a malevolent creature intent on bodily injury, a vampire, say, or a werewolf. The life of the dreamer is in danger in all of them, usually with the prospect of considerable pain.

(7) As a matter of fact, only high emotions exist in dreams, nothing is casual or pedestrian, or if it is then supercharged with feeling. No real features are presented as they are in waking life. In addition to the Poetzl phenomenon of neglected experiences, the ordinary memories have become exaggerated to an extent which gives them another meaning and places them in another context. People in dreams do not behave quite in the way in which they did in waking life but if they do

the meaning is changed. Dreams are not reproductions of waking experiences, they are imaginative transcriptions. Personalities and events have become distorted, as though the scene and the characters had been written over again.

(8) The waking life is an interrupted sequence of episodes having continuity. The dream life is an interrupted sequence of episodes with apparent discontinuity. But is the discontinuity as genuine as it seems? The dreams night after night are happening to the same individual, they contain persons and events composed of bits of actual waking reality disclosed to experience but reassembled in strange and unfamiliar ways. Can it be that they lack continuity, or is it not rather that most dreams are not remembered and cannot be recalled? The discontinuity may be due to a simple failure of inventory.

For each dream seems in a sense to be calling on others for a continuity of meaning, as though they were recounting a continued story from which important pieces were missing. How otherwise explain the consistency which seems to be the property of inconsistent elements? Dreams suffer in their interpretation from comparison with the known continuity of waking life; each is asked to stand on its own feet in a way in which the isolated days of a waking life could not do.

V. THE UNCONSCIOUS

The largest part of the mind is not consciousness but that penumbral area which, for want of a better term, is called the unconscious. Consciousness floats like a top layer on the unconscious and cannot contain nearly so much. The unconscious is like a bottomless lake, to borrow a metaphor from Peirce.[4] Rain continues to fall on the surface of consciousness, but below it and rarely brought to the top are the ideas and images which are suspended at various depths. Much of what enters into the unconscious did not get there by being routed through the conscious mind, the effects of gravitation, for instance.

All that is retained as memory and susceptible to revival is part of the unconscious mind. The memory is a vast storehouse of previous experiences lodged in what – for want of a better description – we name the unconscious. It is more positive than that appellation would indicate, for it is what sanity rests on. No memory, then no person, as we know from those pathological cases of amnesia. Memories are all unconscious

---

[4] *Collected Papers of Charles S. Peirce*, C. Hartshorne and P. Weiss, eds. (Cambridge, Mass., 1935–1937, Harvard University Press), 7.553–4.

but they are available for recall, and when they are recalled they are brought to the level of consciousness. Remembering means in effect rendering conscious what had previously been only unconscious.

Every philosopher ought to be a realist with respect to the acquisition of knowledge and an idealist with respect to the holding of knowledge. The beliefs which an individual has must be rendered consistent if he is to continue to have them. Or at least if not then it must not be to his knowledge; often indeed he does entertain inconsistencies – propositions which contradict one another – but only so long as he remains unaware of this feature. Inconsistencies among beliefs often do exist, and betray themselves only when they issue in conflicting actions. The name 'unconscious' may be a misnomer, for the unconscious is continuous with consciousness and may be the scene of more activity than is usually supposed. There is a certain low degree of alertness in sleep, for instance, and one capable of fine discrimination among stimuli. A mother may sleep quietly through the most tremendous thunderstorm yet awaken at once when her child gives a feeble cry.

That the unconscious is not entirely passive, however, was first pointed out by Freud. He saw that the psychopathology of the adult may be due in many instances to errors of association made in infancy and childhood. Illogical inferences serve as axioms from which theorems are drawn which will later guide actions. The therapy practiced by psychoanalysis consists in directing the patient's thoughts to the memories of those early years when the false associations were first made and the incorrect inferences were first drawn. Only back there, Freud insisted, would it be possible to substitute logical inferences and so change the theorems leading to activity in such a way that there would be no more neurotic behavior.

It would not be possible to construct a complete account of osteology from a study of broken bones. Similarly, a complete account of the unconscious cannot be given when the only data furnished consists in illogical inferences. In addition to that process and to the vast catalogue of memories – according to the neuroanatomists, a catalogue containing everything which ever happened to the individual – there is the capacity of the unconscious to make correct inferences, in a word, to think. There is such a thing as live action in the unconscious, such as takes place when we are made aware only of the conclusions to what must have been a chain of deductive syllogisms. For only the conclusions rise to the level of consciousness. Many innovative and productive geniuses have left accounts of problems solved in sleep, of novel ideas arrived at when the conscious mind was otherwise occupied, usually in the performance of some menial task.

Since most beliefs, both those which are held exclusively by the individual and those which he holds in common with the other members of his culture, are held unconsciously, I have named them the private and public 'retention schemata' respectively. We shall hear more of them later. Here it is only necessary to say that action is dictated by them.

Behavior must conform to schemata, it must be consistent. When instead there is inconsistency, when actions are taken which are contrary to beliefs, then there arises the feeling of discomfort which has been called 'conscience'. The individual who does not do what he believes he should have done, or who does do what he believes he should not have, suffers the pangs of conscience, which may be strong enough to be described as pain. Conscience occurs more often in connection with the public retention schema than with the private, though either or both may of course be involved.

VI. CONCEPTUALIZATION

The same mechanism of preferred sensations which leads to perception operates in the case of conception. Conception arises from preferred perceptions. Previous experiences, including memory traces of perceptions, help the observer to take some perceptions more seriously than others. His peculiar perspective dictates the choice of perceptions and explains why some are preferred to others. Nevertheless, the process of conception exists at a higher level. In conception the universals which were implicit in the objects of perception are contemplated on their own apart from the objects from which they were learned. This requires thought, and thought is that conscious activity which is aimed at solving problems. If the problem is theoretical then thought has as its aim the discovery of truth, but if the problem is practical then thought has as its aim the establishment of a belief which is henceforth available as a guide to possible action. It often happens that, deliberately or inadvertently, the theoretical serves the practical.

It is all that we can do to venture on an interpretation of sense experience, for what the senses report to an observer is meaningless without a certain measure of hypothesis and interpretation. In this connection it would appear that perception is a very intellectual process. Given in simple perceptual terms, a man reading a book makes no sense at all. The observer of the scene would have to formulate an hypothesis as to what was really going on, and then check his hypothesis against the observed facts. He does not 'see' a man reading a book, he 'sees' members of classes with which he was already familiar, namely, the class 'man' and the class 'book'. How can he put them together without another class with which he is already familiar but which he cannot observe? He can only call on the hint in the observed fact that the two members of the familiar class are in such a position that the third supposed class, which we may name as the process 'reading', may also be present, though that third supposed class remains unobservable.

Perception is always incomplete, and conception employs it as a crude material requiring extensive supplementation. Then gradually thought retreats to the consideration of the relations between the classes whose members were once observed but are no longer needed. It is the formulation of those classes and of their classes – the classes of classes – on which thought finally comes to operate.

Conceptualization consists in the extraction of universals from concrete things as we encounter them in our experience. The nominalistic theory of resemblances attempts to explain away universals by claiming for resemblances only what the term implies. We are told that things resemble one another according as they have similar qualities or relations, but that we are not to take such similarities as indicating anything independent. Yet the fact that such resemblances occur among properties which survive the perishing of the material objects in which they inhere, that in a word they recur, would have to be neglected, and it is too important and too prevalent a phenomenon for that. As Price pointed out, the definition of a class of resemblances presupposes having in mind the defining universal.[5] There are such things as universals, and they not only exist in perceived objects but they also ensure in some more permanent way which enables them to return to existence in their original state. The resemblances exist apart from our knowledge of them every bit as surely as do the material objects of which they are parts.

If it is true that concrete things exist apart from our knowledge of them, it is true also that abstract things exist in the same way. We learn about them because they exist, they do not exist because we learn about them. Knowing is not a double method of both learning and producing the things that we learn. Thus we come to the recogni-

---

[5] H. H. Price, *Thinking and Representation* (Oxford, 1946, Clarendon Press), p. 31f.

tion that there is a two-story world, with material things forming the first story, the one encountered by our senses, and abstract things forming the second story, the one encountered by our most general thoughts.

Such a theory, which calls for the combination of a Platonism of abstract things with an Aristotelianism of material things – a position by the way which neither Plato nor Aristotle held completely – is out of fashion at present with professional philosophers and is to be found chiefly among Greek scholars and theoretical physicists. Physics could hardly move for a day without assuming, explicitly or implicitly, an abstract and independent (and permanent) status for its mathematically-formulated empirical findings. That fact should carry at least enough weight to get the professional philosophers to reconsider their prejudices against the theory of universals.

The study of universals is not confined to classes. It begins with sense perception, for we perceive relations in and between material objects. But the study of universals is not confined to relations, either, for it extends also to qualities. We sense qualities and qualities also are universals. The evidence for this is contained in the fact that qualities whenever and wherever they appear are always the same qualities. The particular shade of blue the observer sees in a shirt he sees also in the tropical sky and on the dust cover of his book. That particular shade of blue is a universal, for it is an identity and not a similarity. Similarity may be defined as the identity of parts. Qualities, like relations, are the parts in question. The shirt, the sky and the book are *similar*, but the blue is *identical*.

The mind does not operate in a vacuum when there is thinking to be done. It operates more like a sealed chamber into which nothing further can enter and from which for the time being nothing can escape, as though one were to say to an individual in a locked room, 'see what you can make of the materials that are in there with you'. When something does emerge as the result of such an isolated process, it has remarkable properties. For thanks to the newly acquired insights the conception of the material object now can be penetrated with astounding revelations. The properties of the object as a whole and the depth of its existence may now become known. If the speculations have been at a higher abstract level so that only classes of classes are related and not classes of material objects, then the result may be a new set of logical objects. It is a case of withdrawal-and-return, withdrawal from perception, and return to perception but with much enriched tools of observation. It is now possible to 'see' what formerly had been only an hypothesis with respect to what there was to be observed. It is now possible to 'see' the man reading the book.

Of course we cannot discuss the formation of concepts at this stage without reminding ourselves that they are not always veridical. Errors in concept formation are always possible and indeed often do occur. The wrong things may be put together in the hypothesis, things which actually do not have the relations the observer attributes to them. Error may be the result of the influence of feeling on the understanding, as in what is called wishful thinking. We may want so much to have certain perceptions related in a certain way that we think we see them in that way, when in fact we do not but only something similar. The man may not be reading at all but only 'daydreaming' with his eyes wide open and the book before him. These are the errors of concept formation. We shall see shortly the errors of thought, which are more advanced and sophisticated.

The analysis of conception suffers from the same faulty analysis as frequently happens to the analysis of perception. It tends to be based upon a single instance. Conception is an ongoing process with cumulative effects. The chief effect is the breadth which the concept acquires through repetition. There is in the concept more often than not a depth of meaning which can be explored only be coming at it from different perspectives. Its properties can be explored only by means of a careful study of the results of repetition. In this way philosophers often build better than they know. Accidental ambiguity is a group effort, though it can be the effort of a single investigator over a period of time. Aristotle's multiple definitions of the same term – 'substance' for instance – is a case in point. Did he intend them to refer to a subject matter which is inherently ambiguous, as in Peirce's statements about the unavoidable vagueness of generality, or was it an accident of good fortune which succeeded in penetraticn to the essence of the term? Both kinds employ analogy, intentional or otherwise, the relation of similarity between values which are carried qualitatively. And similarity in this connection, as we have noted, means an identity of parts though not of the whole.

William James thought that concepts were entirely mental and had been invented to meet a particular need.[6] I do wish that were the case, for then conditions would be whatever we conceived them to be, and

⁶ William James, *Some Problems of Philosophy* (New York, 1911, Longmans Green), Ch. IV.

beauty would replace ugliness, the good replace the bad and truth error, all by fiat. Unfortunately, the contents of concepts are no more human inventions than the contents of percepts, although there has been some disposition to recognize the difference. Concepts are classes, and classes are not human inventions. And if similarities are found between classes so that classes of classes can be identified and named, then they are not human inventions, either.

The most empirical of European philosophers have long recognized that material things have forms, everyone in fact from Plato to Locke has done so; but the acknowledgement that such forms are universals did not follow from this recognition. The object, in Locke's hands, became merely a skeletal set of local forms, with no universality and no qualities of its own, only those it was able to borrow temporarily from the perceiving subject. Locke never was able to explain why the qualities fitted the forms so well when those qualities were supposed to have been contributed by the human mind.

James could not get over the impoverishment of the abstract in comparison with the "thickness" of the concrete. Abstractions, he thought, are thin; they come from a rich experience and they go back into service with that experience; but they have no standing in and for themselves. He was incapable evidently of seeing that the richness of the field of mathematics is another kind of richness, and that, while concepts in that world may in a certain sense stand by themselves, they have myriads of connections which twine and intertwine in such a complex way as to make for another kind of thick texture. The knowledge of that abstract world gives us glimpses of it only, enough however to tell us that there is more to it than we know. Bergson was fond of pointing out that the material world is far richer than any of our limited schemes to encompass it. In a similar way, though for an entirely different reason, it is true that the domain of abstract objects also, which was such an obsession with Plato that he could not admit the reality of any other, is richer than our limited schemes.

Epistemology suffers badly from the 'either/or' error. Dewey was convinced for instance that concepts are not independent and fixed essences of the universe but rather means of facilitating and executing all kinds of social transactions.[7] He did not think they could be both. He opted of course for the social transaction theory. There is no doubt about the latter, but in what way would that impugn the validity of

---

[7] John Dewey, *The Quest for Certainty* (New York, 1929, Minton Balch).

the former? Dewey confused the knowledge of concepts with the concepts themselves.

The knowledge of concepts might sometimes – though certainly not always – have its origin in practical situations and prove to be, in a backward look, synonymous with a corresponding set of operations, as Bridgman had insisted, though it is difficult to see how the concepts themselves are eternally bound to the operations. For one thing, the operations are always particular while the concepts are always general. Moreover, similar situations far removed from each other in time and space often fall under the same concept. We operate in terms of particulars and think in terms of generals, and miraculously our thoughts so correspond to our operations that the operations themselves are facilitated. Often the concepts we employ to control operations are standing concepts, much older than the operations themselves. Conic sections were discovered 3700 years before they were first employed in bridge building.

The Dewey-Bridgman kind of thinking has as its aim the admirable one expressed in Occam's dictum: no more entities than are necessary. If possible, universals are to be held down to the cognitive activity of an organism in its efforts to grapple with its natural environment. An admirable aim but a false one. For it happens to be the case that no number of particulars exhausts a universal. Language is incurably general while activity is irrefrangibly particular, so that the latter does not entirely account for the former. Universals seem to have a permanence about them, and a capacity for recurrence, which is not shared by particulars. The roundness of round pennies recurs in a way in which the pennies themselves do not. There seems to be no way to avoid the postulation of a second universe, though, and since it is logical yet we learn about it from the material universe, we are entitled to name it the logical universe and consider it a second story.

Dewey's "instrumentalism" paradoxically cannot explain the concepts which arise from the use of instruments. It is a misnomer for the doctrine that common sense and ordinary experience can account for any concepts which may arise provided they are used in connection with the solving of problems. This theory holds instrumentalism down to the unaided senses, and cannot account for the kind of scientific knowledge which is acquired by means of exceedingly complex instruments. For no one can attribute to the instruments the knowledge acquired thereby. Are the concepts of astronomy, such as background radiation, interstellar gas, and the red shift, functions of the various kinds of optical and radio telescopes employed in detecting them? Given the enormous disparity in their comparative ages, it would seem not.

VII. JUDGMENT

Decision-making, or what I have chosen to call by a more old-fashioned name, judgment, proceeds in much the same way as concept formation, only connecting wider and more inclusive objects both material and logical. To call on our example again, we are dealing not with a man reading a book now, but instead with one acquiring abstract knowledge: and not with a man merely but with a scholar, say, one having a considerable amount both of experience and equipment, and not with a book merely, but with one in which many abstract ideas are expressed, and with reading now as making a connection between two sets of highly complex material objects in which many logical objects are involved and therefore a function more complex still. The man's thoughts may be such as Chomsky has described them in his generative grammar, and the man's equipment might include such a sufficient knowledge of grammar as to enable him to formulate acceptable sentences conveying judgments on his reading; but the man himself would hardly know that.

Simple judgment consists in the recognition of the results of perception. Complex judgment – what is usually meant by judgment and what will be meant by it here – consists in the evaluation of the data, a further stage in the mental proceedings. Every judgment about the external world is an effort to reach some kind of belief about it, and so *mutatis mutandis* for judgments about logical objects. Every mental act, the recognition of a sense impression or of a thought, is performed in support of such a judgment. There is no experience of the underived, but everything that we know follows from axioms of some sort; and this is no less true for our not knowing about the axioms.

The idealists would have us suppose that judgments are always about what is real, and the linguistic philosophers insist that they always involve language. Bradley wanted us to believe that every judgment has reality as its topic,[8] but even Bradley had to admit that there is such a thing as prelinguistic judgments.[9] As to reality, this is to

---

[8] Cf. *The Principles of Logic* (London, 1883, reprinted New York, 1920, G. E. Stechert); *Appearance and Reality* (Oxford, 1930, Clarendon Press); *Essays on Truth and Reality* (Oxford, 1914, Clarendon Press).
[9] *The Principles of Logic*, vol. I, p. 32.

ascribe too lofty a function to all judgments. Most of them are more pedestrian, judgments concerning the choice of ice-cream or of which tie blends with which shirt, for example. Intuitive or insightful judgments are sudden and arrived at without the use of signs. They could and sometimes do occur in this way, but not always, and that is all we have to claim.

It is often forgotten that the bare logical bones of the process of judgment do not give the whole picture. All sorts of other considerations often influence it. Excited emotional states, predispositions, previously acquired prejudices, irrationalisms of these and other sorts often enter into the making of a judgment. An insight, an intuition, a previously adopted axiom, might as easily as not turn the judgment in this or that direction. Often the data are not available to check the judgment, and so it stands as accurate or inaccurate.

One of the commonest sources of erroneous judgments is the result of falling into a disjunctive trap. Judgments reached by denying the existence of other sources when the two alternatives have not first been proved exhaustive, and when for that matter they may not be, is often a fallacious method. 'My friend is not at home and so he must have gone away', is false when the third alternative prevails: he was only in his garden. The law of excluded middle applies absolutely only in the logical domain, not in the material world.

Another common error in judgment is a more sophisticated one. A judgment is reached which looks as though it had been the conclusion of an argument. The steps of a syllogism may have demanded it, and yet they may not have been taken and it may be false to fact. 'All blondes are promiscuous; Susan is a blonde; therefore Susan is promiscuous' might be given as the evidence for the conclusion as a judgment. The argument itself is perfectly valid, though only the minor premise is true, and Susan may appear the victim of a very logical judgment. But judgments are not often reached in this way. The judgment 'Susan is promiscuous' is usually reached *instanter* and as a result of processes that could not be described even afterwards by the individual making the judgment. A judgment is the conclusion of a syllogism reached by one who did not argue from the premises yet could not claim either that it was an intuition or an induction. It was not; it was a judgment.

The process of judgment is one of decision making, but on the basis of what criteria are judgments made? What is reasonable? Many of the scientific findings which rely so heavily upon the use of reason still seem unreasonable. Reason is only partly logical; another part seems based on common sense. But logic may be incorrectly used and common sense can err.

Behind every ideal judgment there stands a rather complex and flexible mechanism. What we 'feel' is right in most instances was not arrived at by feeling. There are unconscious rational processes which are reliable, even though our introduction to their existence came from the theory of psychopathology advanced by Freud. From the fundamental beliefs we hold without recognizing them, or without holding them in consciousness all the time, we make many deductions, some of which lead to further thought while others are followed into action.

Reliance on reason is an instinct, but it is one more cultivated in some cultures than in others. Reasoning has been a matter of consistency with a set of axioms which are held unconsciously as beliefs. The so-called rational individual accepts his axiom set absolutely, and, because his deductions from it are validly derived, regards himself as proceeding reasonably. Yet practice never constructs proofs; the axiom set may be incomplete and as a result inadequate, and the deductions may be false to fact. Thus a methodologically functioning interim doubt is part of the equipment of any one who considers himself rational. He must remain prepared to add to or substract from his assumptions if the actions proceeding from his logical conclusions are not to prove disastrous. Not to be able to doubt means not to be able to think clearly.

VIII. THOUGHT

Definitions are rough affairs only when we are dealing with events, but distinctions are still needed, as for instance to make clear the relation between 'judgment' and 'thought'. A judgment is a single proposition arrived at for whatever reason. A thought is a relating of propositions.

Sometimes it is impossible to tell by inspection whether the conclusion of a syllogism was arrived at as a matter of judgment or of thought, in the senses accepted above. I have shown in the previous section how the conclusion of a syllogism might be classified as a judgment. Here I must show how a conclusion might be better classified as an argument. Some preliminary explanations will first have to be introduced, however.

Thought is a mental event, which is to say, a high-level variety of bodily skilled behavior, and it takes place in terms of images or signs, according as the elements of the material world or of the logical domain are in view. If they are from the material world, in the first instance images remembered are removed from their original context and related by means of resemblances. If they are from the logical domain, then sign-relations are shown abstractly.

It is possible to relate images in accordance with the laws of the syllogism. Let us suppose that I have in my mind the image of a man; he would be for me a sort of abstracted American male, say in a conventional gray business suit and shirt with a four-in-hand tie and brown shoes. I will for convenience of the printer not draw a picture but imagine one whenever I see the words, GREY SUIT. Let us now say that I have in mind also the picture of a Frenchman, one taken from a vaudeville parody, a man with a waxed moustache, wearing spats and a bow tie, somewhat short and stocky. I will call his picture FRENCH. I need one more picture, that of a dead man in a coffin. I will call his picture, COFFIN. Now, employing *these pictures only* and *not the words*, I formulate the following argument.

> All GREY SUIT are COFFIN,
> All FRENCH are GREY SUIT,
> Therefore all FRENCH are COFFIN.

We are all more accustomed to the logical formulation, which provides the same argument but this time in *words*, which are, after all, signs:

> All men are mortal,
> All Frenchmen are men,
> All Frenchmen are mortal.

or, more abstract still,

> All M is P,
> All S is M,
> All S is P.

an argument which symbolic logic abstracts still more, thus,

$$m p = O$$
$$s m = O$$
$$s p = O$$

We have seen in this progression of syllogistic reasonings how images give way to signs, thus losing in the vividity which has nothing to do with logical relationships but gaining in abstractedness which has, a lesson in what Whitehead called "extensive abstraction," in the movement from the material world to the logical domain. That is what has been named deductive reasoning, or thought. But there is another and more elusive type which has also been recognized and named: inductive reasoning or intuitive thought.

What has not been noted as clearly is that the two directions of reasoning employ the same rungs of the ladder, and it is simply a business of coming down the ladder from general premises to less general conclusion (deduction) or going up the ladder from the less general to the more general. In the former exercise no steps are skipped and so the process can be followed very closely, but in the latter steps *are* skipped, often very many, and so the process is difficult if not impossible to follow.

What is suggested is that there is a vast and complex lattice of relationships, and reasonings run down or up on them without disturbing their essential being. The logical lattice exists (Meinong would have said "subsists") and reasoning runs around on it. Thus the distinction between abstract thought and what abstract thought is about is preserved.

The point is best made by reminding ourselves that arguments can be carried out by mechanical means, using for instance the truth tables of logic or the laws of arithmetic. Thought would have to include induction as well as deduction, and it would have to include those unconscious ratiocinations which have proved so valuable in the life work of men of orginative genius. An intuition is not a judgment but a piece of instantaneous reasoning which relies upon the existence of a deductive structure.

As for unconscious thought, perhaps I could say a bit more about it because it has been so misunderstood thanks to the influence of the Freudians. The discovery of the unconscious and the study of its effects on the life of the individual have largely been conducted in connection with a theory of psychopathology. Mental illness has furnished the motive, and psychoanalysis has provided the technique of therapy. This has been mostly to the good, but it does not exhaust the functioning of the unconscious. Not all unconscious thoughts rest on false premises, nor do they all lead to such disastrous consequences as they do in neurotics and psychotics, because not all unconscious thoughts are pathological and erroneous. There are more often than not unconscious thoughts which proceed correctly from true premises to true conclusions, as evidenced in the reports of productive mathematicians and experimental scientists who have declared that so much of their important work, so many of their most brilliant insights, were arrived at unconsciously, for instance either when they were engaged in some trivial manual exercise which they had learned long since and practiced continually, or when they were asleep.

It comes to this, then: thought may be conscious and deliberate or unconscious; and unconscious thought may be either pathological or rational.

Unconscious thought tends to be inductive. Conscious thought tends to be deductive and is by far the most complicated. It can consist in long chains of deductions, as in mathematical reasoning, and now it can rely upon instruments, such as the computer, which operated mechanically at the behest of some conscious thinker who deliberately programs it to produce the answer he seeks, all a quite deliberate and rational process.

The final distinction between judgment and thought is one between the practical and the theoretical or between the concrete and the abstract. Judgments are apt to be practical and concrete, made in terms of material objects. Thought is apt to be theoretical and abstract and made in terms of logical objects. There can be little doubt that Plato and Aristotle were right when they proclaimed abstract thought to be the highest of human functions, and man thinking abstractly to be man at his highest.

It is about here of course that one encounters all the mysticism which gets foisted onto the capacity for abstract thought. For Hegel it was spirit, and spirit has meant some very odd things in its day. The tendency of materialists is to dismiss it, but I would argue that it has a legitimate place provided that we understand somewhat more didactically than usual what is meant by it. The rejection of spirit was based upon an ancient materialism which held sway from Leucippus to Feuerbach but which is obsolete now. To supplant it there has come a new materialism which was the logical issue of the new physics. In that new version of materialism spirit could be a property of matter, and could within that context be defined as "the dominant inner quality of a material thing."[10] There is little doubt that in its highest reaches abstract thought touches upon something else, just as theoretical physics and the fine arts do in their respective ways. But that lies beyond the province of epistemology and so we shall leave it here and return to the role played by thought in the assimilation of knowledge.

IX. VERIFICATION

Verification (or falsification) is a more sophisticated version of judgment, one involving some sort of overt activity and therefore intended to refer primarily, if not exclusively to the material world. It is often

[10] James K. Feibleman, *The New Materialism* (The Hague, 1970, Martinus Nijhoff), p. 14.

necessary to make an investigation of the correspondence (or lack of correspondence) between a proposition (at this stage called an 'hypothesis') and the relevant facts before pronouncing it true or false. Such an investigation could consist in careful observations but it is more likely to involve experiments conducted with instruments.

To verify an hypothesis is not to prove it true but only to support its claim to truth. There is no such thing as an absolute empirical proof, only a measure of statistical support. Thus 'verification' always means verification to some degree of probability less than 1. Falsification, on the other hand, is stronger. Simple logic bears this out. A single affirmative particular will not strongly verify a proposition, but a single negative particular will falsify it. Absolute proofs are reserved for the domain of logic and mathematics.

It should not be necessary to add that verification and falsification are kinds of reference, not of meaning. What a proposition means and what it refers to are quite distinct, as Frege was at such pains to point out. In the sentence 'The moon is made of Danish blue cheese' we know exactly what is meant because we have experienced the moon and Danish blue separately. We have also seen things 'made out of' other things, like toy castles made out of sand. No question about the meaning, then, but the reference is something different. Experience, and particularly the experience of those astronauts who have walked on the moon and returned with samples of the material taken from its surface, can tell us that the moon is not made of Danish blue cheese. The sentence in question, then, has meaning but no reference. 'The surface of the moon contains rocks' has both meaning and reference, and moreover they are identical.

What Wittgenstein tried to do in his *Philosophical Investigations* is to show us how to discover and eliminate the discrepancy between meaning and reference (though this may be a charitable view and he may have intended meaning exclusively). But he leaned over backward and seems to have got himself so involved with meaning that he rarely got to consider reference at all. Yet reference must in the end govern; meaning is valid only when it corresponds to reference. I am speaking of course of the material domain, not of the logico-mathematical domain where meaning is chiefly pursued and the reference if any forgotten.

One of the things that thinkers in a nominalistic age are apt to forget, or if they know about it disbelieve, is that abstract ideas also have a reference. That thoughts, such as those about the structure of the real number system, are concerned with something which is not material yet is part of an abstract logical domain outside the mind, is a proposition which is hard to accept, yet accept it we must if all of the data are to be taken into the account. This is an ontological axiom in the realistic philosophy, and the alternatives to it are not sufficiently explanatory. Religious Platonists have earned the theory of Ideas (since that is what it is) a bad name among empiricists, yet scientists, and especially physicists, are implicitly committed to it in their processes of investigation.

X. BELIEF

Conception, as we have already noted, puts objects together. Similarly, as we have just seen, judgment puts concepts together. And now we will study how beliefs put judgments in storage for later use by adding the preservative of feelings of conviction.

By 'belief' is meant the feeling that a judgment (or proposition) is true. Belief starts with perception; the observer believes that what he perceives is in fact there. More complexly, belief is the name for the more or less permanent impact of a value. Beliefs function as condition-ed responses to stimuli, and have nothing to do with truth. All beliefs are held by the believer to be true, but since all sorts of things are believed in this and other cultures by individuals who do or do not conform to the fundamental beliefs of the culture, it follows that many beliefs must be false. That is to say, they are true as beliefs but false as contents: what is believed to be true is in fact not true. Thus doubt is the security of the thinking man, just as faith is that of the unthink-ing. Ignorance is not the absence of truth but the presence of beliefs with false contents.[11]

Beliefs are hard to come by and can be given up only for reasons, reasons to doubt as well as reasons to believe. The tracing of beliefs back to their points of origin is insufficient to account for the beliefs. The fallacy of reduction must not be allowed to cancel the gains in knowledge made by the individual as he senses, thinks and acts in terms of the knowledge he has slowly accumulated. Put otherwise, in the descriptions made so fashionable in the early twentieth century, true and general propositions about the material world which have been induced from collected experiences cannot be reduced to protocol

---

[11] Aristotle, *Anal. Post*, 79b23.

statements endeavoring to put into language our most primitive and uninterpreted elementary experiences. The starting material contains suggestions of beliefs but not the sum of beliefs; hints as to the qualitative character of the world but not a description of what is known about it. The logical positivists acting in terms of language, as Wittgenstein had taught them to do, sought to put the chicken back into the egg, the tree of knowledge back into the acorn. Most assuredly that will not work.

Belief, said Hume, is "a more vivid and intense conception of an idea, proceeding from its relation to a present impression."[12] He thought, in other words, that beliefs are conscious only. Kant knew better, for he held that there are unconscious beliefs, though it is true that he did not make much of the discovery.[13] Unconscious beliefs comprise the majority of beliefs, for we seem able to hold in consciousness only one belief at a time, whereas thanks to memory we have many beliefs available to recall. Indeed the most tenaciously held beliefs, those which have effected the greatest penetration of the person, begin to approach in feeling the essence of the subject.

The collection of individual beliefs, both those which are conscious and those which are unconscious, are arranged in the mind as schemata. As we have already noted, there are two sets of schemata: those beliefs which are held in common with the other members of a culture, the public retention schema; and those beliefs which are peculiar to the individual, the private retention schema. All alterations which take place in the schemata come under the heading of adaptations. The public retention schema is altered in what the geneticists call 'genotypic modification'. The private retention schema is altered as an act of deliberate belief. They were arranged in order by courtesy of an anterior belief, the belief in reason, which follows from the conviction that if certain logical rules are followed in relating propositions already held, the result will be a set of valid propositions from which the others follow by necessity. That the retention schemata constitute a consistent body of knowledge is the kernel of truth in idealism, and the idealists should be given full credit for their intensive study of its properties.

Belief, James held, is at the mercy of the will.[14] It is possible to will to believe, and indeed he thought that this power has often been used

[12] Hume, *Treatise of Human Nature*, Part III, Section VIII.
[13] Kant, *Critique of Pure Reason*, A 78; A 141.
[14] William James, *The Will to Believe and Other Essays in Popular Philosophy* (New York, 1896, Longmans Green and Co.).

in the service of the good. He cited the example of the belief in God, which helped to bring into the world the divine characters of justice and kindness. This is a highly prejudiced view. Surely even if James was right it is true that the belief in God has brought into the world more war than kindness. Wars of religion have proved to be of the most ferocious sort, and few if any are the religions which have not been responsible for them.

Since Peirce replied to James on the issue of belief by showing that belief, like doubt, was not at the mercy of the will but to the contrary relied upon evidence, that in fact one can no more will to believe against the evidence than one could will to doubt in the same way, it has not been necessary to refute again James' theory of belief.[15] With the best will in the world it is still true that things are as they are and assert themselves in the end to correct those beliefs which go against them for voluntary purposes.

There are levels of belief, arranged in accordance with degree of conviction. At the top, and nearest to consciousness, float those wisps of belief, those evanescent fancies, which hover momentarily, held in the slightest mental grasp. At the bottom and difficult of access lie those unconscious fundamental beliefs concerning the nature of things, metaphysical beliefs, which the individual could part with no more easily than he could part with a vital organ. In between these extremes are to be found beliefs of various strengths, of diverse degrees of conviction. The top beliefs are quite easily changed for others and frequently do get changed; the bottom beliefs are changed, too, though more rarely and only when accompanied by considerable adjustments and dislocations. An individual might believe quite sincerely in the honesty of a political candidate and not be surprised too much when the evidence led him to 'change his mind'. On the other hand, he might believe profoundly in the truth of Kant's philosophy to such an extent that when presented with overwhelming evidence to the contrary almost his entire personality and life style might be involved.

James saw clearly that beliefs lead to actions. There are of course random actions which are not dictated by anything more than the needs of the musculature. But most actions are not of this character, they are more deliberate. We act as a rule either from conscious beliefs, as when we endeavor to carry out a preconceived program, or from

---

[15] *Collected Papers of Charles S. Peirce*, 5.265.

unconscious beliefs, when the hookup between deep-seated beliefs and impulsive actions is routed around consciousness; instinctive actions, we call them.

A conceptual scheme involves a standpoint. It is to Kant's credit that he was the first to point this out so graphically. But he took up the position of the believer. If instead we were to look from the position of the conceptual scheme, we should see that the believer is only a temporary convenience, without the staying power possessed by the scheme itself which later believers will accept. The knower takes his stand on the object, not on the subject. As noted earlier, if he were to take his stand on the subject it would involve a double subjectivity. We need to know the logical generality and empirical support which exists for the scheme, and for this purpose we can dispense with the believer. Belief will have to become more flexible; it will have to become a habit that inadequate schemes, however operative, are discarded and others brought in to replace them. For the sum of the conceptual schemes has a tensor character which if properly reinforced could become the basis for a standpointlessness. This at least ought to be the aim of all belief, though as an ideal it must remain forever somewhat removed.

The limitations of various philosophical positions are what cripple and distort them. Could they be more inclusive they might become more affirmative; but the limitations stand in the way. It is because of not undertaking any position whatsoever that the philosopher subscribing to standpointlessness would be able to abstract from all limitations.

CHAPTER IV

THE DEPLOYMENT OF KNOWLEDGE

In the last two chapters, beginning with the topic of the preconditions which make perceptions possible, and ending with that of belief, I have been giving my version of the successive steps of the cycle of adaptive knowing. The description of that cycle will not be complete, of course, until we have put the last bricks in place. This will involve a description of the condition of knowledge and how it is used for understanding and control, ending with the conative function and with overt behavior.

I. THE CONDITION OF KNOWLEDGE

It is one thing to acquire knowledge and to become familiar with its interrelations and quite another to learn how to bring it to bear upon problems of a theoretical as well as practical nature. A system of ideas is not only a system of explanation but also an instrument of application. The knowledge that was sought because it aided understanding can be turned to the governance of the immediate environment.

The knowledge that we acquire, assimilate and deploy is purportedly a picture of reality, a representation of what the world is like. I define 'reality' in this epistemological connection as 'the immediate knowledge of that which is true', and truth as the property of those propositions which correspond to the facts. More precisely, truth is what describes, or refers to, either a concrete or an abstract state of affairs. That is what is meant by truth in the grand sense, truth with all of the falsity eliminated. I shall employ the term 'cognitive truth' for that which we hold to be true: for so-called knowledge. We do know what we think we know, but what we think we know may not be true. Indeed knowledge as such is usually a mixture of the true and the false where it is not false altogether. Astrology and alchemy contain little if any truth, yet they have been in their time considered the precious possession of the knowledge of many people. The propositions are what constitute knowledge.

The condition of knowledge, then, is that of a set of propositions stored in the unconscious, or memory, and made available when needed for applications. It is held there by convictions of various strengths in proportion to the degree accorded to the belief in its truth. The storage process has rules of its own. The knowledge itself is kept in two ways: as pictures and as non-pictorial signs. Pictures of course are also signs. Since I have discussed them already as images in chapter III, it will not be necessary to dwell on them here except to emphasize that they are signs, too. Pictures are signs because while they resemble the thing signified they are not identical with it but are to some extent abstracted from it; which means in effect that some features are retained but not all. Not only are they abstracted but also they have been selected; not all experiences are retained as images, only some and those the more significant to the individual.

We do not often think of pictures or of images as stored knowledge though of course that is what it is. The memory of a friend's face serves as a guide to path finding. The situation is quite different with non-pictorial signs, for now we are dealing with language, which puts signs together in order to add to meaning. Language consists entirely in signs, and while some individuals know many of the signs in a language, nobody knows them all, which means that a language is the common possession of a people and not the exclusive property of any one person.

It has not been sufficiently recognized that knowledge, at least in amount and kind, and not merely in the fact that there *is* knowledge, is culturally conditioned. What passes for knowledge in the United States in 1973, say, would not be the same as what passes for knowledge in Afghanistan on the same date, or what did pass for knowledge in Paris in 1500. The unit is the community which is adapted to its surroundings through its possession of a certain body of knowledge. But, as with biological evolution, the maintenance of the community can be guaranteed only by the addition of new knowledge, by ensuring the continuance of adaptation. As the material and cultural conditions of the environment change, so must the culture; if it is to survive it must keep pace with them.

The two principal manifestations of culture are: artifacts and languages. Artifacts may be defined as material objects which have been altered by human agency for human uses, anything material in a culture, in other words. It has not been sufficiently recognized that in this sense language also is an artifact. It employs signs in two ways: as modifications of sound waves and as scratches on hard surfaces. The signs themselves either directly or indirectly refer to other material objects. Cultures are stored in many ways, then: in collections of artifacts, anything from buildings to libraries and their contents, and in languages. As knowledge in the mind of man, it is languages with which we shall here be chiefly concerned.

Since languages are sign systems, it might be well here to say what signs are. Signs are material objects which in some established way point to other material objects or to other signs. All signs eventually have a material reference, but some refer more directly than others. Most words have a reference which lies outside language but some do refer only to other language: 'horse' and 'verb' for example. A nod of the head can be a sign and so can a drawing of a pointing hand. The material object which carries the sign is not the sign, but there is no sign not conveyed by a material object. The sign itself is the pointing. Signs point to other signs in mathematics for instance, as when 'i' means '$\sqrt{-1}$'.

Colloquial (as distinguished from artificial) languages are composed of words which function not as signs but as symbols. They are almost never without connotations which indicate the presence of qualities. A symbol is a sign whose leading edge is a quality. Most signs which have been in use for a long time have acquired the qualities which render them symbols. Artificial languages, by contrast, are mere systems of signs. Computer language, for instance, or esperanto, has not had the years of usage which enables a language to transpose signs into symbols.

Knowledge is communicated and even discovered as well as stored by means of signs. These are among the functions of languages. No one can say from our limited fund of information just how the 'natural' or colloquial languages were first invented. This applies to the rules of grammar and syntax as well as to their vast vocabulary which no one individual knows completely. Language is one of the unknowns presently under sharp investigation. Here we are concerned mainly with its connection with knowledge. And knowledge is information stored in the unconscious (or memory) by means of signs; either, as we have noted, in pictures or in language. The discovery of language marked a great advance, for so much can be stored in signs, which are shorthand methods of dealing with information.

The knowledge process, then, is able to refer beyond itself through the use of signs or symbols. The universal nature of most language injects into all descriptions of experience a self-transcending element which must be reckoned with in all studies of knowledge theory. So long as it remains impossible to describe the experience of sensible particulars without the use of universals, this much must remain true.

Here we take knowledge to be a natural fact and we do not seek the information concerning how it first started up in man. For one thing, the data are lacking, and there is the necessity to proceed without them by pursuing another line of investigation. And so we shall consider all knowledge as acquired through experience.

In terms of the prehistoric development of man as having had origins beyond the animal species and back to a time when there was a planet earth but no life, the old and time-honored distinction between 'innate' and 'acquired' knowledge has no meaning at all. What is now innate could well have been acquired at some early stage, perhaps even before man was differentiated as a species from other humanoid types, or back still further before humanoid types were distinguished from the other primates. I have in mind such 'knowledge' as space perception. The ability to locate objects in space, to judge distance and to determine relative size, was developed perhaps somewhere along that early set of stages, so that the inheritance of acquired characters could occur allowing for millions of years, not in terms of knowledge which is handed down but in terms of adaptive structures which were developed to meet the newly acquired means of locomotion.

Knowledge as such is the name for both a process and a structure, it is knowledge as a process that has been mostly considered in the foregoing pages. The process of knowledge is best described as a stage process, with acquisition, interpretation, storage and applications as the stages. The structure is something else; for here we must take leave for a moment of the cognitive subject and confine our attention to what it is that he comes to know. It can be described in two varieties; there are sensed particulars and there are observed similarities. The sensed particulars are tied to date and place and they do not recur. The observed similarities are general in nature and they do recur. Together they constitute a two-layered field which for the purposes here may be described as the knowable. The two layers may be found at every empirical level, as noted in the first section of Chapter II above. For instance, there are both sensed particulars and observed similarities which are purely physical, purely chemical, purely biological, etc. Knowledge comes out of this dual field, and the organism of the knower responds to it. He is dependent upon it because while he can change the sensed particulars he cannot change the observed regularities and he must cope with both, which is what his knowledge puts him in the way of being able to do. The structure of the world would be the same whether he came to know something about it or not, and he would be dependent upon it in the same way in both cases.

The human organism, like all others, is an unstable system which can maintain itself only through a continual interchange with its environment. It must find the materials to reduce its organic needs in its immediate neighborhood, and, for this, action is necessary. The human individual is possessed of a large store of possible reactions to stimuli. Most of those he makes are in the interest of self-maintenance but not all. He does not always act in terms of his beliefs as these are held in common with his fellows. Some may be private, and these may even be pathological, in which case his actions are not in the interest of continued self-maintenance but the reverse: they may lead to his destruction. It is so in the case of criminal activities. But we are concerned in this work chiefly with the average of ordinary behavior.

There would be no action, and hence no need-reduction if there were no knowledge. The human individual must know not only what he needs but also how and where to set about getting it. His needs in this sense fall into two broad divisions. He needs to know, and he needs to satisfy his more material wants. The first we shall examine under the heading of knowledge for its own sake, though it is an organ-specific need of the brain, and the second under the heading of knowledge for the sake of manipulating the environment in order to alter it for human uses. More common names would be *theoretical knowledge* and *practical knowledge* respectively. I propose to examine these two kinds of knowledge in the following two sections.

II. KNOWLEDGE FOR UNDERSTANDING

There are two reasons for acquiring knowledge. The first is that we have an organic need for understanding the world about us; the second is that we have an equally organic but larger need for its control. The acquisition of knowledge for purposes of understanding is in a way the most far-reaching need. It comes to be a great thing when we remember that most of the cosmic universe lies hopelessly beyond our control. Indeed the very idea that we might control segments of the immediate environment is new. The distant galaxies as well as most of our own

Galaxy can surely never be controlled by us. It remains for us then only to gain knowledge, and this must suffice.

Put succinctly, our understanding of the universe as a whole, with everything that we know about its parts somehow fitted into the explanation, must amount to a system of reality, which is to say, a metaphysics. Epistemology serves in this connection to police the method of its acquisition. The process of knowledge is an area in which we can submit to examination the technique whereby all our knowledge is acquired, to be sure that such knowledge is as authentic as we can hope to make it by a process of selection, of acceptance or rejection.

Newly acquired knowledge has to be fitted in as a belief among other beliefs. It has to be organized into propositions which have then to be arranged in an order. For want of a better term we may characterize the order as a system of reality.

The system of reality is not a simple affair. For example, as I have hinted earlier, it is subdivided into a public schema and a private schema. The public schema – what I have earlier described as the 'public retention schema' – is what a believer holds in common with the greater number of his fellows in his particular culture.[1] Woven into this as best it can be done is another schema, the 'private retention schema', which is composed of those of his beliefs which were independently arrived at and are not among the received beliefs of his fellows. The two together comprise the retention schemata made up of his beliefs as they stand together in some sort of system. In that earlier work I was concerned with the retention schemata as dispositional states looked at from the nature of their apprehension. Here I wish to consider them as they are faced forward rather than backward and in the direction of their overt effects.

Before discussing how the retention schemata are held it might be best to review briefly how they are acquired. The brain may be a blank slate at birth, as Locke affirmed, but that description applies only to its contents, not to its form. For it seems to contain an inherent capacity for acquiring knowledge even if no knowledge comes with it ready made. I go along with Locke in the theory that all knowledge is a product of experience. Given a brain with the capacity for knowing, and experience to teach the young animal what to know, the rest follows.

At first no contradictory knowledge is acquired, the pieces are so

---

[1] James K. Feibleman, *Biosocial Factors in Mental Illness* (Springfield, Ill., 1962, Charles C. Thomas), pp. 41, 70, 80, 86–7.

few and so random that the need to put them together comes only after the pieces are too many to contain in any other way. Order is a requirement of storage; it is so much easier to remember things if they can be connected in some way. Now difference is a kind of connection but it is a monotonous connection and leads nowhere, whereas similarity is a useful one and less limited. When the similarity becomes widespread it soon develops that some common assumptions are also present, and so the dim outlines of a system begin to appear. I submit that this happens before there is any explicit awareness of it. The role of consciousness in thinking has been over-played, for although deliberate thought is conscious, the rational processes such as I have been describing are not. Only their conclusions show above the surface where they issue first in explanation and only later in the guidance of action.

Full-blown philosophies, then, occur to the human individual only slowly and almost altogether without his being aware of their nature. The low estate of philosophy currently is based on ignorance of this development. It is impossible for an individual to live and function in the world without his possession of a system of knowledge which can best be described as a philosophy, even though the special language needed to describe it has not yet been acquired by him and in most cases never is.

Bartlett has made the point that most people think in terms of closed systems[2] (my 'retention schemata'). This is true of those who live within established religious or political systems, for example. Only a few are able to struggle outside them sufficiently long to permit the enlarging or revising of the system. Those who are able to do so are engaging in adventurous thinking. Of course to some extent the schemata are open systems, however minimal the openness might be. Some knowledge always does enter or leave the schemata. However stable the systems, new ideas do to some extent become accepted as beliefs, and old beliefs become eroded by wearing against the rough edges of experience.

That is the situation in brief, but there are current theories hitting all around it which I would yet describe as somewhat short of the mark. Noam Chomsky has a theory of how philosophies come about and Claude Lévi-Strauss has a theory of what they are. The name generally adopted for this school is 'structuralism'. We might with profit look at both versions briefly.

[2] F. Bartlett, *Thinking: An Experimental and Social Study* (London, 1964, Unwin University Books).

For Chomsky there is inherent in the mind an innate structuring capacity for languages, that in other words something like the natural or colloquial languages is present at birth, that there is in other words deep in the mind a generative grammar. Knowledge is not acquired through experience based on observations of the external world but instead man imposes his own rational order upon it.

For Lévi-Strauss the myths of primitive peoples constitute a kind of alphabet of beliefs, and to abstract it is in effect to discover the most profound workings of the human mind. The relationships between these myths constitute the elements of a symbolic language by means of which primitive man communicates his fundamental philosophy which includes a theory of culture and how it fits into nature in general. The language is a closed system, it is regulated by law, and it corresponds to the structure of the mind itself.

A little analysis will disclose that structuralism at present can claim only the status of an hypothesis. It may be as Chomsky and Lévi-Strauss say but they have not proved it nor even given any convincing demonstration.

Chomsky's evidence consists in the fact that along with the knowledge of a natural language comes the understanding of the rules of grammar in that language sufficient to generate new sentences. But it is one thing to observe that men have such a capacity and quite another to claim that they were born with it.

Lévi-Strauss' evidence consists in the similarity of myths, but that is no fresh discovery. More than half a century ago Sir James George Frazer, in a multi-volumed work entitled *The Golden Bough*, pointed to the astonishing similarity among the myths of primitive peoples far removed from each other. But it is one thing to say that such similarities exist and quite another to claim that they constitute the form of the human mind. I see no warrant in the evidence we have at the present time for putting Frazer-like findings in the framework provided by Immanuel Kant.

Both hypotheses must await confirmation or disconfirmation, the discovery of data which will in some way verify or falsify the contentions of the structuralists. Meanwhile I should prefer to return to the less elaborate description of the orderly views of the fully adult individual as constituting what in more professional language may be called a philosophy. In the products of eastern and western civilizations, of Asian religions and western sciences I should prefer to argue that the philosophies however dimly and pervasively held they may be are yet more abstract in their character and more nearly approach what we should call a philosophy than what we should call a myth. There is in fact (I have already much earlier insisted) an implicit dominant ontology in every human culture, the outlines of which can be extracted with some patient and painstaking efforts.[3] It comprises a background of understanding against which all candidates for belief are judged and by means of which disparate facts and more limited theories are rendered rational or rejected.

There are numerous surprises and novelties encountered in experience but if they are to be retained by the individual as other than illusions they must somehow earn their reality by becoming included in the wider systems of explanation which exists in the implicit dominant ontology of the particular culture in question. The axiomatic beliefs which the implicit dominant ontology consists in allow for a large range of theorems among which the new candidates for belief may find (or not find) their appropriate places. This is how the individual with his retention schemata functions in the world in which he finds himself. The public retention schema is only another name for the implicit dominant ontology looked at from the perspective of the individual who holds it. His private retention schema is his own business and must be reckoned with in the face of the public retention schema, to be reconciled with it or not. If not, then the situation presents itself, at least to others, as pathological, and calls for systems of explanation provided by abnormal psychology and psychiatry.

III. KNOWLEDGE FOR CONTROL

When *Homo sapiens* first appeared upon the earth his efforts to survive took the form of searching his environment for materials to reduce his needs. He altered portions of the material world that lay within his reach to the extent of his knowledge. In a word, he undertook to adapt himself to the world. The only difference was that he did so by means of tools. Almost as early as there was man, it has been claimed, there were hunting weapons and skin clothing. That situation did not alter radically until some ten thousand years ago, when cities first appeared and what is now called 'civilization' came with them.

Within the last three hundred years, and chiefly within the last fifty, there has been a radical change. Almost all of the immediate material

---

[3] James K. Feibleman, *The Theory of Human Culture* (New York, 1946, Duell, Sloan and Pearce), reprinted (New York 1968, Humanities Press), *passim*.

environment has been altered by human techniques for human uses. In other words, he has largely adapted the environment to himself. There is very little now in the surroundings of *Homo sapiens* that he has not changed; so much is this true that it can now be said that he lives almost altogether in an artificial environment. The result has been a mixed bag of achievements. On the unfavorable side are the undesirable effects upon the environment and consequently upon himself: the pollution of the environment chiefly. On the favorable side is the fact that knowledge –knowledge solely for the purpose of understanding – has greatly increased. So of course has knowledge intended for control.

Man knows a great deal more than he did about the cosmic universe through applications of physics and astronomy. And he has doubled the life expectancy of the individual in all scientifically advanced countries. On the unfavorable side is the unexpected and unwanted extent to which human motivation is ambivalent, knowledge for control in conflict with itself. He has discovered the medical technique for doubling the life expectancy, as we have noted, but he has also and with equal energy increased the efficiency of weapons of war. He has gone from the tent of the shaman to the hospital of the modern doctor, as surely as he has gone from the spear to the hydrogen bomb. Knowledge for control has produced no governance of motivation.

The relationship between knowledge for understanding and knowledge for control is not entirely separate and distinct. One fades off into the other. Not so long ago Charles S. Peirce characterized a belief as that upon which a man is prepared to act. The understanding of the world leads inevitably by a logical series of steps to the efforts to change the world. If it concerns the beliefs themselves then it amounts to control over theory, but if it concerns the material world then it amounts to control over practice. Axiomatic beliefs lead to theorematic actions. Precipitate actions often are directly connected with deep-lying beliefs to which they cannot so easily be traced, and that is why they seem irrational when in point of fact they are not.

Knowledge acquired for the sheer purpose of understanding still leads to practical efforts at control, and it is true also that practical efforts at control often lead to an increase in understanding. That is in fact how adaptive knowing operates, for the lessons of experience have been recognized. The public retention schema, which the individual seeks to apply in practice in the material world, resulted from his encounters with that world in the first place. What practice teaches is what the individual is confronted with, and so he finds in the midst of his struggles that he must alter his strategy considerably. On site improvements in technology are no news, they occur all the time, even though the large improvements come in other ways. They come from studies made with more detachment. It is well known that the biggest advances in the practice of medicine are not the work of the bedside physician but of the biochemist working in the isolation of his laboratory. So the antibiotics and the sulfa drugs for instance; so the prevention of poliomyelitis. It is equally well known that the biggest advances in weapons of war were not the work of professional soldiers. Neither the tank, the bombing plane nor the atomic bomb was the discovery of a military man. Applied science and technology are special fields and employ professionals.

However, I revert here to a distinction made earlier in this section, the one between truth in the strict sense and cognitive truth. It is always cognitive truth that is applied, but to the extent to which cognitive truth fails to be truth (and by definition we are not able at the time to tell by how much) the application of cognitive truth must be unsuccessful. We can only do as well as we know how to do, but we do not always know how to do as well as we think we know. That is one reason why practice may not work. Another reason is of course errors in the judgment of the nature of the problem. It may not be exactly such as it is supposed to be, and our skills in ascertaining goodness of fit between theory and practice may not be sufficiently sharp. We find ourselves in the midst of the material world of ongoing processes and interacting entities, and we presume to interfere and to change the situation in accordance with our knowledge, which may indeed be, and often is, somewhat inadequate. Cognitive truth is all that we have to go by, and if we mistake it for truth, that is understandable; and if we commit errors in action consequent upon errors in judgment, then that is understandable, too, even though understanding in such an instance does not alter the degree of gain if there is a gain or of loss if there happens instead to be a loss.

To the active man the world does not present a perfected situation but rather a series of problems and puzzles which seem to call upon him for much ingenuity and activity. He must regard them as challenges which he can draw on his intellectual resources to help him to meet. He develops as a result a strategy for getting from the deep generality of the retention schemata to the often superficial but always immediate practical problems which confront him incessantly. This strategy consists in the main of habit patterns involving attitudes and perspectives by means of which he encounters and treats the practical problems.

A challenge from the immediate environment must be met by the individual in one of the following ways. If it is too far from his liking he will if possible avoid it, and if he cannot avoid it he will fend it off. If unsuccessful in these strategies he may seek to cripple or destroy it. On the other hand, if he is attracted by it he will seek to join it if he is weak or control it if he is strong. In all of these efforts he will use such knowledge as he possesses. Whether it is to his liking or not will be determined for him by his retention schemata and the qualities associated with them. All this of course comes in a kind of instinctive reaction on his part, without any necessary knowledge of what is involved. The body operates in this way without consciousness much as it does through consciousness. Elements in the environment which cannot be sensed often have their effects on the organism nevertheless, as when for instance carbon monoxide from the exhaust of automobiles causes a man walking down a street with heavy traffic to develop a headache.

The more rational a man is the more his reason operates without his knowing. It affects his tastes and other sensory avenues in such a way as to determine his reactions, instinctively as it were. The impulses of a rational man are such as would have the accord of his reason, just as the impulses of an irrational man would run uncontrolled without them, the behavior of an average citizen of London, England, say, compared with the corresponding behavior of a native of New Guinea.

The more intelligent a man is the more he operates, consciously or unconsciously, from assumptions of an axiomatic nature. His actions are deductively-discovered theorems put into practice. This means of course that if the axioms are false his actions will be disastrous. No one makes mistakes as large as those of the highly intelligent man, for he tends to be faithful to his assumptions and to reason logically from them. A less intelligent man, equipped say with reliable feelings, would tend to be less logical, which means that he would tend to depart from consequences to which he might otherwise be committed. This is no argument of course against intelligence: the great achievements of mankind have resulted from axioms which were carried through in practice into large-scale and long planned programs. The knowledge which is exercised for the control of the immediate environment is to some that of an inherent philosophy but filtered through the habit patterns, the attitudes, and the taste preferences, of the individual while holding it deeply in his memory where it lies unrecognized but available for recall. Much of his knowledge seems remote because it has never been invoked.

What is true of the unconscious memory of the individual is equally true of the culture of which he is a member. Much knowledge remains in a culture unused, often for many decades or even centuries. There is so much more residual in cultures which its individual members have forgotten if indeed they have ever been consciously known. A safe generalization of the relation between abstract knowledge and concrete activity is that there is no useless knowledge, there is only the knowledge which has not yet been used. This was true of conic sections from their discovery in the third century B.C. to their use in engineering from the seventeenth century A.D. on. Lord Rutherford was convinced that there would be no practical applications of his splitting of the atom, and there was none for a brief time but for a brief time only. He never lived to see the vast peacetime uses of atomic energy. The more useful knowledge is, the more social it becomes. Thus scientific knowledge soon passes from the hands of those who have discovered it into the general possession of all of the members of a culture who are able to cope with its technicalities.

The process we are concerned with here lies at a more primitive level and therefore is an individual matter. I only wanted to make the point that the man who seeks through his overt activities to influence his environment does not do so entirely on his own but against the background of socially-acquired dispositional states made possible by the fundamental core of beliefs which I have called above the 'public retention schema' when it lies within the individual, and the 'implicit dominant ontology' when we see it extend over the culture to which he belongs and with influences on him of which he may remain largely unaware.

IV. THE WILL

Philosophers have written a great deal about the will. But, curiously, it is a will which is never exercised! The individual, in their accounts, wills to do things but he never does them, and so the consequences to knowledge of doing them is never considered. The will as it has been regarded in philosophy is an oddly passive affair. We are in need of a more active version.

What is true in philosophy is true also in psychology. The will as an entity has gone out of psychology ever since the behaviorism and the stimulus-response mechanism has been accepted. So few thoughts, feelings or actions are said to be voluntary that there is no place for the term. And yet there does seem to be a residue of choice which can be activated or not, and there is such a thing as resolution which is (as we say) strong – or weak-willed. I should think that the will, as a term of description of that moment of behavior when it is controlled, could be retained. No doubt this contention will require more explanation.

In the older materialism, still supported in some quarters[4] the mind is causally related to the material world through an outward act. This may serve very well as a description of how the will works but it will not do as a description of the relation of the mind to the material world. In terms of the conditions both of the evolutionary development of the species and of the development of the individual, it is the other way round: the mind is causally related to the material world not from the inside out but from the outside in. The will should be the description of a response, not of a stimulus.

Since Hegel it has been the fashion to regard action as belonging to consciousness.[5] This is pretty absurd on the face of it, since action is a kind of physical event if it is nothing else, and the prior process of deliberation does not make it any the less so. When the will is exercised consciousness is often involved of course, though not exclusively: other connections have to be activated, and it can happen that action is initiated in ways not directly attributable to the will. An individual may react instantly to a challenge, but we can hardly deny that the will was either absent or entirely in charge. The close association with the psychology of consciousness to the exclusion of other considerations crippled philosophy for more than a century. Now we should begin to recognize that the whole of the physiological organism has to be counted. An organism is a complex structure which can be brought to bear *in toto* upon the individual performance of any one of its many faculties. There is always movement.

Consider what the integrated organism has at its disposal. The human body has 206 bones and 639 muscles, many though not all at the service of the will. To the extent to which the musculature is a matter of genetic inheritance, it is fair to say that purpose is congenital. The will is instigative, it is in fact a description of the response end of the stimulus-response circuit when that end is considered (erroneously) to be acting independently and *de novo*. But before there is a decision to act and a

---

[4] D. M. Armstrong, *A Materialist Theory of the Mind*, (London, 1968, Routledge and Kegan Paul), p. 129.
[5] G. W. F. Hegel, *Phenomenology of Mind*, J. B. Baillie, trans. (New York 1931, Macmillan), pp. 420–24.

consequent exertion, there may have been a choice of stimuli made in the light of the anticipated consequences of the probable response. There is some freedom of the will so long as there are conflicting stimuli to chose from and the anticipated responses to be sorted over. The subject's initiative, his control, his 'will', consists in choosing in advance just those stimuli which he knows from past experience will produce the responses he requires.

The will, then, is the decision to exert (or not to exert) a force. It is the name for the quality of the controls which turn beliefs into corresponding actions, the collective description of the hooking together of all those mechanisms which exist somewhere between the decision to act and the action itself. Character is strength of will, whether exercised or not.

I think it is misleading to reserve the phrase 'purposive activity' to those acts which are deliberately caused. Quite obviously, planned activities are the archetypes of purposive activities. But in a certain sense all human activity is purposive and that 'certain sense' is when an end is in view. There is an end in view whenever there is integrated action. A knee jerk is not an integrated action, but an action taken suddenly, like something done in anger.

In modern psychology, motivation has come to replace the will as a term of explanation. It does not do good service as a substitute, however. Motivation describes the reasons why a subject would wish to act or try to act. In an earlier chapter I argued that most human motivation is organ-specific and occurs in terms of needs: food for the stomach, water for the tissues, sex for the gonads, information for the brain, activity for the muscles, security for the skin. But this is not the will, which presumably can trigger actions leading to the reduction of any of the needs. Both motivation in terms of need-reduction and the will are concerned with objects, with acting so as to alter them or to refrain from such action.

The freedom of the will has been played down in recent thought, although its probable decline has been based upon the determinations which the physiological mechanism displays. Freedom versus determination has been around for a long time, and the controversy these alleged opposites have engendered has been one of the more challenging. It may be, however, just one more of the many problems which vanish in the face of the empirical nature of the integrative levels of analysis.

Freedom seems to be one integrative level above determinism, mechanism one level below 'purpose'. The subject has a choice, say, between taking this step or that, and he is intensely conscious of its importance, so much so that Sartre wishes to place reality on the moment of choice. This is before the fact, however, and covers only a very small territory. After the fact and taking in a larger territory it may become obvious that what the subject did he was compelled to do by his own preceding experience. Whether it is claimed that he had a genuine choice when he made it, or that he only thought he had one when in fact he did not, resolved itself into the question of when the reading is taken.

The will of man is contrived to aid him in the reduction of his needs. I see the need for security as a need of the skin covering the whole organism, and represented for instance in primitive religions as contagious magic. The kind of security involved here is for survival but not mere immediate survival – that is taken care of by other needs – *ultimate* survival. The most important if not the most importunate of the needs is the need for ultimate survival. To achieve ultimate survival he would have to extend his control over the whole of the cosmic universe or identify himself with its cause. Now, he does have the will to do this and the necessary degree of aggression, but he does not have the strength or the staying power. And so he has fallen back upon a kind of symbolic representation of it in the institutionalized religions. What kind of knowledge the 'world' religions represent, if indeed any, is at least debatable. One thing is certain, with respect to knowledge they offer deep and serious contradictions, for they agree on very little of what they deem significant. But in any case, this final example of the will takes us beyond the bounds of our present investigations, and so I will leave it for discussion in another place.

V. ACTION

When philosophers undertake to analyze experience in the search for reliable knowledge, it is their own experience to which they address themselves. I venture to suggest that this approach may not disclose anything typical. Philosophers by and large are sedentary folk, and they do not engage in overt activities quite as much as do many other people. It would be possible to read the writings of the British empiricists and of many subsequent epistemologists and never know that any one did anything more than sit in a chair and think about what he saw, or at most take a short walk. The approach to philosophy advocated by the followers of Wittgenstein fits in very well with this sedentary method of inquiry. It may tell them a lot about the ordinary speech habits of their uninstructed fellows but if taken by itself it will not necessarily inform them about what the world is like. If I may reach back into history for a comparison, they are still refusing to look through Galileo's telescope.

The conception of knowledge theory acquired in this way is sure to be grossly misleading. To come to philosophy, for professional and layman alike, is to find oneself in the middle of the hurly burly of the busy world of affairs, chiefly as a result of the need to earn a living. Violence is in some measure so large a part of most human lives that we will have to consider it typical and ask ourselves whether it does not have some bearing on the acquisition of knowledge. The normal life of the average man is one long struggle for a living, an effort that pits his energy against existing conditions and more often than not commits him to a contest with others. Such knowledge as he can call on to aid him is acquired, assimilated and deployed in the midst of his most strenuous activities. In its extreme form aggression is either constructive (helping to build cities) or destructive (helping to burn them down), and knowledge must be acquired along the way to make such efforts a success. Thus action occupies more of a central place than we have given it credit for, and we must undertake to examine the important part it plays in coping with knowledge.

I will pass by the special case of scientific method where the laboratory procedures of experiment and control disclose sources of knowledge not hitherto even suspected to exist. Experimental science makes out a strong argument for the acquisition of knowledge through action, but I have discussed it at length elsewhere. Here I should prefer to follow the traditional practise of deriving knowledge from common experience. Action has been neglected in that tradition, despite the many well-known aphorisms, such as 'the burned child shuns the fire', 'the early bird gets the worm', etc.

Making inferences from particular instances of behavior is how in fact most learning occurs. The presence of retention schemata can be derived from what the individual does. For events contain both universal and particular properties. Events are particular but forces are not and neither are qualities and relations, they are universal. It is not ordinary knowledge or even abstract knowledge that I am taking about this time. I have already discussed them. Here the kind of knowledge to which I refer is that possessed not by the brain alone but by the musculature. The skills of western culture are overt and outward-bound:

how to play a musical instrument such as the violin or the piano, how to fly an airplane, or how to ski or ice skate. The skills of eastern culture are inward-bound and aimed at gaining control over the organs which are normally operated by the autonomic nervous system: how to control the heartbeat, the pulse, the bowels. It should be obvious that these two disparate sorts of skills are the result of the application of cultures having quite different implicit dominant ontologies.

Events can as a matter of fact be followed in both directions in time. They can be traced back to assumptions which are axiomatic by nature, and they have consequences which can be read as deductive theorems. Events are of course made up of material particulars, but they imply universals, and it can be seen with a little examination just what universals they imply. In other words, it is possible to argue back from present events to the axiomatic assumptions which led up to them. Social events may have followed from individual beliefs or they may have followed from metaphysical assumptions lying deep in the culture. In any case they do have meanings and the meanings are susceptible of exposure and analysis.

Events can also be traced forward to their theorematic consequences. By deduction it should be possible to see what will happen or at the very least what could happen as the result of the prior happenings of events. The importance of both the events and their consequences are proportional. Actions have consequences and important actions have important consequences. It is possible therefore to tell something about the importance of an action from its consequences. Now many events took place in the past but they have consequences in the present. In so far as a man performs actions which had not been anticipated yet are the results of his past actions, he changes the importance of those actions in the present (obviously their importance in the past cannot be changed). Knowledge can be derived from actions, and actions follow from knowledge.

Learning from experience is a well known phenomenon, though what is not so well known is how primitively it begins. It may prove to be true that ordinary crude sense perceptions, such as those which disclose color and shape, are learned, not innate. See for instance the evidence of those who as adults are cured of blindness for the first time.[6] Learning from action is not new, for Plato mentions it.[7] But as an explicit formulation it has had to await the practice of science and the doctrines

[6] J. Z. Young, *Doubt and Certainty in Science* (Oxford, 1951, Clarendon Press), p. 61.
[7] *Apology*, 32 A.

of the pragmatists. We learn by doing, in Dewey's phrase. The more technical formulation in terms of animal experiment is Skinner's "operant learning." Extreme forms of behavior mark the limits of human capacity; sexual license and total abstinence, for instance, are both in their separate ways instructive.

The importance of the part played by action in epistemology has been very much neglected. The field has been left principally to perception and thought. We shall see in a later chapter how this has worked out. Action consists in deliberate movement by a subject among objects and forces. Epistemology is not necessarily a study of passive and static relationships. The connection of knowledge with the subject as actor is involved, too. Action is participation by the subject as itself an object in a world of objects. For him there is touch, as the sense most immediately involved, and there are pressures and there is resistance. Condillac considered touch to be the most important of the senses. The arena in which such relationships and qualities exist is that of space and time. It should not be forgotten that external relations are the structures of forces and that force is a quality.

The effect of actions is entirely to destroy the absolute claims of subjective idealism. The subject moves among genuine objects which resist his movement so much that he must attend to them. They clearly are not creatures of his fancy, those material things and forces which if unnoticed impede his progress toward his goals. The consequences of random or aimless actions are unpredictable. Given the number of separate material things and forces interacting, it follows that surprises and novelties are bound to occur. This is not quite the case with deliberate actions. If, as Peirce declared, the meaning of a proposition is the sum of its possible consequences, then as McCulloch observed, action is "a proposition on the move."[8]

The world we live in is a confused state of affairs about which we seek the truth. There is an assumption common to all reasonable men that all truths form a system and that therefore a single system can be assumed for all knowledge. The paradox remains that while there are many contradictions in the material world, the truths derived from that world are consistent. This is the paradox we live with, and no solution has been found for it. All the power we acquire over the material world has been gained through the acquisition of the knowledge of its laws, and so there is some evidence that consistency is dominant

---

[8] Warren S. McCulloch, in L.A. Jeffress, ed., *Cerebral Mechanisms in Behavior* (New York, 1951, John Wiley and Sons), p. 32.

over contradiction. This is a strong argument though not necessarily a conclusive one.

All action involves both thought and feeling, yet activities can be classified according as they feature thought, feeling or action, while involving all three. Mathematicians are occupied primarily with thought, artists with feeling, and men of affairs, such as industrialists, farmers, politicians, with action. Now it happens that mathematicians are concerned with consistency, with systems of ideas, while men of affairs are more oncerned with the world in which contradictions occur and are common. Scientists, too, are men of action, for scientific experiments after all are planned actions; but their findings, which are continually increasing at a rapid rate, must be fitted into mathematical systems. Philosophers will have to reconcile these differences and show them all to be parts of a whole. Theirs is a contradiction-containing consistency, such as Hegel claimed for all being. To the extent to which philosophers have failed to recognize this feature their explanations have failed.

PART II

SPECIFIC ISSUES

CHAPTER V

KNOWING, DOING AND BEING

In this chapter I will not talk about knowledge theory but only try to put knowledge theory in the proper perspective. Knowing is not the only activity of the human individual, and if we start by seeing it in relation to his other activities we may gain a better approach to it.

Accordingly, I will begin by applying the theory of Pavlov, Hull and Skinner, to the interpretation of human behavior. My efforts will require certain modifications in the original theory as suggested by the work of Loeb and Tinbergen. Also, the argument moves off in a direction somewhat different from that taken by Watson in his efforts to extend the theory of behaviorism to man, since it includes activities ordinarily considered social or cultural. The extended theory is so altered as to be hardly recognizable, and none of these scientists would necessarily approve of the use which has been made here of their work. Behaviorism is a naturalistic theory, but nature is proving more complex than was formerly supposed. If my theory is successful, it should be possible in this way to account for all of the widely disparate phenomena of human behavior, everything from table manners, say, to the philosophy of existentialism.

Man is an animal very much like the others and so a highly specialized part of his environment. Structures of energies make up the differences. We may be able to explain more about human behavior if we regard it as ecological and examine the individual from the viewpoint which assumes that organs have needs and that their activation consists in responses to stimuli from the external world, many of which man himself originated. Let us look upon him, then, as a primate with added properties, one who has been using tools for more than a million years, and let us see how much of him we can account for in this way.

First, however, a few definitions are in order. By 'behavior' we will mean the movement of organisms so far as it has any pattern or structure, and by 'animal behavior' any movement aimed at reducing a need. A 'need' is what a material object can supply to an animal which is necessary for its or its species' survival.

All animals have much the same needs or drives and all behave in the same way with respect to them. The needs are of course many, but we shall discuss here only the six principal ones mentioned before. They are divided into two groups, remember, as they serve immediate or continued survival. The primary needs are for water, food and sex. The secondary needs are for knowledge, activity and security. In addition to these there are of course dozens of others, such as the needs for authority, for prestige, and for self-esteem, to say nothing of subordinate needs such as the need for toilet training of the young, for a calendar, and for some form of weather control. The six principal needs are more basic, however. It is possible that they are subdivisions of the one great drive of aggression, here defined as the drive to dominate the environment.

Since the behavior of the animal is roughly uniform with respect to the needs, we may take as a model the first of the primary needs, the need for water. It is ordinarily supposed that behavior begins by a lack felt by an animal: he is thirsty. The rhythm occurs in bursts, not steadily or continuously. He hears the sound of a running brook and executes an orienting movement in its direction. This is called a tropism. He sees small waves upon the surface (cue) and this impression activates a feeling of dryness in his mouth, stimulating him to move toward it (taxis). The bending of his head toward the surface, the opening of his mouth and perhaps also the protrusion of his tongue, are called preparatory responses. The drinking of the water is the consummatory response; the need is reduced. Pleasure of a positive sort accompanies all drive-reduction.

The behavior of animals in reducing the need for food and sex is not very different from what it is in reducing the need for water. With the secondary needs, however, there are some changes. The capacity of animals to acquire knowledge is very small indeed. Some, like the porpoise, are said to have signalling systems, but no external technique for storing information. Doing something means making something, as for instance the beaver dam or the bird nest, but in such cases the behavior is stereotyped and results in the same kind of construction. The need to survive is negative in animals, and takes the form largely of escape from threats of danger – the need is for immediate survival.

Now as it happens the account is similar in the case of human behavior. The life of the human individual consists in working out the reduction of his principal needs. When an individual finds that his need is confronted with a tropism, he behaves accordingly: the need becomes a drive, and he moves toward the source of the stimulus by means of a response to its emitted cue. But there are some things that he handles differently from the animals. To make these differences clear, we shall have to return to our account of animal behavior and point out some of its more special features.

There is one peculiar feature of human behavior which is the source of drastic effects on the character of human life. Let us call it instrumental self-conditioning. In order to understand the term it will be necessary to contrast it with classical and instrumental conditioning in animal behavior experiments.

According to the law of effect in psychology, learning takes place only when there is a reward or punishment. In the classical conditioning of Pavlov, the animal learns to respond to a conditioned stimulus. A dog confronted with food will salivate in anticipation of being given it to eat. If now a bell is rung every time the animal is fed and this is repeated a sufficient number of times, then when the bell is sounded without feeding, the animal will salivate. In the modification of this experiment known as instrumental conditioning and introduced by Skinner, the animal is first isolated by being placed in a box which is empty except for a lever and a nearby trough. In the course of its explorations it will accidentally depress the lever which is wired to a food container in such a way that a food pellet is delivered to the trough. The animal eats the pellet and soon learns to press the lever when it wants another food pellet.

In the case of the animal experiment, someone else – a psychologist – provides the box. In the case of human behavior the situation is more complex. The peculiar feature of human behavior is that man himself builds the instrument he wishes to be the source of the stimuli to which he can respond. Moreover, what in the case of the animal was an experiment, in the case of man is a way of life! For the fact is that almost any sequence of human activities would serve equally well as an example. For instance, man builds a restaurant to which he can repair with gustatory reward, or he paints a picture to which he can then respond with aesthetic enjoyment. In this sense, he is the engineer of his own fate. But not entirely. For with each new type of construction he produces in himself altered responses, and among these altered responses are still newer types of construction, so that the process becomes a semi-automatic and cumulatively self-perpetuating one.

Let us look at the changes made in the pattern of animal behavior when it becomes the behavior of the human individual.

For man as for all animals drive-reduction is the end of action. But for man there is the additional factor of terminal goal-achievement. Man, unlike other animals, often does care what effects on the immediate environment are the results direct or indirect of his efforts at drive-reduction.

Again, for all of the needs the step we have called the preparatory response is enormously more developed. Some animals are able to 'put something by' for a rainy day as squirrels hoard nuts for the winter, but it is characteristic of man in connection with all of his needs that he anticipates them and endeavors to prepare for them. Again, in the case of the primary needs his preparatory responses are elaborate. Usually he does not drink water from a brook but from a cup at a table. He does not kill his food and eat it raw but cooks it. Finally, he surrounds his consummatory responses with elaborate ritual and executes them with tools designed for this purpose, dining room, cutlery and table manners.

In the case of the secondary responses, the changes are even sharper. It is here in fact that his humanity begins to show itself so clearly and marks him off as superior to the other animals. He has constructed elaborate techniques for conducting inquiry, established great operant reserves of knowledge, and designed elaborate sign systems to communicate what he remembers.

So much for the need to know. For the need to do, he has equally elaborate resources. For this need he has developed tools and technologies as complex as his sign-systems, and he can make large artifacts. Man is naturally constructive. When he undertakes to reduce his need to do, buildings rise through his efforts, and capital cities accumulate. He is, however, equally destructive, and can reduce his need to do also by fighting with his fellow man. Unfortunately, for reducing the drive to do, destruction works faster and more effectively than construction.

For the need to be, he has adopted two important changes. First, he makes a positive rather than a negative response. He alone seeks positively to protract his existence. Shelters and clothing and the medical arts contribute materially to this need-reduction. Secondly, he has extended his need to be beyond his death. Through the establishment of religion he has sought to insure ultimate security – the continuance of life after death.

But human behavior is not simply a matter of extending animal responses. The signs and tools man has made in order to help him with his need-reductions are very complicated, and require skills. He has had to learn to use languages and to operate complex machinery. The results are far different from what one might suppose.

In order to examine them, let us learn to consider both signs and tools in their advanced versions, languages and machinery, as species of artifacts. By 'artifacts' we shall mean henceforth material objects which have been altered through human agency for human uses. Thus 'signs' are material objects employed to refer to other material objects and 'tools' are material objects employed to move or change other material objects.

Human individuals are responsible for the existence of artifacts, but the effect is not all one way. Not only does man make artifacts but in a certain sense artifacts also make him. He remains a stimulus-bound animal and largely at the mercy of the external world. But there has been one important change: a large part of his immediate environment is filled with artifacts to which he is compelled to react.

Partly, of course, such reactions are desired, planned and expected. A work of art, for instance, is an artifact which is made for the sole purpose of affecting in a definite and intended way those who come into contact with it. But some artifacts often have effects which were neither sought after nor wanted, such as occupational diseases, while many others have effects which remain largely unknown. What man has built up over many years as his material culture for instance now threatens to control his evolution. His adaptability actually puts him at a disadvantage. The automobile not only has determined the structure of our cities but also has influenced courting habits and social life generally. Behavior is an activity of drive-reduction, need-instigated, object-consummated, which alters both man and material object. All effects produce alterations in the human individual, who responds by altering the artifact, initiating a cycle of effects and countereffects which continues indefinitely.

Thus there comes into existence a feedback from artifacts, and the individual is compelled to a continuity of attention which is not the case with other animals. He is able to build upon the work of his predecessors, thereby producing for himself and his fellows an environment which is, so to speak, an integral part of him and without which he would not be human. If we remember that languages are sign systems consisting in marks on paper or modulations in sound waves, and therefore just as much artifacts as the tools we ordinarily consider material, say spades and ships, then we can understand that the continuing cycle of interactions, what the engineers call the reverberating or reentrant circuit, includes both human individuals and artifacts in a closed organization. There are so many variables involved at this point that nobody has been able to predict what will happen.

Now that we have at our disposal an understanding of human needs, the way in which the individual goes about reducing them, and the effects of a continuity of such need-reductions both upon the external world and upon the individual himself, let us turn back to an examination of need-reduction in more detail, particularly as it concerns those features which are more prominently human. We have noted already that the peculiar way in which man plans for the reduction of his primary needs for water, food and a mate marks him as different from other animals. In man the primary needs are importunate, as indeed they are with all animals, but the secondary needs are important. When we examine the secondary needs for knowledge, activity, and survival – to know, to do and to be respectively – we find that their differences and extensions in man are far-reaching. Perhaps it will be best if we devote some time to an examination of each of them separately.

The need to know is a natural development from the primary needs. All animals are inquisitive, and they must be if they are to find those particular kinds of material objects in the world which can offer them need-reductions. Approach-and-exploration behavior is familiar enough. A chimpanzee or a kitten will move toward any small object to examine it. The object may after all be good to eat, but if not it is usually discarded. In the same way the human individual approached knowledge: it may be useful; but if not, in his case it is not discarded. For he has learned that what is not useful directly may be useful indirectly and so be worth saving.

Knowledge which can lead directly to need-reduction is called concrete knowledge. That the raw cassava root contains a poisonous sap but when dried and cooked is good to eat, is an example of concrete knowledge. Knowledge which does not necessarily lead directly to need-reductions of the primary needs is called abstract knowledge. That the square on the hypotenuse of a triangle is equal to the sum of the squares on the other two sides, is an example of abstract knowledge. Abstract knowledge can of course lead indirectly to need-reductions by providing information necessary to concrete knowledge. But abstract knowledge can lead also to need-reductions directly in connection with the secondary needs. This becomes clear when we remember that the first of the secondary needs is the need to know.

What attracts the human individual to abstract knowledge is its durability. The abstract objects to which the words and sentences of abstract knowledge refer cannot be destroyed, because they are logical objects and as such properties of material objects. The material objects possessing them can be destroyed and they may disappear along with those objects, but then they can be found recurring as the properties of other, and similar, material objects. They are man-discovered and afterwards man-known, but they are not man-made, and that is why we are justified in calling them 'naturally occurring relations'. The similarity of shape of two trees, the difference in color of two rocks, for instance. The stimulation of the similarity leads the individual to recognize the existence of classes, such as classes of trees and classes of rocks. And the stimulation of the differences between two material objects leads to the recognition of them as separate and particular objects.

When it is understood that the knowledge of naturally occurring relations can be abstracted from particular material objects without disturbing them, and further can be combined in statements by means of which it is possible to represent absent as well as present objects, the extreme value of abstract knowledge is recognized. Such knowledge exerts a compulsion upon the knower to deal with it in proper fashion, and measures are taken for its acquisition, development and preservation. The acquisition is called learning, and, in its regulated social form, education. The development is carried out by mental processes of association and dissociation, and is called thought. It is preserved in two ways, subjectively and objectively: subjectively in the memories of individuals, and objectively in books and libraries.

Let us call the naturally occurring relations when they are in the mind of individuals 'true ideas'. The individual, we say, is in possession of certain information. Knowing is a kind of owning. There are then three and only three mental operations: the recognition of true ideas, the discovery of hitherto unknown relations between true ideas, and the invention of false ones.

Knowledge is reinforced by the pleasure which attends understanding. There is a kind of comfort in the permanence of knowledge. It leads to belief, the feeling that a statement is true. Not all beliefs are conscious. Those beliefs which are necessary to other beliefs are retained by the individual without his specific awareness of them. The operation of learning repeated in the way demanded by the feedback of the reentrant circuit leads to complex beliefs consisting in systems of ideas. The larger of these are conventionally called 'philosophies', elaborate response systems encompassing all of the possibilities of behavior lying within a certain range as determined by belief. Such philosophies exercise a kind of determinism over the behavior of the human individual, resulting in adaptive knowing.

'Adaptive behavior' in general means meeting or producing modifications in the special ways in which man sets about obtaining the reductions of his needs, a kind of continuously revised self-conditioning. By 'adaptive knowing', then, is meant adaptive behavior applied to knowing: continuously meeting or producing the new conditions brought about by the possession of knowledge. It is the endurance of artifacts and their own often unexpected properties which force an extended continuity of behavior upon the human individual.

Man reacts to the world in accordance with what he knows about the world, and, in accordance with the reactions he makes, what he knows about the world also changes. New instruments make possible new observations, and new observations suggest still further modifications in the instruments. Thus philosophies are enlarged to include new information or exchanged for more efficient ones. Philosophy is an activity, an enterprise of inquiry, a method of improving the consistency and completeness of response systems.

But there is another and less desirable side effect of philosophies. To the extent to which they are consistent and complete they tend to shut off further inquiry. To know means to seek knowledge no longer. The analytic philosophy of ordinary language is based upon the attempt to circumvent the blocking of inquiry by means of a temporary displacement. If the fundamental response system of a philosophy is deeply imbedded in the language, then it must be recovered before its limitations can be dissipated. The requirements of communication must be satisfied by an inspection of knowing, and the degree of distortion the language entails recognized. Only in this way can there be a successful resumption of inquiry as a method of reducing the need to know.

Such a procedure has the support which the disparity between any response system and the corresponding environment it purports to represent must always constitute. The world is always larger than any conceptions of it, and eventually some of its neglected features must intrude themselves upon the tidy neatness of any absolutely accepted philosophy, forcing its abandonment and the consequent resumption of the fundamental inquiry. Clearly, then, something more is needed. Knowing is passive, but there is also an active aspect to be developed. This is called doing, and it too works to reduce a need.

The need to do is the animal need for activity. All needs involve activity of some sort, and there is always a background of alertness in the aroused animal. But for the need to do the activity itself furnishes need-reduction. The very existence of the material object is a challenge on cue. Obstacles must be overcome if struggle is the means by which the individual is to reduce his need for activity. Thus both construction and destruction are capable of reducing the need, which takes many forms: power over men and property, and acquisitiveness, but also building, scientific investigation and even war. Somehow, the aim is to combine a certain measure of violence with permanence, for the effects sought are anything but temporary.

The reduction of the need to do is often preceded by plans. Activity as achievement requires careful preparation. Work is not a random affair but must be meticulously laid out. Thus engineering diagrams, architectural blueprints, travel guides, and schedules for industrial production are proposals to follow certain courses of action. Athletic contests and spectator sports lead the drive into harmless channels and anticipate vicarious participation in the need-reduction of doing.

Skills, which are the combination of practical knowledge with mechanical aptitude, belong to the preparation phase of the need to do. 'Know-how' means the knowledge of technique either for reducing a need or for doing something which contributes indirectly to a need-reduction. Scientific agriculture is a kind of 'know-how'; as for indirect methods, the man who can play a violin very well may in this way be earning the money to feed a family.

Part of the need to do is what is commonly described as self-expression, the need to say. This may take the form of writing or speech. Speech is that form of activity intended to affect present persons, writing is aimed at affecting absent persons. Both are accomplished by altering materials: by printing or by modulating sound waves. The reference is usually some material object to which the language calls attention, a communication usually having some action in view.

Whatever the result of activity may be, there is a certain satisfaction in mere doing, an element of spontaneity in the release which exertion affords. The exercise of the muscles brings with it its own keen sense of enjoyment. Hence the popularity of play, which may have as its aim the transformation of no material object except the organism itself. So far as the individual alone is concerned, there seems to be as much need-reduction in raw, overt aggression as in some more positive form of achievement, destruction is as satisfactory as construction, and it is quicker. The reward of the need to do is furnished by activity itself or by achievement: either in the sense of muscle tonus, the feeling of relaxation, or a material object altered, a sense of accomplishment. Doing is more intimate than knowing because the individual has interfered with the object physically and changed it in some way that is peculiarly his own.

It often happens, however, that in the need to do the response is blocked. Some obstacle has been interposed between the individual and the object he aims to alter. Activity is inhibited, and as a result the circuit continues to reverberate with the entry closed. Emotion is the response of the whole organism to the blocking of behavior, just as water is raised above normal levels by dams. The emotion of rage, when it does find an outlet is apt to be destructive. It is short-lived, whereas love, say, is reinforced by finding an outlet.

Doing is a kind of having, because struggle to some extent puts the individual into physical contact and possession. The most organized construction is a government or an experimental science. A government is a security system designed to provide relative security only, within the limits of action absolutes. That is to say, it allows for action by restricting the area of action. A science is a response system limited to quantity and structure in a particular empirical domain. Such a response system exercises a determinism over those who can operate it and compels the individual to respond with adaptive behavior.

By 'adaptive doing' is meant the special ways in which man sets about obtaining the reduction of his need for making. The protracted existence of the altered material object forces revisions and extensions in the individual's continued dealings with it.

Man reacts to the world in accordance with what he does in the world, and, in accordance with what he does in the world, his reactions to the world also change. But there is an undesirable side effect. To the extent to which he has accomplished something, his need for accomplishment abates somewhat. However, there is always more to do than has ever been done, and the challenge to activity recurs. Both governments and sciences are limited affairs, dealing with finite security only. But there is also the question of greater survival. Clearly, another need is involved and hence another reduction required. This is furnished by being, which also can be counted on to reduce a need.

The need to be is the need for ultimate security, the need for self-preservation extended through death. Immediate security belongs to the primary drives, ultimate security to the secondary. Both knowing and doing may be called on to contribute to the preservation of being. Ultimate security is an extension of immediate security which is obtained through a supply of water, food, shelter, clothing, etc. The lower animals express the need for ultimate security negatively, in escape and defense reflexes, but man does so positively in the search for a secure object to which he can attach himself or with which he can be identified.

The need to be means of course the need to continue to be. Since being here means 'being-in-itself', continuance of being can be attained either by aggrandizement of the self, by achieving what Homer called "immortal fame among mortal men," or by immortality, the survival of death.

The secure object is usually a large or faraway object which exhibits the property of permanence (understood as persistence of being). The Greek gods lived on Mt. Olympus, Triton was the deep sea god, the Egyptian Re was a sun-god, and there have been sky gods, a moon god and the universal God of the Hebrews. In each case, there is often a nearby symbol of deity, such as an icon, a talisman or a cross, symbolizing permanence beyond the life of human individuals.

The prospect of distant objects exhibiting permanence of course evokes a response, and the response is proportional to the extent of the supposed threat to existence. The need for personal security takes the form of a craving for transcendentals, a search for association with the supernatural. The preparatory response is the guarantee of duration contained in the acceptance of an absolute security system, a religion. A theology is a qualitative response system promising survival. Need-reduction can be obtained by visiting the inner essence of being in the shape of the nearby self, a concentration on the core of consciousness through mystic states, as a method of making direct contact with the faraway god.

The consummatory response of the need to be consists in ritual observance. Since negatively the security of the person is guaranteed by the absence of touch, positively the skin is the organ of security and there must be some kind of physical contact, such as contagious magic or the participation in a sacrament with its transfer to the chosen goal-object. But the goal-object in such a case is merely a symbol of the faraway object so the behavior is with the stimulus absent – operant behavior. The repetition of the ritual reinforces belief.

If religion is a response to the world-quality, this quality is apprehended in little in the parts and wholes of existence, in short, in ethical and aesthetic objects respectively. Ethics is the theory of the good, and goodness the quality of the bond between wholes. Aesthetics is the theory of the beautiful, and beauty the quality of the bond between parts. Goodness is the affective aspect of completeness; beauty the affective aspect of consistency. Although secular codes of conduct and artistic movements exist, every religion contains an authorized morality and seeks support from works of art.

With the fully completed response to the need to be comes a sharp reversal of roles. For whereas with the other needs the object was at the service of the subject, with the need to be there is an attempt to have the subject serve the object. In place of assimilation *by* the individual there is the dedication *of* the individual. Self-transcendence is a need. The aggrandizement of the ego is satisfied by identification with a much larger object.

The reward of the need-reduction is the consequent feeling of ultimate security which is promised in return for the combination of faith with ritual observance. Faith may be defined as absolute belief. Beliefs less than absolute have to be supported by evidence, whereas faith is belief without evidence.

All faiths are comforting, and tend to reduce the anxiety of the need to be. The truth of such beliefs does not have to be known to the believer. Indeed they may be stronger when they are not known. One believes in something, not in the knowledge of it. Belief is a feeling which aims straight through to the object of belief, without the evidential indetermination of knowledge.

Membership in a church means subscribing to a religion which offers faith in the efficacy of ritual to achieve identification of the self with a faraway object exhibiting the permanence of persistence. Religion exercises a kind of determinism over the individual and compels in him the development of adaptive being.

By 'adaptive being' is meant the special way in which man sets about obtaining the reduction of his need for ultimate security. It is the remoteness of the goal-object and man's continued failure to attain to it which compels renewals and revisions in his efforts.

Man reacts to the world in accordance with what he feels about the world, and, in accordance with the feelings he has, his reactions to the world also change. He becomes aware that his is a short-range self and that his need to reach out to a remote goal means existing-for-another. Thus a certain plasticity of behavior is called for beyond the rigidity of a permanent kind of response which is poorly adapted to the aspirations of the short-range self. A permanent whole of being can be constructed of changing parts, and it is not merely to the whole that the self must adapt but also to the parts.

There is, however, a less desirable side effect on religions. To the extent that they are consistent and complete they tend to shut off inquiry. To feel secure is to end the search for security. But the universe is large and never entirely encompassed by feelings. The neglected aspects intrude themselves upon the individual; and the search for ultimate security, whereby he found a security system in the first place, must be renewed.

It sometimes happens that instead of being shut off, the drive for ultimate security is displaced. The displacement may take many forms. One of the more familiar is asceticism. A failing concentration on the need to be is reinforced by inhibiting the primary needs through the practice of fasting or chastity, or retreat or vows of silence.

Other and even more drastic techniques are common. One of these is the result of the need to encounter death. What is mostly feared – namely, death – is challenged, in order to end the fear. An adversary who has won can threaten no longer. The playing of dangerous games, which never go begging for participants, includes a wide variety: from bullfighting, jousting and fencing, to stunt flying, auto racing and border skirmishes. The hero of a possibly fatal sport has always seemed exceedingly romantic, and this is equally true whether he has died in the bull ring or fighting the Pathans on the northwest frontier of India. We tend to look up to anyone who has had the courage to escape from our petty concern with mere personal survival by demonstrating that he himself does not care. The death we fear most he defies, and in the struggle for ultimate survival he has proved himself a conqueror.

Another displacement of the need to be is represented by its reversal, the turning of the drive to be into the drive to not be. Being is as rare an occurrence in the vast extent of nonbeing as matter in space. An individual who contemplates his own existence as it might be after his death in terms of what it must have been before his conception and birth is sure to understand that being lacks the pervasiveness and the persistence of nonbeing. He would conclude that ultimate security lay in identification not with being but with nonbeing. Both Hinduism and Buddhism seem to incorporate some of the consequences of this argument. The *nirvāna* of the Hindu and the desire for nonexistence of the *Hīnayāna* Buddhist are examples.

A third variety of displacement is that which occurs when the short-range self is substituted for the faraway goal-object of the need to be. This conception of being is described by the existentialists as the encounter with nonbeing. If the experience of nothingness produces dread, and the individual feels the loneliness which results from his having been cut off from the whole of being, then the insecurity which results from identification with nothingness must be turned into security by recognizing that man has been given over into his own custody. Ultimate security is to be found only in the self itself and responsibility in the moment of choice. The anguish of despair is a recognition of reality.

In general, then, human behavior like animal behavior can be accounted for by the search to reduce the drives. With the primary drives the case is the same as it is with the subhuman animals, except that the human individual with his foresight makes elaborate preparatory responses. With the secondary drives the case is the same, except that the human individual with his knowledge of death seeks something permanent: abstract knowledge, a material construction, and finally, association or identification with a large, faraway object possessing enormous powers of persistence. The exceptions are crucial and the entire behavior discloses an integral pattern.

The search begins with material objects in the immediate environment and ends with the whole universe of being. The entire sequence of need-reductions, from the first primary need for water, to the last secondary need for the ultimate security which seems to be possessed only by the whole universe, rests on the transformation of material objects, either by the human individual's assimilation of them or by their assimilation of the human individual. Man is always part of the material universe and in his every thought, feeling and action exhibits characteristic behavior in relation to it. Human behavior can be accounted for only through considering as biological motivation the efforts of the individual to reduce his needs by obtaining for himself a larger share of the world in which he is contained.

Earlier in this presentation I pointed out that man differed from the other animals in that he had not only their interest in drive-reduction but also a correlative interest in terminal goal-achievement. The relation of man to his immediate environment is that of a sensitivity-reactivity system of energy levels. The immediate environment, containing as it does both artifacts and other individuals, consists in the same set of levels; only it is customary to call them integrative levels when referring to their existence in the environment. The complete development of the individual is possible only within an ecosystem which is physical, chemical, biological and cultural, one in which his goals can be attained and his needs reduced. Man however primitive lives in a world composed largely of artifacts. Very little of his environment is as it was before he made alterations in it; certainly not the earth on which he stands or the very air he breathes. The earliest history of man is also that of his tools and signs; he cannot have existed apart from them. The fact that without men there would be no artifacts has perhaps blinded us to the companion fact that without artifacts there would be no men. Artifacts have enabled men to develop upright posture, unusual skills, brains, languages, roles, institutions, entire cultures.

Human individuals are voluntarily conditioned by artifacts. They will respond with chain learned behavior to the stimulus of the artifact. The voluntary part of this procedure is the extent to which the individuals submit themselves to such training. The method is one similar to that of the natural selection Darwin has made familiar in organic evolution. In a process of selective responses, the individual learns to repeat only those ways of operating the tool or sign which prove most effective, and not to repeat the others. Due to the peculiar construction of both kinds of artifacts they can be dealt with only in certain preferred ways. Thus they condition human behavior. Their intractability is a brute fact with which such behavior must reckon.

What then does this mean in terms of human evolution? All students of human nature as it has developed from primitive archetypes over the last million years have acknowledged the prevalence and persistence of artifacts. The man who stood erect in the Olduvai Gorge in Tanzania some million and a quarter years ago had flaked tools, and, like all fossil hominids, the tongue muscles. We have been told for a long time about the genetic nature of organic inheritance. But there has been an epigenetic inheritance of no lesser importance, the inheritance of artifacts and of the techniques involved in their construction and use. The genotype is the result of genetic mutation and internal inheritance. Acquired characters are not biological but cultural. The inheritance of acquired characters is an external inheritance, and has taken place by means of artifacts. Both human organisms through their internal inheritance and artifacts through their external inheritance have grown in extent and complexity. In order to find evidence of the earliest hominid it is necessary to go back to the Australopithicine remains. Even though Stone Age man survived as late as 7,000 years ago, *Homo sapiens* appears to be between a quarter and a half million years old.

Human artifactual culture of any degree of complexity is, however, very recent, going back hardly more than ten thousand years. Its effects will be swiftly felt, as evolutionary time is measured. In place of the cave man we have metropolitan man: in place of the stone axe we have the nuclear reactor. But only a one-way series of effects has been noted, the effects of man on artifacts, while the effects of artifacts on man have been neglected almost altogether. Thanks to the horse and carriage and the automobile, the contemporary American cannot run as fast or as long as the nomadic plains Indian once could. But he can do more mathematics with his brain and computer.

What has happened of course is that man has taken a hand in his own evolution and the result has been to accelerate it. Some contemporary authorities are of the opinion that the artificial environment has put a stop to the evolutionary process, but the evidence can quite easily be read to the contrary. Like Frankenstein, we are at the mercy of our own technological monsters, and we do not know where they are leading us – forward, we can only hope. The signs read that way, because our skills have increased. We need to do less with our muscles because we can do more with our brains, an increase in complexity that has been traced backward in organic evolution. And so we find ourselves becoming more what we were about to be. But we have not increased our foresight as fast as we have our mastery. It may be just as well. For we might not have liked to surpass ourselves had we understood altogether what this would mean.

The perfectly reasonable man is one who has subordinated the drives in their proper order so that disadvantageous reinforcements and frustrations are avoided. Elsewhere I have tried to exemplify the many aberrations which can and do occur in the drives, chiefly those of excess and defect. But then what man is perfectly reasonable? In most investigations of human nature we have concealed from ourselves as well as omitted from our reports the many ugly truths, which, however, continue to reassert themselves in consequences. The evidence is strong that the earliest men were cannibals, but how much has the situation changed? The psychology of the carnivore is still very much in evidence among us. The killing of animals remains a favorite sport, and human suffering in certain quarters is still enjoyable. Men have grown more subtle but not more soft. They still prey on each other. There is still a very pleasurable type of need-reduction to be found in raw, overt aggression. And it is an historic fact that wars are desired (though not desirable), that rape is popular (though not moral), and that competition is stimulating (though partly disastrous).

There is no reason for despair. The first step in grappling with a problem must be to recognize its existence. Half a century ago William James sought a moral equivalent for war and thought he had one when he proposed to send the Harvard undergraduates to work camps in the summer. But at least he saw the problem. The needs are still what they always were, because they are those of the animal, even though the drives have taken specifically human form. If it is possible to tame any of man's behavior, it will be the drives rather than the needs. There is hope in the fact that it is at least possible to reduce a drive without reducing the corresponding need, by inducing one drive to cut across another. There is hope, too, in the possibility that increased communication and transportation facilities might compel increased cooperation in larger and larger social units. Although men remain aggressive outside the group, the group itself increases in size and they become more cooperative inside it. If we know that the phenotype is affected by life in a world so largely composed of tools and signs, could we not put that knowledge to better advantage? Perhaps such investigations are only just beginning, and it is through them that the most intelligible promise might be followed.

CHAPTER VI

ABSENT OBJECTS

I propose to study here some of the problems which have been raised about the character of the disclosures of sense experience as these are made in the knowledge process. No situation is entirely open and this is especially true of problems which are restricted in scope because they carry with them a range of possible solutions. In difficult cases – those which are found in epistemology for instance – it is important for the investigator to know just what he is dealing with, for once it has been well stated his task is nearly at an end.

I have perhaps made things sound too easy. The best approach is through successive definitions, in this way reducing the statement of the problem by revisions until a final formulation is found which can lead the way through many of the possible solutions to that special one which might be of value. I suspect that if this study contributes anything, it will lie in that general direction.

There can be no objection to giving the game away at the beginning provided only that a development of the position be quickly offered, with adequate explanations of what is involved. The theme of this study, then, is that some kind of basic platonism is forced on the observer of a material object by reason of the incomplete character of his immediate experience as this reveals itself to his genetically-developing consciousness. Knowledge sharpens awareness; the more he knows, the greater his capacity for learning. It is a richer and more complex world than he will ever succeed in encompassing and the potential increase in his capacities is therefore without limit.

I shall try to examine as naively as possible the kind of happening that we have come to call 'having a sense experience', and in this way to set up a first stage in the analysis of knowledge. The knowledge relation itself is a delicate one, and so easily disturbed by any examination that the results of deliberate observation are apt to be misleading. Just as in physics according to the principle of indeterminacy light interferes with the study of photons, so in the analysis of knowing it is necessary to become self-conscious, and this distorts the accuracy of the description of the awareness of the external world. The process operates in much the same way that getting control of the autonomic functions distorts them. If one thinks about breathing, the regularity is upset and any conclusion about its frequency is almost sure to be false.

Every sense experience is an encounter between a human individual (to be called 'the observer') and a material object, and it is this encounter that I want to examine. Let me quickly comment, then, first on the observer and next on what he observes.

As to the observer, the term will be employed to describe the outward-faced aspect of the experiencing subject as he stands in some relation to a material object. But this is only another way of talking about a perspective, and perspectives belong to objects and are carried about by them. The table seen from directly above it will be the same wherever the table is. A perspective must be understood as a view made possible both by the angle of vision and by the equipment of the observer. What can be experienced from some particular perspective is the arrangement of the world with respect to the peculiar angle of vision.

But the equipment of the observer is relevant too, and contributes to what can be experienced from the perspective. Thus a man standing in a valley from which he could see the rock face of the side of a mountain would not 'see' as much as a geologist standing in the same spot. The difference is not only mental, however, for what is true of the two men would be equally true of a camera with two kinds of film. Thus a camera with black and white film would not apprehend the same impressions as another in the same position but with color-sensitive film. It is clear then that we are talking about aspects of a material object, not about those appertaining to an observer, for what we are dealing with is not the object in relation to an observer but the observer in relation to the object; for the purposes of knowledge the dependence has shifted.

In this way we widen the considerations though they remain an affair of knowledge. Epistemology itself has always been a kind of subjective interest but that is unfair to a field of inquiry, as unfair as identifying metaphysics with idealism. It is as though a class were to be confused with one of its own members. While it is true that knowledge theory always concerns the observer in some way – either his relations to knowledge or its relations to him – that is no reason to neglect another and equally significant aspect, namely, the centrality of the material object without which there would be no knowledge. All we need to do to alter the emphasis is to remember that in the connection which occupies our interest the subject is an observer and we are concerned with him chiefly in this way. Whatever else he is or is not is relevant only if it bears, directly or indirectly, upon his functioning as an observer.

That is why realistic epistemologies have been so poorly developed: they are not needed, because the objective existence of the world together with its immediate knowability are axiomatic for realism; and since axioms cannot be proved within any system there is no particular point in their detailed examination. A mere statement of realism in knowledge theory was considered enough for Aristotle.[1] But such a cursory statement lends itself to neglect in the grand economy of his whole philosophy, and so it has not been too often assumed even for an understanding of Aristotle. Evidently, more is involved than has been formerly analyzed in the realistic version of epistemology, and with the addition of the new materialism more must be said.

So much then for the observer to start with. As to the material objects the observer encounters, the term, matter, will be employed generically to describe both material things and events, the static and dynamic states of matter. In this way I shall avoid adding more terms than necessary; for example, 'substance', which is often employed in this way. 'Matter', meaning either material entities or material events involving energy (or both), will serve as a convenient shorthand. We should note that since matter accounts for the resistance to muscular effort, the best indication of the presence of matter is action.

I should add quickly that I have selected the most general case, because in this way I do not have to give special consideration to the encounter when the material object is another human individual. The second individual, in this context at least, is another material object. When there is an encounter between two minds, it is also one between material objects; for minds are parts of human individuals and human individuals are themselves at least (though not only) material objects.

But, more complexly, the encounter generally involves a third material object such as the sounds of a spoken language or the marks of a written one, but the examination of this additional factor would

[1] See, for instance, his *Categories*, 7b27–8a12.

complicate our problem and require analysis at a higher level of organization. And so in the interests of simplicity and of first-level analysis I have deliberately ruled out all consideration of the encounter with other minds, although I do recognize its importance.

Before entering upon a discussion of the details of the knowledge relation I had better talk about it in general. For it is only fair to point out that I am approaching it from the point of view of a framework in which it appears as an example of the 'Method of Induced Subjectivity'.

Let me explain. To take the point of view of a subject at first glance would be a most easy and natural one since we are all subjects. Unfortunately, this is not the case. We are subjects and so we *have* the point of view of subjects. But to *have* the point of view of subjects is not to *take* the point of view of subjects. And to be aware that we are subjects and that as subjects we have the point of view that goes with them is to take a second-level subjective view, not by any means an easy or natural thing to do. This is a neglected assumption and it makes for concealed difficulties in most of the Kantian epistemologies from Cassirer to C. I. Lewis. In a realistic approach no such assumption is made, and that is why I have thought it best to call attention to the alternative. It consists in deliberately remembering that the observer is a subject and that he falls naturally into the subjective point of view. As a matter of fact, it means viewing the subject and the object of knowledge as though they were two different sorts of objects.

Subjectivity is a tricky affair, and it can be induced in several ways. Not many have noticed that there is a difference between the inner-induced and the outer-induced varieties, but the distinction is crucial.

For a description of the inner-induced subjectivities, consult the main accounts of Hinduism and Buddhism. The religious cultures of Indian Asia have been largely devoted to inner-induced subjective states, while the secular epistemologies of European countries have been occupied with the analysis of outer-induced subjective states. The latter can be made eventually to give way to a concentration on the object toward which it was originally directed, that is to say, to the object as being.

The assumption underlying outer-induced subjective states is one which is frequently forgotten or overlooked in the kind of analysis of knowledge so popular in England in the seventeenth and eighteenth centuries. It is that the subject in this context is dependent upon the object and conditioned by it, and not the reverse. The dependence on the object is forgotten because the observer is always able to shut off further sense experience, to close his eyes, say, and to concentrate on what he has already seen and which still exists for him as images. Subjectivity is merely the subject mentally digesting what he has taken in previously through his sense organs in the way of impressions from material objects. But that does not alter the fact of the origins of what he is experiencing: it came to him from the external world and is not dependent for its being upon his knowing. There is, then, strictly speaking, no such thing as 'subjectivity'. What is *called* subjectivity in any one of its varieties, not excluding solipsism, is only some form of objectivity closed or open, and, in the case of extreme subjective states, usually closed.

When we act in accordance with the belief that the objects of our perceptions exist independently of those perceptions, more often than not the objects will respond accordingly; and such behavior on their part reinforces our belief in them. So that it is action rather than passive perception or equally passive thought on which we must rely in the last analysis to support our belief in the external world. Hume hinted at this and so did Reid, but because Kant was the more powerful commentator the point was passed over, and all the efforts of the American pragmatists to show that activity is a source of reliable knowledge, despite the powerful evidence for it which could be accumulated from centuries of experimental science, have not received their due in credence from the philosophers.

Anyone who is motivated by a passionate desire not to make any statement in philosophy which cannot be proved must first of all confine himself to epistemology and in that field to a subjectivism which if it does not fall into solipsism at least borders dangerously on it. If epistemology is to be pursued for its explanatory value, then the philosopher must make an inductive leap to a system of ideas which he can thenceforth support by adducing to its aid all available evidence from whatever source, and then in addition argue for its plausibility.

We shall be interested here only in outer-induced subjective states. Knowing, on this approach, appears as a special case of being, the being of being-known, or being from the outside. Knowing-as-such is being from the inside. The somatic organism of the observer has a peculiar meaning for epistemology. It is the locus of the equipment for knowing, at once a complex and movable perspective. It is the ground where the knower and known meet under the conditions it provides. It is not the subject but instead that special part of the external world used by the knower to view the remainder. Subjectivity, then, at least to a realist of the outer-induced variety, is an awareness of an object among objects. For there is objectivity inherent in the very fact that the subject is able to recognize himself as a subject.

Since Hume it has been acknowledged that any direct experience of the self is of course impossible. There is no accurate self-observation and certainly no verification of hypotheses arrived at in this way. Introspection has its severely limited aspects. It is no doubt true that I can know that I am knowing, but a recognition of this sort sometimes fails and there is no special method of verification. That is why when we are in search of reliable knowledge we say that the self can be studied only as an object and by others. It becomes an authentic and genuine datum only when it becomes an object. The proper approach of philosophy to knowledge theory, therefore, is to take its stand on the object, not on the subject, and to consider a subject only as an object experienced against a background of other objects with which it is constantly interacting.

But if we are to take a stand on the object we would do better to choose a proper object and not the subject as object. The subject would be a poor choice of object for this purpose because of its inherent passivity in the knowledge process. That we do not perceive our perceptions or experience our experiences is as Herbart saw a strong argument against being limited in our theory of knowledge to what we can perceive and experience. The observer does not see his eyes but only what his eyes see, and the content of his experience is objective to both of them and indeed must be independent of them since they cannot be changed in this way. It is not without good reason that the physicist prefers his instruments to his body, relying upon the vibrating membrane rather than his own ear, the thermometer rather than his own skin, employing physical optics in which his eye is no longer needed. Evidently we shall be obliged to debit the observer with an inability to explain the content of experience by means of the act of experience. It is necessary to look elsewhere for an explanation.

The theory of knowledge was initiated as a study by Kant, and ever since his work was published it has been interpreted as the conception of the world (in so far as it could be known) immersed in the knowing mind. The present study reverses this interpretation and endeavors to present the outlines of an epistemology in which the knowing mind is immersed in the world. It is true of course and always will be that the world as we know it is the world-as-known. But to suppose that the world-as-such is bigger than the world-as-known, as indeed we must if we admit that from time to time there take place important and sometimes surprising additions to knowledge, has important consequences to the theory of knowledge. For the world-as-known is dependent upon the world-as-such, in the same way in which a part is always dependent upon the whole of which it is a part, if the world-as-such is to present to the knower the world-as-known.

Knowing is an accidental, not a necessary, property of things known. They would exist if they were not known and knowing them does not change them. That this proposition cannot be demonstrated as a matter of knowledge has been the main argument of the subjectivists. The counter-argument would seem obvious, however, for the proposition that what we do not know we cannot know is equally indemonstrable as a matter of knowledge; it cannot be proved in the process of knowing. We may know that we know, but we do not know also that we produce our knowledge in the course of knowing and there is no evidence of this sort available.

That things known stand in some relation to the knower would seem to be a trivial tautology. The things known, however, have other relations which are not open to the same charge. The chair as I see it stands in some relation to my visual perception, yes, but more importantly for the purposes of being a chair it has relations to other chairs with which it shares class membership, to the floor which supports it, to the roof which keeps the rain and snow from destroying it, and so on. It is this broad picture into which the observer must fit himself.

The point is that what is peculiar about the observer is his ability to add to his experience of objects by relating himself to a different and quite separate kind of experience: the experience of some objects in relation to each other. Is it possible to deny that there are interactions between the things that the observer experiences? He cannot claim that all things stand only or even chiefly in relation to him and not to each other. If the observer were to see a man and a horse, he might if he wished suppose that their existence was dependent upon his experience of them, even though this would seem to be stretching things a bit, but it would be even harder for him to suppose that when the man mounted the horse and rode off, his experience was responsible for this too. To call such an event an experience is an admission of what the observer owes to its content. What is always involved between the observer and the material object which he observes is that it is a function of two variables, both changing in time; the observer as a dependent variable and the object observed as an independent variable. The encounter has two phases, one static, the other dynamic.

I propose to call the static phase a passive conditioned encounter. It is passive because the observer is helpless to alter his impressions as he receives them. Moreover the encounter is brilliant and it is insistent. The observer cannot get away from it or avoid its impact upon him. It will have its way so long as he exposes his sense of sight to it. If he sees the yellow full moon, he is powerless to see it as red or square. The only activity involved has been the exposure: the observer has placed himself in the position of seeing the moon by looking up at the sky on a clear night, but then the situation immediately turned passive, and he has no influence over the terms of his impression. The moon was yellow and round and that was that.

The observer does tend to get experience itself confused with the description of experience. He does not describe his experience until there has been a recognition of the objects experienced. But if the objects are too large to be grasped in a single act of experience, the recognition may have to come later. Experience may be of simpler elements: a color or a shape, when he knows and conditions his experience upon knowing that there are such things as colors and shapes that are not the colors and shapes of material objects. But he begins less primitively with experiences which are describable, and then in his description the class of material objects is as primitive as the singular material objects themselves because it is the class which enables him to describe his experiences.

So far there is nothing either novel or notable in any way about the account; it has been set forth many times by epistemological realists. But I do wish to introduce a new note, and without it there would not have been any point in writing this chapter. The new note is contained in the word, 'conditioned'. The passive encounter is conditioned by many factors. I shall choose the most important one. The object encountered is a member of a class.

It is possible to say of the class when its membership is denumerable that it is extensively finite, but we are more concerned here with the class which is extensively infinite. But it is not possible to say of it when its membership is nondenumerable that it is extensively infinite even though it may be. A class of material objects does not give us a clue as to the number of its absent members. For that, we have to go to logical objects, which do. How many planets are there in the material universe? We do not know, but we do know that the number of circles is infinite because the class 'circle' is inexhaustible. But it is possible to say in any case that one of the conditions set by the encounter with material objects is for the observer that he is confronted by a class. Confrontation in sense experience means the encounter through the present members of a class with that class.

So we shall see that the encounter with a logical class, i.e. one whose members are classes, is no less a confrontation, and we shall be led to the conclusion that there are two kinds of objects, material objects and logical objects. A logical object is a class which has as its members either properties of material objects (forms or qualities), classes of material objects, or classes of classes of material objects. One of the unique features of this analysis is the classification of qualities as one kind of logical object.

But we are concerned for the moment exclusively with the class whose members are material objects. The yellow moon, then, is present to his senses because he is passive in the encounter and conditioned by the experience. Not only is the moon there and now, it is also the member of an indefinitely large class. Its presence can be considered from two aspects, the one particular and the other general. Let us consider the particular aspect first.

The important thing to note about the particular aspect is that it is capable of calling upon all his powers of apprehension though not necessarily all at one time. To begin with he sees it. Then if it were any material object closer than the moon he could if he liked touch it but that is not all of the senses either of sight or touch, for if he could walk around it he would be able to see and touch other sides of it. This brings into play the dynamic phase of the encounter referred to earlier. For it is only as an entire man that the observer is able to plan and execute his further experiences.

For as an entire man the observer is capable of having three kinds of experiences. He can feel by means of his senses, any or all of them; he can engage in actions, either casual and unassisted or planned and assisted by instruments designed for the purpose; and he can think, again either casually or in a calculated manner, also the former unassisted and the latter assisted by instruments of logical or material provenience, say a canon of deduction or a computer. Being present in a particular way, then, means being present to all of him, and this requires already a sequence of events since the exposure to his senses cannot be accomplished all at once.

The observer does not exist in the world whose single faculties operate separately and one at a time. There is no one who has ever been dependent for his acquaintance with the external world only upon a single sense, such as that of sight. The contacts with the external world come in terms of all three faculties interacting together. He deals with the world as though he were a whole individual, not a fragmented one. The senses, aided by action and thought, present the observer with a conception of the world, and it is in terms of such a conception that he is able to conduct his life successfully. His very success at living constitutes a kind of pragmatic reinforcement of the conception. The composite nature of his experience (for that is what every experience is) is organized into a synthetic unity by means of a stereoscopic representation which is true to the facts. He sees things in immediate perception at least partly as they are, and he supports this with a conception of how he knows them to be.

There is much more to be said about this aspect of the kind of happening we have agreed to call 'having a sense experience'. I have deliberately omitted a number of subjective conditioning factors which are quite essential, such as the degree of alertness. Since wakefulness seems to depend upon a level of cortical activity which has to be maintained by a continual stream of incoming sensory impulses, it would seem that consciousness depends upon the external world and not the reverse. Admittedly, there must be a capacity for receiving and registering these impulses, but the capacity could be there without being exercised. The existence of consciousness, then, can hardly be adduced as evidence that the mind has a mode of being which is separate from the material organism. There is also an element of abstractiveness involved in attending to one material object which has to be discriminated against a background of other material objects in which it essentially belongs and with which it can be apprehended in a larger chunk of experience encompassing a wider field.

Resemblances recur, differences perish. The way in which material things resemble each other will be encountered again, but the ways in which they differ will be lost and their places taken by other differences. Substance *supports* the similarities but *contributes* the differences. These are the facts the observer has to face in the data disclosed to him by his sense experience; and they are facts so insistent that he is compelled to recognize a recurrent order of similarities and a persistent sequence of differences. Similarities provide continuities while differences are responsible for discontinuities, but the similarities and differences can be combined, and indeed they often are, as can be observed in any cycle: the seasons, for example, or the face of a clock. The differences are salutary and as it happens their abruptness has furnished the discreteness necessary for discrimination in the first place. And that is why we have come to regard continuities as unobserved even though they too are observed.

Earlier I said that the present object can be considered from two aspects: the one particular, the other general; and now I want to concentrate more importantly for the moment on the more general aspect. Our example, if you recall, was the presence of the moon. The important fact about the general aspect is that the other members of the class to which it belongs are absent. They are absent in time and they are absent in space.

Planets are absent in time because they last for a great while even though not forever. No one knows the exact age of the material universe but everyone who has studied the question agrees that it has been here for a very long period, some 13 billion years, at the very least. In all that vast duration there have been many planets, most of which no longer exist but all of which will have to be counted as members of the same class even though they are not present.

Planets are absent in space because the material universe is an exceedingly large one. A million galaxies are known to exist, and how many more it is impossible to guess. As far out as the telescopes reach, there are still galaxies. Thus we may say that in space as well as in time the absent planets are to be found in very great numbers, in numbers so large that it is almost impossible even to imagine them.

How do these facts bear on our example of the encounter of the observer with the moon? It raises the question at least of whether what is encountered is a unique individual or a member of a class. The moon is a unique individual, no doubt of that. It has properties which it shares not only with no other planet but also with no other material object. It has features which are peculiar to it so that no other planet looks exactly like it, and it occupies a spatio-temporal region occupied by no other astronomical body. Yet it must be admitted that its uniqueness, though it is a fact, is overwhelmed by the further fact of its membership in a class having very many members. It is the sole *present* representative of the class, and this is so meaningful that it tends to overwhelm every other facet of its existence.

It is at this point that I find it necessary to establish the importance of the class as an element present in the encounter of the observer with the moon by making two moves. One is to acknowledge the operation of a kind of 'Principle of Class Presence'. The presence of a class is a characteristic which will have to be included among the essential elements in any happening sufficiently formal to be called an encounter. What the individual is meeting when he encounters a planet is the member of a class, and one of the salient features of the encounter is the power the class has and imposes on him through its present representative. And because of the prevalence of members throughout the vast reaches of time and space the class is of the utmost importance, of more importance in fact than any member through which the observer may come to know it. Every individual exists in part as the only present representative of the class of which it is a member. So that knowledge is not merely particular but also general, and every experience contains general elements whose representative nature is the most prominent thing about it.

This brings me to the second of the two moves. The first was the introduction of a 'Principle of Class Presence' mentioned above. The second is the recognition that every encounter is a primary confrontation.

In every act of experience there is evidently a complex situation. There is the encounter with the particular material object, and there is the confrontation with the objectivity of the class, with the present representation of absent objects. Here the three capacities for thought, feeling and action, which I have been at pains to show together, must be separated, though this time with a different intent. When the observer thinks about his own thoughts, this at its best is mathematics; when he feels keenly about his own feelings, this at its worst is neurotic. The individual recognizes at some point that he has met with two distinct but related kinds of resistance. Not only is the individual powerless to render his experience with the particular other than it is, but he is powerless equally to alter the class. Logic has its own kind of stubbornness on a par with the stubbornness of particular material objects.

Confrontation in knowledge theory may be defined as the encounter through the present members of a class with that class, and through the class with the absent members of that same class. Put otherwise, it is possible to say that there is a confrontation with both a class and its absent members in consideration of the encounter with present objects.

This is the situation which must be remembered when we are analyzing sense experience. It means that no human individual ever encounters a material object just so and entirely limited to itself. For the act of experience involves the recognition of the class and through the class of its absent members. In the traditional terminology of knowledge theory, the encounter between present particulars (e.g. the observer and his moon) is conditioned by a confrontation involving present universals and absent particulars. Classes are interpolated concretely, and knowing is a way of being confronted. Universals, on this interpretation, consist in the representations of absent objects.

One strong implication of the above analysis is that the new materialism does not imply nominalism. The older materialism assuredly did, for in the classic definition of nominalism as the sole reality of physical particulars classes had no residence except the mind which recognized them. And although this brought about the difficulty that the same mental act which recognized universals also brought them into being, it remained the stock explanation. The new materialism necessarily requires the existence of genuine objective classes, and so nominalism no longer fits but instead a variety of realism is required.

In traditional knowledge theory, this situation has been given a subjective explanation. It has been said that an element of conception enters into every act of perception. No doubt this is the case; but another interpretation of it can be made, one more compatible with the point of view I have been taking and the kind of analysis I am trying to make from it. I can say, then, not merely that a conception enters into every act of perception (although it does) but also that there is a perception of generals. Universals can be seen, heard, smelled, tasted in the very perception of particulars. A particular material object discloses its nature as a member of a class to the observer who in the very act of recognition is working with the class which he professes to see in it. When the observer looks at the moon and *sees* it as *a* moon, that is what is occurring. He is remembering the similarity between it as a material object and others of the same class that he may have seen or known about on previous occasions and now recalls. So long as in the actual presence of the material object he is aware of the class to which it belongs, he has recognized the class externally, and he does not need to back up his sense perceptions by mentioning the additional and extraneously introduced fact that he is capable also of conceptions.

So far, so good; but the recognition of the external existence of the class has difficulties of its own with which the observer must cope. If there were a single and clear-cut specification of the material object the difficulties might not exist, but the description would then be a very impoverished affair. It would do nicely for mathematics, indeed it is desirable in mathematics. But the actual world of material objects which are continually interacting and changing has dimensions which are not to be encompassed so simply or so easily. For no description has ever been given which exhausts the properties of an actual material object. Until we can find some kind of calculus of qualities, philosophy cannot be reduced to mathematics or wholly expressed in the language of mathematics.

And so an unacknowledged but effective remedy has been found in the device of multiple definition. Aristotle has given one of the best examples of it. A reader may think he knows what Aristotle meant by "substance" when he studies the first account, but what happens later when he meets many more definitions and descriptions of it is that his self-assurance vanishes. Yet the situation however confused does not show a net loss. There is here a situation which may best be described as the breadth of the concept. Multiple definition means a class turning its face in a number of directions. Philosophical concepts are qualitative and disclose different aspects when seen in different contexts. Each may be partially correct and together they may reveal a richness which none indicated separately. Hegel like Aristotle used the same term in different senses and in a somewhat different way also employed the breadth of the concept.

If some ambiguity inevitably results from the practice of such a method of explanation, why then we must ask ourselves whether this is by design or by accident. If it is by design then we may refer to it as analogical ambiguity, where 'analogical' refers to the relation between values qualitatively expressed. By contrast accidental ambiguity refers to nothing or at most to a very confused situation which exists in and between the observer and his object. Analogical ambiguity is intended to show the breadth of the concept. It refers to an object which is inherently ambiguous. It is obvious now that we must consider the classes to be permeable, transparent and flexible, as well as richly endowed, and get rid of the notion that they have fixed, rigid and limited boundaries or that they are narrow, unmoved and precisely definable.

I promised earlier to touch upon a second kind of encounter, which is the encounter with logical classes. In addition to primary confrontation, there is a second and more sophisticated kind. Secondary confrontation consists in moving up one level of abstractiveness. The observer recognizes through his apprehension of the class to which the material object belongs that there are other classes similar to the class apprehended. He is conceiving now, if you like, instead of merely perceiving, but if so he is conceiving in a chain sequence which starts from the level of the single material object. An abstract idea is also an encounter with a material object, for as philosophers of the nominalistic persuasion from Descartes on have argued, an idea is always accompanied by an image, and the image is a material object. But the image is a material object with a different function; for, unlike other kinds of material objects, it represents a class and stands in thought for it. Thus the observer is brought into the domain of classes, which is the domain of logic; and there he cannot help but notice the relations which exist between classes and which present their own kind of stubbornness.

The first kind of confrontation was material confrontation, the second kind may be called logical confrontation. The observer encounters logic through his own processes of conception when he studies the relations between classes, and he encounters material particulars by means of perception. But because logic is perfect, and because the world, being imperfect, does not conform absolutely to logic, he thinks it follows that logic is mental. He forgets that he knows logic as he knows the world: through an encounter; and when he remembers that the encounter is also a confrontation, then he ought to be able to pick up the fact that the failure of the world to conform to logic is no evidence that either is mental. Indeed the distinction between his own often fallacious processes of reasoning and the logical relations he is endeavoring to follow is evidence of the objectivity of logic.

The entities and relations disclosed by thought, like the materials and events disclosed by sense perception, fight back when any attempt is made to read them as other than they are. Both logical manipulations and material adventures offer resistance and present the observer with surprises. That is why mathematical discoveries are possible; the sequence of primes, for example. And when something happens that the observer could not have predicted from what he knows, then he can be sure that there is an external world which exists whether he knows it or not, and exists moreover in a state of considerable indifference to him. This is what I referred to much earlier as the inner-induced recognition of subjectivity, and it results in the outlines of an objective epistemology, based largely on a demonstration of outer experience. For now, thanks to the sorting out of the various threads of encounter and confrontation, there is a recognition in what I choose to call inner experience that there is an outer experience.

A number of points can be made by drawing inferences, tangential or otherwise, from the foregoing account of the act of experience. I would like to state them first as three graded yet interrelated theses and then comment on what I think that together they lead us to in the way of conclusions.

The three theses are:

(1) that what is sensationally immediate may be perceptually obscuring;

(2) that what is intermediately vague (distant, yet apprehended through images as partly perceived and partly conceptual) may recede into conceptual generality; and lastly;

(3) that what may be too distant for perception in time and space may contribute materially to conception.

The acquisition of knowledge begins with the encounter with a single material object which is discriminated against a background and in this way recognized for what it is. But such acquisition does not stop there, chiefly because the object encountered was not a valid isolate. Just as the observer comes to the encounter with equipment on his side: with the lessons he has learned from his previous encounters with members of the same class, for instance, and with the knowledge that there are other classes to which that class is itself logically related, so the single material object brings to the encounter all of its close relations with absent objects. It may be discriminated against a background, but this is possible only because the material object encountered differs from the objects in its immediate neighborhood. The object has differences with other present objects but immense similarities with enormous numbers of absent objects of the same class, objects absent in time on the one hand and in space on the other.

Now when both the material object and the individual encountering it have such complex other relations, it is hardly to be expected that the knowledge which relates to the individual on his side of the encounter would end there. And it does not do so, either, but goes on to similar situations in the universe, situations in which there are other material objects and it may be other human individuals encountering them in much the same way. Knowledge is always limited, but the limits recede as knowledge advances.

It is in this way that we are entitled to speak of the 'Fallacy of the Local Present'. There is nothing merely local about the present, neither in space nor in time, for everything which is peculiarly related to it participates in it even in the most primitive aspect of sense perception. Thus the kind of happening we have come to call 'having a sense experience' is the beginning of an accumulation of knowledge which always exceeds the immediate occasion.

Another point might be stated somewhat as follows. Considering the dependence of the observer on his environment – on his physical environment for air and shelter, on his biological environment for food, and on his social environment for beliefs and language – it could fairly be said that he himself consists in an arbitrary selected segment of an environing natural world. There are no valid isolates, each is part of all; and so all of the effects of material objects upon that other material object which is the knower must be counted as fundamental. Consciousness is from this point of view the center of the impingement of the world upon the observer, who is an uncommonly sensitive mechanism for sorting out tropisms and for integrating influences.

The observer is both a material object and a knower with a view of himself and of the world with which as a material object he interacts. So much is plain; but there is sometimes more. For subjectivity can also mean the condition of being in a position to observe both that object itself from the inside and some limited portion of the environing world from the outside, both under the dictates of a judgment which renders the view of the object from inside more real or more important than the view of the environing world. It happens that this judgment is wrong. The self is a point and a focus, nothing more; not anything in and of itself. There are no objects in the mind, neither material objects nor logical objects, only the knowledge of objects constructed in terms of images and ideas. The objects of which minds have knowledge must be independent of the minds which know them for there to be knowledge at all. Mind is simply matter in a condition to be aware of itself and of the world beyond, including the representations of absent objects.

Finally, it can be categorically asserted that there is nothing in the mind that was not first in the external world, except error. The mind has two capacities: to apprehend truth and to create error. Strictly speaking, error is not 'created' but consists in a false selection and arrangement of genuine elements. The observer's organism was constructed out of elements selected from the world and put together in such a way as to accept the world. It is his perspective – not only the angle from which it is taken but what lies within it – that gives him back to himself as a self. For the self is not to be found through internal concentration but rather by deducing from the world the peculiar perspective from which it is being observed, that part of the world which can be apprehended from the self. The self itself is only a point-instant from which it was possible to make a world selection.

THE MIND-BODY PROBLEM

I. CONTRA

It often happens in the history of philosophy that problems which cannot be solved are dropped. This may come about when due to the advent of access to additional information a problem turns out to be not a genuine problem after all but only a pseudo-problem, or when interest shifts from a problem which proves to be either undecidable or of less importance than had been thought. In any case it means for some philosophical assumptions that they lead to trial runs which need not be made.

If assumptions are axiomatic beliefs which compel theorematic behavior, then the contentions of present day logic and mathematics that we are unconcerned with the truth of axioms is not the case. We may not be able to demonstrate their truth within the system in which they function as axioms, but when we have reason to suspect their falsehood we are done with them. And this situation can be dealt with more easily when adequate substitutes are available.

I submit that this is the case now with respect to the mind-body problem, and I propose to point to the substitute which, having already been discovered by others, stands ready and waiting on the scene. The assumption which is at issue here is that the distinction between mind and body is an important one.

The mind-body distinction was first brought into prominence when Descartes changed "form" to "mind" in the Aristotelian categories of form and matter. The change was both fundamental and radical. Aristotle's categories had been ontological ones and the distinction was basic to his system. The change which Descartes proposed marked a radical shift from a metaphysics with epistemological implications to an epistemology in which is embedded a metaphysical universe of discourse.

The exact terms of the Cartesian distinction were "thinking substance" (*res cogitans*) and "extended substance" (*res extensa*). Evidently, the mind which knows matter was henceforth to be as important as the matter which is known by mind. In the case of the human individual mind was to be taken more seriously by philosophers on the assumption that matter could well be left to the physicists. That men had minds as well as material bodies struck them immediately as meaning that their minds were the more important of the two, for everything had bodies, and not only other animals (scornfully described by Descartes as mere automata) but even plants and boulders. The new emphasis accordingly led the way to the investigation of knowledge theory and of how the mind worked – in short to epistemology and psychology. No one was interested any longer in metaphysics, but the science of psychology was probably a result. Paradoxically the Cartesian distinction proved useful in getting psychology started but held it back after it was firmly entrenched as a science. Only with the behaviorists did psychology begin to get away from the strictures and limitations of the conception.

The Cartesian distinction has had no effect on the sciences other than psychology. The physical scientists pursued their objective experiments to determine the nature and properties of matter in the direction in which they had been aimed ever since men like Robert Grosseteste, Roger Bacon and Galileo had first correctly outlined the scientific method of investigation.

The success of the scientific empiricists needs no elaboration or emphasis here, but the route taken by the philosophers might be traced.

The effect on philosophy was nothing less than paralyzing. Subjectivisms of all sorts, which were ancient even in Descartes' time, were given a new authority and a more substantial residence than they had ever had before, and the trend is by no means over. The continental rationalists after Descartes, with their reliance on reasoning rather than logic, and the British empiricists, with their exclusive concentration upon sense experience rather than fact, have had their followers and continue to have them still today. The strongest arguments against the Cartesian position were those launched by C. S. Peirce,[1] but they have been relatively neglected and in any case have not done any serious damage to the Cartesian tradition. The subjectivisms are more in control today than ever outside Marxist countries. Consider for

---

[1] See the references in my *Introduction to Peirce's Philosophy* (New York, 1946, Harper and Brothers), Chapter 2, Section E, pp. 69–75.

instance the subjective implications of illness in Kierkegaard's feeling of isolation, the subjective version of phenomenology as propounded by Husserl and Heidegger, and the subjective interpretation of linguistics which Wittgenstein's followers understand him to have taught. By means of these tortuous efforts the philosophers have sought to describe mental events which they believed to be quite independent of matter.

It occurred to very few philosophers except Peirce to reject the distinction; it occurred to many to grapple with it as though it were an irrefrangible given of experience. The result was a number of alternative choices: the reduction of matter to mind (idealism); the reduction of mind to matter (crude materialism); the less popular parallelism which accepted the equality of mind and matter (Malebranche) or a one-way effect of mind on matter (Descartes), a one-way effect of matter on mind (Feuerbach), or a refusal to admit any interaction (Leibniz); and, finally, a kind of identification of the two which yet retains the distinction by regarding them as different ways of obtaining the same thing (Feigl). In addition to those who retreated to the study of the mind, there were others who endeavored to cope with the Cartesian heritage *in toto*.

The mind-body problem, aptly so-called, makes more difficulties than it solves, and anyone who had examined these impartially would have been justified in rejecting the whole conception. Most of the difficulties centered around the problem presented by the "forms" of Aristotle which had been displaced by "mind" in the Cartesian distinction. Because of the undeniable being of the forms, the matter-mind distinction fails to meet the requirements of every fundamental pair of categories: that they be mutually exclusive and exhaustive. They can be exclusive if we classify the central nervous system and the brain with matter; but they cannot be exhaustive so long as the forms held in the mind by thought and held in the past by materials do not exhaust the forms. For both of these are examples of actual forms, whereas there are forms too which are possible: the form of the tree, of the house, of the crater, tomorrow, all have to be accounted for; and it can be shown that more forms are possible than actual, for there always are many ways in which every actual thing could have forms other than the one it has.

Conceived as a kind of epistemological dualism, the mind-body distinction dies hard. It is still found in the most unexpected places, as for instance in symposia or information processing,[2] where the attempt

---

[2] *Proceedings of IFIP Congress 65*, vol. I (Washington, D.C., 1965, Spartan Books, Inc.), pp. 45–49.

is made to bring together mental events and physical events which should not have been distinguished in the first place. They are not on the same level of analysis, and therefore any attempt to equate or oppose them is misleading. Attempts to solve the "mind-body puzzle" on the basis of their equivalence have not met with any greater acceptance.[3]

The mind-body distinction lurks under other terms in such a way that it often gets by as new knowledge. Since each account is a special one, no formula can be provided for recognizing them. Perhaps the example of one such account will suffice to make the point.

Talbot Waterman recognizes "two major components" which can be "analyzed for understanding biological systems. One of these comprises all the elements relating to the acquisition, transfer and utilization of *energy*. ... The other consists of everything functioning in the detection, processing, retention and utilization of *information*." The first concerns the work of the organism, the second its control.[4]

Now I submit that the distinction simply will not do as a description. Energy is acquired and transferred partly by means of the channels of information, and on the other hand the processing and utilization of information requires the expenditure of a certain amount of energy. The areas laid out by the categories overlap in a serious way which robs them of their effectiveness.

The error no doubt arises, as we saw at the outset, from the attempt to give ontological status to what is essentially only an epistemological distinction. Our categories of being could come from distinctions about knowing provided that what is, is, because it is known. Differences in logical orders ought to be sufficient evidence to refute the confusion; the order of knowing is *not* the order of being, and what is learned is not ontologically structured in the same way in which it is learned.

II. PRO

There is no need to argue against the mind-body distinction any further, except as such arguments may be needed to make the contrast with the analysis which replaces it. For the chief aim of this essay is to show not what cannot be done but what can. A line of inquiry has been opened

---

[3] Satosi Watanabe, "A Model of Mind-Body Relation in Terms of Modular Logic", in Marx W. Wartofsky, ed., *Boston Studies in the Philosophy of Science* (Dordrecht, Holland, 1963, D. Reidel), pp. 1–41.

[4] Talbot H. Waterman, "Systems Theory and Biology – View of a Biologist," in M. D. Mesarovic, ed., *Systems Theory and Biology* (New York, 1968, Springer-Verlag), p. 1.

up recently that could have a bearing on the mind as much as it has had already on the body.

The persistence of the mind-matter (or mind-body) distinction ignores the development of the experimental sciences, and, more particularly, of knowledge concerning the relations between the segments of nature investigated by those sciences, an area now named the integrative levels. In brief, the picture looks somewhat as follows.

	Scientific Field	Entity	Energy
E	Culture (anthropology)	society, artifacts	ethos
D	Psychology	human individual	awareness
C	Biology	organisms, cells	life
B	Chemistry	compounds, elements, molecules	valence
A	Physics	atoms, nuclear components	nuclear gravitational electromagnetic

FIGURE I

The integrative levels contribute a hierarchy of multi-level structures in a continuous series, in which a number of functions can be discerned. For instance, each level includes organizations belonging to the level below, plus one emergent kind of energy or quality. Each level finds its mechanism at the level next below and its goal (end, purpose) at the level next above. At each level upward, control is increased and power decreased, evolution is increased and entropy decreased. Still other integrative level laws are known.

Now let us consider not the integrative levels in general but rather the integrative levels as they exist in the human body. The human organism participates in a number of levels. Individual man in fact shares all of the levels except the highest, and on his social side he is part of that one.

For the human organism is a complex structure, having many natural divisions and constituents, beginning with the physical and ending with the psychological but including the levels between, such as the chemical and the biological.

Integrative		Entity	Energy
E		Neurons: awareness, memory	Motivation
D	Mind	Organs: control mechanisms	Self-direction
C		Organs: functional mechanisms Cells	Reproduction
B	Body	Biochemicals: carbohydrates, liquids, proteins	Self-repair
A		Physical chemicals: water, salts, sulphur, iron	Integration

FIGURE 2

First off it should be pointed out that the integrative levels within the organism, like those in the actual world, given earlier, are gross levels, listed briefly and only for purposes of illustration. Actually, each of the levels can be subdivided many times. For example, I have not listed macromolecules, or the various kinds of cells which are more complex and therefore higher than others in the series of sublevels.

It should be clear from the foregoing that the mind-body distinction is no longer acceptable. The integrative levels within the body consist in a continuous series with qualitatively graded breaks, just as they do outside the body, and so there is no justification for considering one break more important than the others, or for reifying the two sides of the break as though they were categorically different things.

The integrative levels (Figure 1) can be matched by levels within the individual organism (Figure 2) as the capital letters indicate. What is called 'body' comprises the three lower levels, A through C, while what is called 'mind' consists in the two upper levels, D and E. After C and D the arbitrary break, which has been assigned unwarranted importance, occurs between organs which are functional mechanisms, e.g. the heart, and those which are control mechanisms, e.g. the brain. The 'body' is properly speaking the name for the entire human organism, and the 'mind' the name for that part of the body which controls its thoughts, influences its feelings, and dictates its movement.

The mind is an arbitrary setting off of the upper levels of the body, and not a separate entity which can be considered on its own ground. Mind with respect to body simply means that the controls of the organism are built into the organism and are more elaborate than those which thus far have been built into any other machine. The mind is a set of functions of the body, intimately related to it and difficult to conceive without it.

Consciousness (or, alternatively, awareness, attention, wakefulness, alertness), is chiefly what 'mind' means to those who entertain the mind-body distinction, though sometimes 'mind' is employed to designate a more comprehensive conception which includes consciousness but may be extended to include also those processes which lie below consciousness and are accordingly described as 'unconscious' or 'subconscious', such as memory or unconscious thought. In any case consciousness, or the mind, interacts with the elements of a number of structures which are external to it: (1) with the material environment, containing both non-human nature and artifacts; (2) with lower levels of the somatic organism; (3) with memory, through recall; and (4) with the unconscious thought processes. We may glance at them in that order.

(1) The reification of a pair of categories such as mind and body raises many questions as to the implications of the distinctions. Neither the human mind nor the human body was always in its present state; both were instead the outcome of certain evolutionary developments. And both the mind and the material world with which the mind interacts through the medium of the body have been altered as a result of continual interchange.

At first and for hundreds of thousands of years the interchange took place between the human individual and his nonhuman environment. He could change it very little and was therefore obliged to adapt to it in order to survive. This called for changes in him but not in it. In more recent millennia, however, he has been able to make over parts of his material environment by constructing artifacts or tools, earlier described as material objects altered through human agency to serve human needs. In this way he has forced what in effect amounts to an adaptation on the part of the material environment, which in turn reacts back upon him.

The intellectual stage to which the human mind has been brought did not occur in a vacuum. It has resulted from a long genetic evolution, affected as much by the complexity of artifacts as by anything else.[5] For it was the invention and use of tools which accounted for an increase in the size of the brain and its consequent tremendous capacity for abstract thought. The complexity of high abstractions, of mathematics for instance, kept pace with the increased complexity of tools. It is a

[5] Ernest Caspari, "Selective Forces in the Evolution of Man", in M. F. Ashley Montagu ed., *Culture: Man's Adaptive Dimension* (London, 1968, Oxford University Press), pp. 159–69.

long way from early man to modern man, but no longer than it is from the stone ax to the intercontinental ballistics missile. And during that time the speed and intricacy of the interaction increased proportionately. Man no longer adapts only to a crude material environment. Surely he does this too so long as he drinks the water, breathes the air and walks on the ground. But he also interacts with that part of the material environment which consists in artifacts. As Warren McCullough has argued,[6] the feedback loops of the central nervous system extend to the environment. This interaction has produced in the environment tools at every integrative level.

But now a further and more sophisticated interaction takes place: the human individual interacts with the tools to produce an altered individual. Henceforth the problems which he undertakes to solve must be worked on by means of the tools which are specific to their solution; and all of his efforts to reach goals are mediated by tools. This is what is meant by saying that he has become a civilized man, for his achievements either consist in tools or have been brought about by tools.

Integrative level:		Tools:
Culture	(E)	civilizations
Psychology	(D)	books, schools
Biology	(C)	agricultural implements, animal husbandry
Chemistry	(B)	chemical industry, processing plants
Physics	(A)	water purification plants, airplanes

FIGURE 3

(2) That consciousness interacts with the somatic organism through its outer levels is now well known. Psychosomatic effects are too numerous to list here. Suffice to say by way of illustration that according to the theory of reverberations a disturbance at any integrative level within the body has echoing effects at all other levels. That anxiety states can affect digestion is a familiar fact to the psychiatrists, as familiar as the fact that tranquillizers can reduce anxiety. Certain diseases are accompanied by characteristic traumas; people with tuberculosis are usually optimistic about their future, those with

[6] *Embodiments of Mind* (Cambridge, Mass., 1965, MIT Press), p. 144.

carcinoma pessimistic. A disorder at any level is sure to have its effects upon consciousness.

(3) Through association the contents of consciousness are apt to provoke recall in a way which changes those contents. The memory is a storehouse of past experiences any of which may be revived and in this way influence consciousness. We are to that extent what our past has made of us, and our present and future are affected accordingly.

(4) Freud has made us familiar with the pathological aspects of unconscious thought processes. And if there are pathological aspects there must be normal processes, and as it develops there are. Who is not familiar with the unsolved problem that we decide to 'sleep over', on the assumption that we will awake in the morning to find the problem solved? Many a scientist and mathematician has reported that important discoveries and valuable insights have occurred to him while he was doing something else of a trivial mechanical nature, such as boarding a bus or shaving.

To the four separate sets of feedbacks we have just enumerated, it is necessary to add their interactions, which amount to some ten varieties of permutations and combinations. Moreover, the simplistic description we have been giving probably falsifies the account of the situation. For the feedbacks occur at times intermittently, at other times without interruption, so that any flat description is bound to be to some extent misleading. The combination of orders with disorders is confusing, but one fact stands out. Consciousness is a kind of thin Dedekind cut between memory and current events; between events which, having happened, were recorded, on the one hand, and events which are still happening, on the other. If consciousness seems aimless and undirected, no wonder then when we consider all of the forces which continually play upon it. It is after all a state of tension brought to bear upon a loose consensus. The primacy of consciousness which, as Peirce noted, stands behind the Cartesian distinction between mind and body, is hardly justified by the facts.

THE KNOWLEDGE OF THE KNOWN

It is the thesis of this chapter that the adjective 'known' adds nothing to our knowledge, and, by extension, that epistemology is very much less important than is currently believed.

In order to support this contention I propose to make three arguments against the value of the assertion 'X is known' which will hold whatever X may be. Let us begin then by assuming that there is something which is named X. Let us further assume that it is legitimate to assert that 'X is known' whenever anything is known about X. (It will not be argued in this paper though it can be shown that it is never the case that everything is known about X.)

First Argument. That X is either known or unknown involves in the former instance a redundancy and in the latter a contradiction. Let us consider these two propositions separately.

If 'X' is known, then to assert that 'X is known' would be to assert the same as 'X', for 'X' could not be asserted unless it were known. Therefore to add 'is known' to 'X' would mean to bring about a redundancy, and so it would not be necessary to assert that 'X is known', only to assert 'X'.

If X is unknown, then to assert that 'X is known' would be to assert the contradictory and hence a falsehood, while to assert 'X' would be only to utter a sound, not even to enunciate a sign, since we would not know what it was we were asserting. Thus we could not assert 'X is known' or even 'X'.

It remains to ask whether under the circumstances that X is unknown we could even assert 'X is unknown'. The statement is self-defeating, for X is known to the extent to which we can say anything about it. Yet what we are saying denies this, and so X is known, at least to the extent to which we assert that it is unknown.

If the charge of equivocation be levelled against this argument, on the grounds that I have confused the name of what is unknown with the thing which is unknown after the manner described by Quine in the distinction between "use" and "mention,"[1] it can be contended that in all instances we are dealing only with the name but always on the assumption (made equally in all instances) that the name is the name *of* something just in case there is something to be named. In some cases it is something unknown beyond the fact of being known to be something, and in all cases it is unknown whether there is something which is unknown or simply nothing at all.

Several further comments in extension.

There is no need in this chapter which is a study in the logic of epistemology, to complicate matters by introducing a psychological reference. It would not help and would only make the argument confused. Thus to assert of something that it is unknown is meant here *simpliciter* and without reference to person, and what is unknown without reference to person is of course unknown by anyone.

Again, the lack of knowledge contained in the statement 'X is unknown' is a lack regardless of whether what is lacking is knowledge-by-acquaintance or knowledge-by-description: the negative category is inclusive of everything except its contradictory.

Second Argument. The assertion that 'X is known' involves an infinite regress. For if it is true that 'X is known' then to assert it is to imply something else, for if I can draw on my knowledge to say 'I know that X is known', what I am implying is that "'X is known' is known."

How far does self-consciousness penetrate? If we know, then we have knowledge of ourselves knowing. But does anyone have knowledge of *that*? If I do, then what is to prevent me from taking a further step? Not only 'I know' and 'I know that I know' but also 'I know that I know that I know' and so on? But if not, then the lack of validity tumbles back down and I cannot assert that "'X is known' is known" nor for that matter that 'X is known', and perhaps not even 'X'.

Subjectivity is evidently a wholly artificial viewpoint, one which can be stated abstractly but which nobody actually assumes and for which there is no logical or factual evidence. Ordinarily, the knower is concerned with *what* he knows, not with the fact *that* he knows. The former is rich in distinctions and differences, and therefore rewards attention, while the latter displays only a trivial similarity. The former

---

[1] W. V. Quine, *Mathematical Logic* (Cambridge, Mass., 1947, Harvard University Press), Chapter One, 4.

is communicable, the latter, in its quality of knowing, is not. The pro-
spective recession to a point-instant of the consciousness of knowledge
is entirely private and must remain so. It cannot furnish a topic for
discourse by means of which one knower seeks to persuade another.

Third Argument. By the principle of excluded middle, either 'X is
known' or 'X is unknown', at least that is the situation in logic; but in
actual material existence excluded middles abound. For while logic
does apply to existence it does not apply absolutely but always with
mediation and through extenuating circumstances. Thus it may happen
that while logically either 'X is known' or 'X is unknown', materially
X may be partly known and partly unknown, depending upon the
degree of penetration of the knowledge and upon the degree of alteration in that which is either known or unknown. Given the richness of
existence and the poverty of knowledge, it can safely be claimed that
the knowledge about a thing is never complete, and that we do not
know how much of the thing our knowledge covers or for what length
of time the knowledge we do have remains reliable. That is to say, an
ambiguity may arise from the falsity of the knowledge when a part is
allowed to represent a whole, or when something known changes and
therefore is known no longer, i.e. when what was known has become
once again unknown. This is the case with every scientific hypothesis
temporarily, and it is the case with every comprehensive system of
philosophy permanently. The best that can be offered in these instances
is that the evidence in support of an assertion that 'X is known' has
such and such a force.

We have already noted at the end of the Second Argument that the
statement 'X is unknown' is self-contradictory; for we saw there that
to the extent that X is unknown we are in no position to assert that it
is unknown, for we could not possibly know that; while, on the other
hand, we must know that in order to assert it. In short, to assert that
'X is unknown' is to assert that in some sense it is known. Therefore we
cannot assert that 'X is unknown'. But if we cannot assert that 'X is
unknown', then the assertion 'X is known' adds nothing to our knowledge. It does not add anything to our knowledge to assert of what could
not possibly be false that it is true.

The separation of the known from the unknown is not accomplished
nor knowledge increased by studies in epistemology. Indeed difficulties
of various sorts about the degree of knowledge contained in statements
often serve as the occasions for important discoveries, for they may

prompt us to seek in concrete situations for solutions to the problems they pose. The use of false propositions is a common occurrence in scientific investigation. Examples may be found in many instances where a false argument has led to a true conclusion. As Popper has pointed out,[2] when a scientist discovers an hypothesis he has reason to suspect is true, he tries to prove it false, and if he fails this is considered evidence for its truth. Maxwell invented a model of idler wheels and gears functioning in space, and with its aid deduced equations concerning electromagnetic phenomena. The idler wheels have never been accepted by subsequent investigators but the equations have been shown to be true.

The proposal to consider that self-contradictory statements *can* be employed in the interpretation of concrete situations is obviously one calculated to horrify any logician who may chance to read it. The argument in defense of this proposal would take us too far afield. Suffice to say here perhaps that self-contradictory statements in logic are represented *mutatis mutandis* in the domain of matter by events. Conversely, incompatible situations among events are the material counterparts of contradictory logical propositions.

I might cite two examples, one trivial, and one so serious it has shaken the world of physics.

The material equivalent of the logical paradoxes is exemplified in an amusing way by a small box which an old lady who died recently left among her effects. It was labelled "String Too Short to Save."

The incompatibility of material events is exemplified in quantum mechanics by the phenomena which exhibit themselves in one connection as a wave and in another as a stream of particles. The "wave-particle duality" of Heisenberg was in fact gradually elevated through his "uncertainty principle" and Pauli's "exclusion principle" to Bohr's principle of "complementarity" in which, under the influence of his teacher Hoffding who had been heavily influenced by Kierkegaard, the ambiguity came to be regarded as inherent in the human mind, from which the physical situation could never be divorced. In the end von Neumann insisted that quantum mechanics could not be formulated without reference to human consciousness.

Einstein did not agree, de Broglie does not agree, Vigier does not agree, Bohr does not agree. What strikes one most forcefully is that if Bohr and von Neumann are right, then it is difficult to see how quan-

---

[2] Karl Popper, *The Logic of Scientific Discovery* (London, 1959, Hutchinson), p. 40.

tum mechanics can be distinguished from anything else the knowledge of which enters the human consciousness, such as shoes and ships and sealing wax, or how the physical world with its waves and particles ever existed before the advent of man.

Bohr's and von Neumann's contention is subject to the same objections that can be raised against any claim respecting the knowledge of what is known. The observer is not part of that which is observed. But even if he were, then who is to observe the observer, and who is to observe the observer observing the observer, and so on? Suffice to say here that subjectivity is a wholly artificial viewpoint which no subject ordinarily experiences and nobody can demonstrate. And if there is no evidence for it, and if assuming it in quantum mechanics points to a similarity which confuses it with other things known with which it has nothing significant in common, then why hold it?

The argument for subjectivity in quantum mechanics is made even weaker when we remember that there it is not the observer we are talking about, in any but a secondary sense, but the observer's instrument, which is, by the way, a material object and not a conscious subject even though it is employed by the conscious subject who makes use of its pointer readings. An experiment conducted by means of instruments is a planned and controlled effect of one material object upon another, one which is no less material because designed and interpreted by a human being. Human consciousness no more enters the picture in such a case than it does in other, less scientific undertakings. Thus when von Neumann concluded that the formulation of quantum mechanics could be completed by the inclusion of a reference to human consciousness, Einstein, Podolsky and Rosen insisted that it was in its present stage of development inherently incomplete. The latter answer is more likely to be the correct one. For in von Neumann's formulation we have a clear instance of the reference to 'known' as a difference when is it in fact only a similarity.

The last distinction makes the case in point. For any two things that may be said to be known, whatever they are, have similarities and differences. The class to which a thing belongs is defined by its similarities with other things of the same class, while its uniqueness is specified by its differences from them. These distinctions are significant because they contribute to the understanding of the thing. But the further and broader proposition that any two things that are known have in common *that* they are known is not significant, for while it points to a similarity it is not accompanied by a requisite difference and thus tends to obscure knowledge rather than add to it.

It is no help to assert about the things that are known that they have 'being known' in common, for, apart from acknowledging the process of knowing itself, it is the differences which are full of surprises and not the similarities. We have come to recognize that the differences are found in the object while the similarities, at least those with respect to being known, are found in the subject. In the examples already given, there is no way in which we could evaluate separately – and differently – a piece of string on the one hand and the wave-particle duality of quantum mechanics on the other, certainly not by asserting that both were known.

To locate the fundamental error of epistemology we must penetrate deeper than the mere examination of a central problem. We must reach down for and find the assumptions upon which the standard positions in epistemology rest. Chief among these is the assumption that the question, 'What is there?' can be satisfied by the answer to another question, 'How can anything be known?' The equation which states that water is composed of two parts of hydrogen to one part of oxygen

$$H + OH \rightarrow H_2O$$

is not meaningfully expanded in the expression

$$\text{known } H + \text{known } OH \rightarrow \text{known } H_2O$$

The expansion is made on the assumption that being known is the most important relation of being, as though the limited human knower were on a par with the universe which partly at least he knows. I have tried to show that this assumption is false.

The reason why knowing adds nothing to knowledge is that epistemology itself is inherently subjective. Whenever the question of what can be known is raised, the condition is immediately set that whatever the answer it must include a contribution from the knower. But there is a circularity in supposing that the knower only gets back his own. In the end under this limitation he is bound to confine his curiosity to his own processes of knowing, which makes knowledge, in the grand sense of knowledge of the world, impossible to obtain, and produces only a monotonous scepticism.

The realist makes a different assumption concerning knowledge. He inquires in order to learn what exists apart from him and even without him. The assumption of the realist produces an emphasis which can be satisfied only by a study of what there is, with the further assumption that if the study is successful its results will become known. The human limitation is for him one of selection rather than distortion. His material objects are accompanied by a large, possibly an infinite, set of perspectives which belong to the object necessarily and are occupied by a knower only accidentally. In this way inquiry is returned to the object, and ontology replaces epistemology.

CHAPTER IX

THE SUBJECTIVITY OF A REALIST

Ever since experimental science, which is a cumulative cultural enterprise, first appeared upon the social scene in western Europe in about the seventeenth century, the philosophers, in order to avoid the sense of defeat and discouragement which its successes gave them, have felt crowded out of the public world and have retreated to a defense of their own sensations. Although themselves guided by a scrupulous adherence to fact and logic, they have been concentrating upon the subjective end of the knowledge relation, on the assumption that nobody would be able to disturb them there. The microcosm of feeling seemed to be a refuge from the macrocosm of the world where measurement and instruments are employed far and wide without limit. And the harder the philosophers become pressed by the progress of nearby sciences, such as neurophysiology, the more they concentrate on the privacy of the subject when he is alone with his feelings.

What I have said applies, of course, primarily to the idealists. The realists, like the materialists, have thought their enterprise reinforced rather than supplanted by the sciences. Subjectivity traditionally has been the province of the idealists in philosophy, under various and more specific names such as 'mind' or 'consciousness'. The object of knowledge has been left to the realists. But the idealists must also account for the object and realists for the subject. Both have done so hitherto in only summary fashion. The idealists, in extreme cases such as Kant's, have even dismissed the object as inherently unknowable; and the realists, with a like casualness, have insisted that the subject does not exist except as a reference point, a contention in which they have had the support of the sceptics, Hume, for instance, who could find no experience of a self. Objective philosophies, such as realism or materialism, have had great difficulty in establishing the subject as it must be conceived when it is independent of the very object which has disclosed it to itself.

The one-sidedness of the philosophers continues to be a prominent feature. There is the subjectivity of the existentialists and the phenomenologists who refuse to concern themselves with the independent object, and there is the objectivity of the Marxists who refuse to concern themselves with the private subject.

Subjective philosophies, such as Kierkegaard's or Husserl's, to name but two, have difficulty in establishing the nature of the object as it must be when it is conceived as independent of the experience which discloses to the subject his own existence. They did not discuss the object at any great length but only concerned themselves with how to escape from it into subjectivity, where alone the truth resides. The result is that lacking a valid theory of the object the subjectivists fail in their own domain also, for the epistemological starting-point of subject and object requires, for an adequate description of the development of the functioning of either end, an acceptable theory about what goes on at the other.

Kierkegaard, the existentialist, was concerned with the subject as an actor for whom the truth is subjective, not as a mere spectator. The quality of subjectivity for him was the anxiety prompted by the necessity for choice, a negative quality, to be supplanted by the leap of faith in God. Thus he considered as qualitative the insupportable feeling of dread which was to be avoided because it issued from the lost feeling of freedom which is negative in the sense that it is unlimited and unbearable. But such feelings, while subjective, are related to the outer environment; and the second was judged better than the first for external reasons, not, in other words, a true subjectivity, only a methodological one, and replaceable by the feeling that God exists.

Husserl, the phenomenologist, tried to observe and describe the elements of the inner environment by first setting off that environment, defining it through the technique of excluding from it everything that does not belong to it, and, secondly, classifying the elements common to groups of individual things, such elements as their qualities. He ended by seeking the truly universal and not the quality as it is in itself.

These two subjectivists, in short, were not subjective enough; they merely sought in the subject the determinants for action respecting objects. They wished to heal the alienation which gave rise to subjectivity and not to continue it. Husserl sought the essence of subjectivity – but in terms of a ground, a foothold for removing the self from the outer environment and placing it in a subjective state where the ego could observe its contents. Kierkegaard sought a subjectivity – but one made real by decisions, one which relied upon the reality of the moment of choice, where choice related to the external world. Neither thinker, in the end, was concerned to isolate and concentrate upon true subjectivity for its own sake.

If the subjectivists avoid the object and so fail to burrow their way into true subjectivity, it is also true that the materialists avoid the subject and so fail to set forth a self-sufficient theory of the object.

For the Marxists, for example, all subjectivity is solipsistic, and any halfway station, such as pragmatism or instrumentalism, is only another variety of solipsism. The part played by the individual is for them reduced almost to nothing. Subjectivity is inherently anti-Marxist, and that is enough to condemn it. Idealism is bourgeois and a bad thing. Proletarian partisanship, on the other hand, sees subjectivity as truly objective in character because it is a faithful reflection of the objective world. Thought follows the object so faithfully that it is only necessary to study the object.

In a word, for the Marxists all is subjective which is not material. But matter was conceived by them only in relation to the senses: for Lenin matter was that which acts upon the sense organs but remains independent of them, and for Marx it was an object of practice rather than of contemplation. There was no disposition on the part of the Marxists to account for, or in any way to deal with, quality as such; it was a thing that changed and that could be exchanged for quantity, and that ended their interest in it. So far as the Marxists are concerned, there is no legitimate area of subjectivity for them to explore, only one to regret – no aspect of it which could be mentioned with approval except reflection, a function which adds nothing.

And yet somehow this is a conception of objectivity which depended upon its separation from the subject. The Marxists seemed unable to define matter or materialism on its own, apart from the necessity of demarking it from the subject. A true materialism, however, can be stated on its own in metaphysical terms, and does not have to be defined by means of an epistemological contrast. If the Marxists intend by the object a material object, as they assuredly do, then it should be possible to define matter, after the physicists, as mass (inertial force) or energy (kinetic force), without reference to any theory of knowledge.

I may end my brief survey of those who accept the epistemological conception of subject and object as foundational. By pointing out that they would be unhappy to learn that in divorcing one end of the knowledge relation and clinging to the other, they have much in common, more than would allow either to have an exclusive hold on the truth or even an independent part of it. Thus we may conclude that the subjectivists are not good subjectivists because of their failure to develop an adequate theory of the object, and the objectivists are not good objectivists because of their failure to develop an adequate theory of the subject.

And yet a complete account of the process of knowing must include a serious description of both subject and object, whatever the assumptions of the investigator. In this chapter, then, I hope to make a start toward correcting at least half of the oversight by establishing the subject as a legitimate topic for inquiry by the realist.

What is subjectivity for a realist? It will be advisable to begin with the picture of the subject as the realist sees him when he is busily engaged in the acquisition of knowledge. For this purpose I will not look at him as though I were he but as though I were observing both him and the object of his knowledge from the outside. First of all I will talk about what the realist assumes about the object of knowledge and then about his own peculiar perspective.

The position of the realist toward the existence of objects capable of being sensed but existing independently of such sensations is too well known to need more than a brief statement here. The object is material, consisting in some form of matter or energy. It exists in the material world independently of the property of being known, which is for it an accidental and not a necessary property. Every object in the course of being experienced (which is only another way of talking about some of its many interactions with its neighbor objects) turns now one and now another of its faces towards its neighbor. But the face is always that of some aspect of quality.

It is too often neglected in the analysis of sense experience that the object, like the subject, moves its position and so shifts its relations with neighbor objects. Let us here consider for a moment what the movements of objects mean to perception. Later we shall discuss subjects in the same connection.

The realist theory of sense perception is criticized on the assumption that it takes its objects to be fixed and absolute. I will give two stock examples, both from visual perception. The straight stick partly immersed in water which appears bent at the water line, is perhaps the most familiar. My second example will be a green dress which looks blue under fluorescent light. The answer in both cases is that they have the appearances they have under conditions which are set by their surroundings. Material objects are no doubt conditioned in many such ways by objects in their immediate environment. But the stick can be removed from the water and the dress can be taken into sunlight, and both observed again. Now the stick will appear straight and the dress green.

But which are they *really*, the idealists ask. Are they really bent and blue or straight and green? The realist's answer is that he makes no distinction with respect to reality; all appearances are real appearances. The fact that the straight stick and green dress check with other tests is irrelevant to the question of real appearance.

The error which lies behind the idealists' charge against the realists involves an assumption that the realist wishes to consider his material objects absolute just because he considers them independent. But he does not. The properties of material objects are partly determined for them by their exchanges with other material objects in their environment – in the above cases, water and fluorescent tubes. The realist is not an absolutist with respect to anything in existence, that is to say, in the world of matter and energy enduring in time and extended in space.

But if the object of the realist shifts and changes, why the subject does, too. For the subject also can be moved about and often is. As he moves his perceptions are altered; every movement substitutes one perspective for another and with it the material objects perceived. And these changes have to be taken into consideration in the epistemology of the realist. Every subject is a unique individual occupying a perspective which is unique with respect to his entire equipment for perceiving, including not only his sense organs but also the contents of his memory as well as alterations in his somatic organism, and his habit patterns, a perspective sensitive to other material objects in his immediate environment which are capable of exerting an influence upon his experiences.

The movements of the subject have a direct bearing on his perceptions. For he is both active and passive in the act of perception. He is active to the extent to which, so to speak, he takes his sense organs around with him wherever he goes and exposes them, active in determining where and when they shall be exposed and to what, though this last not entirely, since there often are surprises. And he is passive to the extent that he is compelled to experience whatever is present to his senses. Put the subject near a man blowing a horn and he cannot help but hear it; immerse him in water and he cannot but feel wet; chain him before a green wall and he can shut his eyes but he cannot keep them shut forever, and when he opens them, unless he is color-blind, there is the green. Thus activity only determines the framework of the subject's experiences while passivity submits him to its impressions.

So far our description sounds as though the subject has his sense experiences piecemeal. Yet he does see and then hear, or touch and then smell, but somehow he gets an impression of them together. For remember that the realist understands how everyone is attuned to the stereoscopic nature of the material objects of perception. Kant's "synthetic unity of apperception" attributes the wholeness of the object to the conditions set by the experience of the subject, whereas for the realist the subject is merely adjusting himself to what he knows to be stereoscopic objects.

The adjustment in question is itself a product of experience, and consists in the fact that the sense organs work together even though one usually leads the others. If I see a horse from one side I know it has another side which might appear somewhat differently; and I know from my previous experiences with other members of the same class that I can expect a certain smell, a certain feel if I touch it, a certain sound if it whinnies or neighs. The stereoscopic perceptions of the entire man are adequately adapted to receiving impressions from solid material objects; and since those objects, or at least others resembling them in the same respects, existed before man and his senses were formed, it is the objects which determine the mode of their perception and not the reverse.

Now that we have sketched out something of how the realist views the object and the subject of sense perception, we are ready to approach the topic of how in his understanding the process of sense perception itself takes place.

I will begin by considering what happens in feeling. A feeling may be looked at as a quality of a material object which has been received by a subject. It is not a faithful reproduction, however, but only a close approximation, a restoration at the cortical centers after a pattern transmitted through the nervous system. It has a character of its own which it acquires through the peculiar processes of its reception, and to this extent it is privately owned and will be privately used.

I want to make a distinction between the sense data or qualia and the report of the sense data which the subject makes to himself. The sense data are given in perception, and, of course, they are in this connection private even though there are good reasons to suspect that this is not their only condition of being. But that is by no means the entire account of the connection. For in addition to the sense data there is the report which the subject makes about them to himself. This is what the epistemologists have conventionally thought of as the interpretation which the subject puts upon his experience, but I mean something else. I mean the extent to which the data are permeated by the contents of the report about them, a report which is also private.

There are, then, in this situation three separate elements: first, the sense data; next, the interpretation of the sense data which is a product of the subject's past experiences from which he has learned what to expect of sense data in general; and, finally, the private report of the subject to himself concerning the specific sense data which he has received.

The interpretation which conditioned the reception is not necessarily identical with the private report. It is the last which will determine how the particular sense data are to take their place as available for the later interpretation of further sense data as these are received on some subsequent occasion. The private report has been recognized, but in another connection and under another terminology. It has been present as an element in the interior dialogue. Interior dialogues take place all the time, as reports of the individual to himself about his experiences and about how they shall be remembered.

I am now in a position to state something of the meaning of subjectivity for a realist. It relies upon that attitude of the subject when he temporarily cuts off further perception in order to shut himself up with what is inside already. The data acquired from previous perceptions are regarded as owned, and there is no reference to their origins, they are inside and available to the private report and so they, too, are private. For the subject to face himself insofar as the feelings are involved is what subjectivity amounts to – to terminate further stimulation for qualitative reasons. (To do so for quantitative or structural reasons would be to think, but I shall not here be concerned with that more sophisticated level.)

The attitude of subjectivity is a function of the inner environment. The outer environment is the world in which the subject lives and moves and interacts with other material things. The inner environment is whatever part of the outer environment has been perceived and retained as recorded images. It is the background with which the feelings merge without boundaries. No one has ever successfully assigned a place to the inner environment except vaguely to associate it with the subject. I do not use the term consciousness because consciousness is a

subjective conception which allows its contents to be considered separately and, to this extent, objectively. The inner environment presumably comes already unified, complete, and simple. It is where and
how a feeling exists.

The balance of attention between the inner environment and the
outer environment is a function of the efficiency of the adaptive control
mechanism of the subject. It depends upon the extent to which the
subject is able to direct his attention. If he attends deliberately and to
a large extent to the contents of the inner environment, this has the
effect, within limits, of shutting off further reception.

A very loud noise or a hard impact will shift the attention immediately from the inner to the outer environment, in the search for a source.
Such a search has one or two motives. If the stimulus is intensely pleas-
ant, then the search will be conducted in the interest of securing a
repetition. If the stimulus is intensely unpleasant, then the search will
be conducted in the interest of avoiding a repetition. For, in the end,
perhaps we live for the sake of certain subjective feelings, and we go
outside only to procure those that we want. But for this we have to
know a great deal about what is going on outside.

In order to shut off further sense perception, techniques are needed.
There is special equipment at the physiological level: the eyes can be
closed, but not so the ears. Beyond that – and it is the exception among
the senses – the subject must rely upon his control over attention. When
he first feels something, the feeling comes to him amid other impressions and sensations: he is attending to a field of experience in which
there are other elements. The limits of the feeling diminish toward other
feelings, ideas, and activities.

To attend to a feeling in this way might be called 'feeling objectively',
for it is the outward-faced variety of feeling. But there is also a subjective variety of feeling, and that is the one under consideration here.
Subjective feeling or 'feeling subjectively' is the inner-faced variety. An
immediacy and a vividity are among its most prominent and insistent
characteristics. Feeling is difficult to describe because it is a quality.
No one has yet succeeded in describing a quality, only some of its features, such as vividity or insistence. Hume only was intent to establish
that impressions and ideas are all that is experienced, but he did not
attempt to describe particular impressions. Those feelings which are
neutral to pleasure and pain might be called the pure feelings because
they remain almost uninterpreted to sensation.

Feeling subjectively means feeling without awareness of limit –

shapeless feeling – the feeling of the feeling itself, unexamined, unaccompanied, and uninterpreted. Feeling as such is neutral; and whereas feeling objectively is, as we have noted, active, feeling subjectively is passive. The feeling itself is allowed to take control, and the feeler makes himself passive before it.

To feel is to have a simple, uncomplicated experience. Now it is precisely because nothing follows from it that no one has been able to build on it. Pure subjectivity does exist, and it consists in a feeling. To go further with it would mean to introduce the element which I have referred to as the private report. But then the subject has departed from the pure feeling which I have named 'feeling subjectively' which is all by itself whatever it is, without addition or remainder.

To be left alone with his feelings, this is a demand the subject cannot successfully make on further feeling. For further feeling invites comparison, and at once he is in the domain of reasoning. No, feeling to be left alone must be singular, particular, and individual – in order that the subject may attend to its contents. Every material thing in the world can be shown to contain an outer form and an inner content. The envelope is dealt with by reasoning; and if the subject wishes to deal with an item by feeling, then he must be in a position to concentrate on it. The concentration is active, but it is more of the nature of self-control; he must resolve not to think or do anything, only to let the feelings permeate, for feelings are in themselves pervasive. They have their natural effects through a process of flowing.

Attention to a feeling is private and hence subjective, more subjective than a thought or an activity because the thought may correspond exactly with something in the outer environment and the activity is a direct and immediate interaction with things in the outer environment, whereas feeling lends itself to confinement within the inner environment. Feeling *qua* feeling can be pure subjectivity.

As a consequence, subjectivity does much to foster the emphasis on uniqueness. Each individual is unique to some extent even though this may not be the most valuable thing about him. But it is something that can be protected and cultivated under the most favorable circumstances of the outer environment. A man who has lost his social connections, a man in jail or living in a fragmented society, can occupy himself with himself in this way. He can live in the microcosm of the self with all its illimitable, if unfathomable, depth, at least for a while, on the assumption that it constitutes all the macrocosm he needs. Hence its immense appeal.

Subjective feeling is not a state that can be maintained for very long. It is not the normal condition of man in the midst of his environment. To remain in a state of subjective feeling is to introduce a pathological element if the state is pursued indefinitely; for as it intensifies, the subject becomes locked into it and can no longer escape. That is why the psychotic is often so hard to reach; his attention is not on his outer environment but on his inner environment, content with what it already contains.

Thus for a normal subject the privacy of feeling is difficult to maintain and in the end impossible. For while the feeling, or at least a certain aspect of it, is private, it becomes, as we have noted, more pervasive the more it is attended to. Now, there are no restrictions on pervasiveness beyond those imposed by the limits of the organism. What an individual feels may permeate his entire body and, in this way, its effects extend beyond the narrower limits of his attention. Thus the privacy of a feeling is at best a brief state.

There is evidence of an outer environment which does not depend upon our experience of it for its existence; but since such evidence is not sufficient to constitute a proof, the statement must stand as an assumption, worth retaining only for what it leads to. There is no retreat into subjectivity which would take us away from the necessity of making such an assumption, short of going all the way to solipsism. It is a kind of refutation of the very possibility of proof in philosophy to admit what has been admitted so often: that while solipsism is the only demonstrable position, it is also an unbelievable one. The idealist can manage quite nicely with the privacy of subjective feelings because he does not need to accept an independently existing outer environment, but the realist does and so he cannot manage in the same way. It is my thesis that the positive feelings of privacy are those which the realist can claim in his interpretation of subjectivity. The privacy is a genuine privacy, and the feelings are genuinely subjective feelings.

At some stage in a feeling it comes to an end, for, as I have pointed out, feeling subjectively is not a state which under normal conditions can endure. At this point the subject leaves his privacy, and the transition is made by his recognition, dimly conceived, that while his attention to the feelings wavers, the feelings in some sense do not; they exhibit a stability he cannot sustain and so must depend upon something other than him and must extend beyond his privacy. They must, in short, have relations other than those to his attention. This is the point at which there occurs a translation from 'I feel blue' to 'There is blue' or to 'Blue is there'. And it occurs in some way in which this translation cannot be made for some other feelings, such as the one expressed in 'I feel fine'. The subject assigns the former to an outer environment and the latter to an inner environment but both to an environment and not to his own attention, no more than he does for 'I have a blue feeling'.

Once the recognition of this sort occurs, it is quickly followed by others; the recognition, say, that there are other blue occasions and that blue of whatever occasion has closer relations with red and green than it has with odors and sounds. I need follow the development in this direction no further, for obviously it must lead to the construction of a complex outer environment, and that in turn to the existence of a world which is not only external to the subject but independent of him as well. This is a many times told tale, and so I shall return to another aspect of my topic which the development in this direction also discloses.

For now the subject has a contrast between himself and a world consisting of objects. When he was alone with his feeling he tended to become one with it in some indistinguishable fashion that did not permit him the recognition of himself as subject. 'I am my blue feeling' had an all-at-onceness to it which inhibited distinctions of any kind. If there are objects, then the subject is a subject only in relation to them. He is related to them in one way and cut off from them in another; for he is not one of them but only aware of them, which is something quite different.

Thus the first degree of subjectivity which is identical with feeling subjectively is succeeded by a second degree of subjectivity which I have earlier called feeling objectively and which is an outer-faced variety. This is the domain in which there are recognitions (qualities resembling those previously experienced) but also novelties and surprises. The existence of life in the inner environment is not cancelled; it is only set aside as a portable possibility which is carried about with the subject in his adventuring among objects in the outer environment. And so, in this way, he comes to learn that although he visits the inner environment, it lacks the staying power to sustain him; and he learns that he can live in the outer environment for longer periods of time.

Alternating periods of objective feeling, by means of which new contents are introduced into the inner environment, and subjective feeling, by means of which the new contents are digested, is perhaps the best arrangement so far as its effects are concerned. The subject leaves the outer environment to attend to the inner environment, but only in order to be able to contribute more to the outer environment, to change something, in it in such a way that it will produce in him again the feelings he has had and liked, and to produce in others the feelings that he himself has felt. In proportional amounts and under the proper controls, subjective feeling can be very productive. A certain amount of such private indulgence may have its results in works of the imagination, of a sort in many instances which is eventually objectified in literature and in the plastic arts.

It is legitimate to conclude, then, that not only is subjectivity genuine for a realist but also it is necessary. Realism has a legitimate place for the subject, his feelings, and the inner environment in which he confronts them. If the inner environment is furnished with materials taken from the outer environment, that does not make them any the less subjective. What has to be abandoned in the subjectivity of a realist is only the absolute claims made by the pure subjectivist of the idealist variety. He would, it seems to me, have to claim something which not only cannot be shown but which cannot in the meanwhile even be plausibly accepted. He would have to claim that what is native to the subjectivity of the subject was initiated by the subject within the inner environment. There is no warrant for believing that, and there is some evidence against it – if for no other reason than that the contents of the inner environment resemble the corresponding segment of the outer environment, and that while the contents of the inner environment can be dismissed from awareness by shifting the attention elsewhere, the contents of the outer environment are stubborn and will not go away when asked.

If the idealist would modify his claims, then he would have no quarrel with the realist. For what is at issue is not the nature of the contents of experience but the location to which those contents are to be permanently assigned. But the idealist would have to admit, what he perhaps cannot bring himself to admit, namely, that subjectivity is the gift of the object and not objectivity the gift of the subject. We do not begin by being aware of our own awareness; that is a sophisticated perspective which must be painfully acquired. We begin by being aware of the object, and only later do we become aware of who is aware and under what circumstances, and of what the awareness is.

Once this distinction is made and recognized, we are in a better position to see how the claims of the realist concerning perception can be supported. The idealist is anxious to show in defense of his position that what the subject experiences is peculiar to the subject. And he points to the peculiarities in it which are not found in the outer environment. The examples already given above will suffice again: the appearance of the bent stick which we know to be 'really' straight, and the blue dress which we know to be 'really' green.

One of the most difficult of tasks in all those formal disciplines which seek universal principles is the evaluation of the data. Even when agreement concerning what the data are is not hard to come by, the evaluation of the data is still a very tricky business. For the evidence of the bent stick and the blue dress is better evidence for the objectivist than for the subjectivist, since it shows how misleading the subjective evidence can at times be.

Among the most certain things in the world are facts; there can be no doubt about that. What is doubtful is just what the facts are. Only on the hypothesis of a certain world of fact is it possible to construct an uncertain world of appearance – in a word, of a subjective world which is certain with respect to its experiences of an inner environment but largely uncertain with respect to its experiences of the outer environment. The former never needs correction; it is what it is. But the latter calls for constant correction, for an unending set of revisions, if it is to approximate the truth. Thus the very existence of error, of falsity, and of misleading appearances calls for an authentic subjectivity and for not attempting to read it necessarily as a true report of the world.

CHAPTER X

ACTIVITY AS A SOURCE OF KNOWLEDGE

I. INTRODUCTION

There is no division of human life which has not been touched upon and altered by science, and this is no less true of philosophy than it is of other concerns. The experimental method of the physical sciences in particular has been and still is the part of science which has influenced philosophy the most. Elsewhere I have tried to argue that philosophical empiricism though developed in imitation of scientific empiricism differs from it sharply.[1] Scientific empiricism is objective while philosophical empiricism is subjective. Scientific empiricism has tried to verify by means of the disclosures of sense experience the regularities which it hypothesizes in nature; philosophical empiricism has tried to verify by means of the sense experiences themselves the meanings which they have for the subject. The result is that science has begun and continues to develop a description of the world, while philosophy remains behind debating the various alternative interpretations of sense experience.

There is another point of comparison which may be relevant. While science worked with the experience of the entire man employing all of his faculties, philosophy has tried to get along with some of his faculties. It is very well known that the Continental rationalists, Descartes, Spinoza, and Leibniz, for instance, sought an explanation of the world in terms of what could be constructed primarily by means of the reasoning faculty. Alternatively, the British empiricists, it is equally well known, sought to discover a source for indubitable knowledge in the isolated deliverances of sense experience.

It is difficult not to ask why such narrow efforts were undertaken. The Continental rationalists inherited the scholastic method but with

---

[1] "Philosophical Empiricism from the Scientific Standpoint," in *Dialectica*, Vol. 16 (1962), pp. 5–14.

a new freedom from dogma and a new empirical interest. They were in a way the closest of the philosophical enlightenment to the period which had gone before. If science touched them in a philosophical way it did so with a light hand. The British empiricists, by comparison, were uncompromising in their efforts to follow the lead of the scientists. They worked hard at making primitive beginnings in sense experience, and if they did not advance as far as the scientists went beyond those beginnings it was not for lack of rigorous efforts. Their enterprise was not less uncompromising because they were themselves mild fellows with no wish to upset the apple cart, and in some cases, that of Berkeley for instance, exceedingly conservative in religious matters.

If the entire man is one who is able to think, feel and act, as we have known since Plato's *Republic* if not much earlier, then why is there assumed to be an advantage in endeavoring to found reliable knowledge upon less resources than the entire man has to call on? Why try to get along with one faculty: reason or sense experience – there is little to choose? Common experience, which is able to operate only at the gross level of ordinary objects, still refutes such specialized appeals, and it is significant that one protest to the method of single faculties came from the Scotch common sense school, led by Thomas Reid.

Hume working with the experiences of the senses alone (and neglecting the importance of the fact that he was thinking about them in so doing) posed the most serious problems to the pursuit of reliable knowledge. He himself has been misinterpreted, and it is one of his ablest commentators who makes the point that Hume's conclusion is not necessarily a sceptical one. N. Kemp Smith has contended that for Hume the source of reliable knowledge is to be found in belief rather than reason, and that it was this positive source in belief which was what Hume had maintained rather than the purely negative scepticism with regard to knowledge which is usually attributed to him.[2] As Hume himself remarked, "The great subverter of Pyrrhonism, or the excessive principle of scepticism, is action, and employment, and the occupations of common life."[3] Belief is yet to receive its due of analysis either from the philosophers or the psychologists. But it remains true that the refutation of Hume properly consists in a consideration of the grounds he adopted for forming his conclusions. The failure to discover a genuine external world and a self was based upon sense experience alone. Had he included action as a source of knowledge, he might have found the

[2] N. Kemp Smith, *The Philosophy of David Hume* (London, 1941, Macmillan).
[3] David Hume, *An Inquiry Concerning Human Understanding*, XII, 11.

external world to be real. For if knowledge is to be derived from experience, as most philosophers as well as all experimental scientists now
pretty well agree that it is, then it must be the whole of experience,
experience in all of its parts rather than only in some, that is meant.
Action must be included as well as thought and sensation.

II. THE PRAGMATISTS

A complete empirical philosophy must await a complete use of all of the
faculties of entire man engaging together in the pursuit of reliable knowledge. Perhaps this is yet to be formulated. It could not be accomplished
through an assemblage of the component parts, as we know from other
discoveries, for that is not how discoveries are made. They are made by
single inductive leaps to the knowledge of systems which can then pain-
stakingly be tested against the relevant data. They are made by first
making hypotheses and then testing them. Two sorts of philosophers are
required for this task, just as in science two sorts of scientists. The great
synthesizer is necessary, the man whose dreaming is of possible systems,
but so is the patient investigator. Neither can do much without the other,
even though the terms of mutual respect based on a common complementarity have not yet been agreed upon.

    In the meanwhile, however, the consequences of adopting certain
principles of procedure must first run their course. It has been for some
time the practice to assume that some single human capacity holds the
key to reliable knowledge, first rationalism and then sense experience
or philosophical empiricism. But there is a third human capacity which
has not yet been included in the catalogue of the method of single inference from single capacities. This is: action. It would have to be true
that some school of philosophy would have had to take its turn in the
succession by exploring how much reliable knowledge could be obtained when employing only the human capacity for action. In this way
it might be possible that philosophy would make a new start more in
keeping with the actual procedure of science which relies upon the
united and integrated capacities of the entire man.

    The American pragmatists have not often been looked at from this
point of view. They have not ordinarily been supposed to have explored
activity as a source of knowledge. Rather have they been thought of in
other ways, and the relationship has been turned around. The pragmatists have been interpreted, not without some reason, as having
concerned themselves with the verification of meaning in terms of

practice. If you wish to understand propositions, they tell us, then consider what practical effects such propositions would have, and this is their meaning.

But suppose we do look at the pragmatists in the way I have suggested, namely, as having tried to explore activity as a source of reliable knowledge. It does not necessarily follow that such a thesis was deliberate or conscious with them or that they understood in this fashion their place in the history of philosophy. I assume that philosophers for all their strenuous efforts to understand what they are taking for granted are like all other people in not being able to attain to the degree of detachment necessary in order to comprehend the first principles from which their thinking proceeds. Moreover, philosophy, unlike other disciplines has the additional problem of the meta-axioms. Its adherents understand very well the axioms from which its theorems are deduced, and even the rules of inference by which such deductions are made. But what it often if not usually misses is the existence of a set of meta-axioms by which its axioms themselves could be established; or, if the very absence of procedure is entailed here in the terms of the existence of a philosophy, then of the inferential existence of meta-axioms. The existence of meta-axioms in mathematics belongs to an allied discipline, the study of the foundations of mathematics; but to what discipline does the study of the foundations of philosophy belong? That there is such a discipline dimly discerned has been noted, as for instance in Aristotle and by Boas.[4]

It will be the aim of this paper, then, to examine briefly some of the writings of the American pragmatists, Peirce, James, Dewey and Mead in order to determine whether they can be interpreted together as having endeavored to found reliable knowledge upon activity. All were philosophers, all concerned themselves with action, all were related, and all wished to understand the relation between propositions and the relevant practices.

III. PEIRCE

The greatest of American philosophers was also the founder of pragmatism, Charles S. Peirce. It is too often forgotten that Peirce was a metaphysician as well as a practicing physicist and an empirically-minded man, and the reason for this is the failure to recognize empi-

[4] George Boas, *Some Assumptions of Aristotle* (Philadelphia, 1959, American Philosophical Society).

ricism as a metaphysics. Metaphysics has been identified with one particular metaphysics, that of idealism, although generically there is no warrant for such an exclusiveness.

Peirce had a philosophical system. His ontological categories were: firstness, secondness and thirdness, or, in other words, quality, reaction and representation. In secondness or reaction he recognized the bruteness of the hard fact of resistance and effort, and gave it a prominent place in his theory of reality.[5] He did not distinguish altogether between a fact and an activity; facts are, among other things, activities (*CP* 1.427–440). Secondness is force (*CP* 1.487). It is the prime characteristic of all existence, whose very nature consists in opposition (*CP* 1.458).

When Peirce came to pronounce his methodological doctrine of pragmatism, however, the relations between concepts and activities got somehow turned around, so that pragmatism became a theory of meaning rather than a doctrine of activity as a source of reliable knowledge. Peirce gave seven definitions of pragmatism. I will quote the most familiar. "Consider what effects, that might conceivably have practical bearings, we conceive the object of our conception to have. Then our conception of these effects is the whole of our conception of the object" (*CP* 5.2).

Pragmatism has been more generally associated with the name of James than with that of Peirce. But James himself freely acknowledged his debt. The term and the conception of pragmatism had their points of origin in the thoughts and writings of Charles S. Peirce. For Peirce, pragmatism was a method of determining the meaning of those concepts which are peculiarly concerned with objective fact (*CP* 5.467).

Pragmatism was designed by Peirce to be a method of logic (*CP* 5.14, 5.465). It is framed in terms of conceptions and of practical effects, and states that conceptions of the practical effects of an object constitute the whole conceptions of the object (*CP* 5.2).[6] Activity is implied as a source of reliable knowledge, but it is certainly not explicitly stated. There is no such thing as practical effects without activity, but the pure experience or the abstract conception of activity is missing. It could be elicited from the pragmatic conception and is very close to it but cannot be identified with it. The consequences of a conception and their part in the defining of the conception is, one might almost say, logically adjacent to the derivation of reliable knowledge from activity;

---

[5] *Collected Papers of Charles Sanders Peirce*, 8 vols. Cambridge, 1931–58). References indicated in terms of volume and hereinafter referred to as *CP*. *CP*, 1.322–325.

[6] See also *CP* 5.9; 5.18; 5.467; 5.438; 6.490; 5.412.

but the connection is too close between conception and consequences. Activity must first be conceived independently of its role as a source of reliable knowledge, if it is to be productively thought of in that connection. Activity does not exist because it is a source of reliable knowledge; it is a source of reliable knowledge because of its independence from its effects upon knowledge. And just in that and in nothing else lies its value to knowledge. Peirce repudiated the Kantian epistemology from which he had learned so many of the problems of philosophy.[7] The relativism of knowledge in a way cancels the authenticity of the claim of pure activity to be a source of reliable knowledge because of the extent to which in that relativism the activity itself is tied in with the process by which the knowledge is elicited.

The promise which Peirce had made in his metaphysics, in which activity was one of the three primary ontological categories, is not fulfilled in his methodological theory of pragmatism. There is no room in pragmatism for quality, and reaction is inextricably intertwined with representation. Toward the end of his life, Peirce specifically repudiated any interest in activity for its own sake, and insisted that he had meant pragmatism all along to be a theory of meaning. Not "doing" but "rational purport" must be considered as the product at which pragmatism is aiming (*CP* 5.429).

Let us revert now to the categories of Peirce's metaphysics. These are, we may remember, firstness or quality, secondness or reaction, and thirdness or representation; subjectively: feeling, effort and thought. Strictly speaking, reaction (resistance or force) is not the same as activity though belonging to the same generic category. But even without this conception there is a discrepancy between Peirce's metaphysics and his pragmatism. Peice's doctrine remains a theory of meaning, not a method of deriving reliable knowledge from experience. It was, however, as we shall see, suggestive in this connection to others.

IV. JAMES

In an address to psychologists on radical empiricism, James sought most vigorously to place activity upon a respectable philosophical footing.[8] In an earlier essay in the same volume, James had described

---

[7] See the reference in James Feibleman, *An Introduction to Peirce's Philosophy* (New York, 1946, Harper), Chapter II.
[8] William James, *Essays in Radical Empiricism* (London, 1938, Longmans, Green and Co.), Chapter VI. Hereinafter referred to as *RE*.

radical empiricism in terms of pure experience, without the emphasis on activity (*RE* Ch.II). In his celebrated pragmatic maxim, James had laid the foundation for a theory of practice. "To attain perfect clearness in our thoughts of an object, we need only consider what effects of a practical kind the object may involve – what sensations we are to expect from it, and what reactions we must prepare. Our conception of these effects, whether immediate or remote, is then for us the whole of our conception of the object."[9] The closeness of James' formulation of pragmatism to that of Peirce is painfully obvious. To be perfectly fair, it is one which James himself freely acknowledged. The practical effects of an object can hardly be construed as otherwise than an activity. And so it is from the activity of an object that we are instructed to gather its meaning.

James was an epistemological realist, as he asserted more than once. He "posited reality *ab initio*"[10] and insisted that he meant that "ideas should be true in advance of and apart from their utility, that, in other words, their objects should be really there" (*MT* 207). However, he did say that by "practical experience" he meant that the experience must be particular rather than active (*MT* 210). Agreement with reality: that touchstone of epistemological realism, stood James in good stead. Truth means agreement with reality; agreement with reality means verifiability; verifiability means ability to guide us through experience. Thus "the possession of true thoughts means everywhere the possession of invaluable instruments of action" (*P* 202).

But the presence of activity is pervasive in his thinking nevertheless, and he returns to it again and again. James more than the other pragmatists saw in activity an important philosophical category.[11] He was concerned with it as a pure experience and he was concerned with it for its connections with the pragmatic method.

James the philosopher is a familiar figure in philosophy, but it must be remembered by philosophers that he was also and often primarily psychologist. In discussing the types of decision under the general heading of the will, James wrote – in italics – "In action as in reasoning, the great thing is the quest of the right conception."[12] He came closer than most pragmatists to enunciating a theory of truth in terms of

---

[9] William James, *Pragmatism* (London, 1940, Longmans, Green), pp. 46–7. Hereinafter referred to as *P*.

[10] William James, *The Meaning of Truth* (New York, 1932, Longmans, Green, p. 195. Hereinafter referred to as *MT*.

[11] *A Plurastic Universe* (New York, 1932, Longmans, Green), Appendix B.

[12] *The Principles of Psychology*, 2 vols. (New York, 1931, Holt), Vol. II, p. 531.

activity because he saw the intimate connection between statements regarding the truth and the relevant activities. His conception of the correspondence theory was a dynamic one. However, he was as much concerned with meaning and particulars as he was with statements and activities, and he wavered between the various combinations of these four interests. The practical man cognizant of affairs and the psychologist took precedence over the detached concerns of the scientifically-minded philosopher in search of a source for reliable knowledge. The result was that he sought primarily a workable theory of meaning as it applied to practice. "Pragmatic method asserts that what a concept means is its consequences."[13]

It happened as often in James' thinking that conceptions were selected in order to bring about practical results as that practical results were employed in order to derive reliable knowledge. The effort to influence action is practical; the effort to employ action in order to determine truth is theoretical. Theory has more far-reaching effects on practice than practice itself approached immediately and directly. That is certainly the practical lesson to be learned from 'pure' science. And so James did not formulate as precisely as he might have a verification theory for statements in terms of activity.

V. MEAD

Of the pragmatists, Mead perhaps best understood the nature of activity as a source of reliable knowledge, and he set up the most adequate model for it. His shortcoming was that he never followed through with an examination of concrete experience in terms of his model, and so he never succeeded in completing the projected ambition and in illuminating knowledge in this way. He left behind him, however, an intriguingly suggestive conceptual scheme.

His model is best explained by beginning with its sources. He proposed to consider a human individual as suggested by the psychological behaviorism of John Watson in a world as outlined by Minkowski. The link between them, as we shall presently note, was what Mead called "contact experience."

Let us begin with the behaviorism. This is best outlined under the heading of social behaviorism. The conduct of the human individual

[13] Ralph Barton Perry, *The Thought and Character of William James*, 2 vols. (Boston, 1935, Little Brown), Vol. II, p. 444.

studied within the behavior of the social group[14] and not confined to
that part which can be externally observed is what Mead meant by his
"social behaviorism." But the role is not merely a passive one, for the
"organism goes out and determines what it is going to respond to"
(*MSS* 25). The "bodily structure can be stated in terms of behaviorism
– *à la* Watson."[15] As we shall see, Mead intended a stimulus-response
system but with the emphasis upon the dynamic response.

Now let us turn to the model of the world as Mead envisaged it. Here
he relied almost entirely upon the *a priori* character of the four-dimen-
sional continuum of space-time and events as set forth by Herman
Minkowski. The Minkowski world, according to Mead, is important in
the human context because it is a stable world "back of our action,
even hurried action ... a world that hypothetically endures both in
its structure and in its rhythms of recurrence" (*PA* 179–180). It is
paradoxically "a world lying beyond any possible experience" (*PA*
609), but in which "we have the experience of continuous passage,"
(*PA* 635) "a world that assimilates space and time" (*PA* 524) but which
also is, through "space-time ... the condition of the change" (*PA* 63).

The Minkowski world, for Mead, is a "world where all stimuli are
spatio-temporally away from them (i.e. those who live in it)" (*PA* 143).
It is, in short, "a world of stimuli and responses" (*PA* 147). We now
have a description of characteristic human behavior and of the world
in Mead's model. We have now to describe the conduct which connects
them in order to complete the model. But the stimuli are not present
in any contiguous sense. Mead recognized that the individual lives in a
larger world than he can ever comprehend, and that the effects of this
world upon the individual are far greater than the effects of the individual upon the world (*PA* 21). The perceived object is a distant object.

Perception thus leads to action, for experience of the object certainly
involves a closer approach to it (*PA* 12). For "distance experience of
any sort is of a different sort from that of ultimate contact" and so
"the ultimate reality of the distance experience is to be found in that of
contact experience" (*PA* 16)

Our exploration of experience, then, means either that we can move
around the object or that we can move the object around by manipulating it (*PA* 16–17). Reliable knowledge may be considered a by-pro-

---

[14] George H. Mead, *Mind, Self and Society* (Chicago, 1934, University Press), p. 6. Hereinafter referred to as *MSS*.

[15] George Herbert Mead, *The Philosophy of the Act* (Chicago, 1938, University Press),
p. 659. Hereinafter referred to as *PA*.

duct of the adaptation of the human organism to its environment (*PA* 312), through a kind of adaptation which consists in substituting "contact observation" (*PA* 22) for distance (*PA* 144). And so it is not surprising to learn from Mead that "the ultimate experience involves not only contact, but it also involves manipulation" (*PA* 226).

"The act is an impulse that maintains the life-process by the selection of certain sorts of stimuli it needs" (*MSS* 6)." The distant object has a reality which waits upon the completion of the act" (*PA* 175–176). Acts become conduct by means of various degrees of deliberation, until conduct becomes the key even to the knowledge of the self (*PA* 65).

The act becoming conduct for the individual in a social world in which he must move toward the material object in order to establish "contact experience" with it makes the sense of touch the important one for Mead. "If we present a distant planet, its matter is presented as we would actually sense it if we could place our hands upon it" (*PA* 20). He emphasizes the point again and again. "The round solid coin in the hand is the ultimate fact of every oval of vision" (*PA* 281). "Things," he confidently assured us, "are not real as seen or heard or smelled; they are real as actually or potentially experienced through contact" (*PA* 364).

The objects with which we have "contact experience" are material objects. "From the standpoint of the perceptual judgment of reality, that of manipulatory contact, these physical objects are there in independence of the acts, and they were there before the organism arose and will continue after its disappearance" (*PA* 453). "That which appears in contact experience is matter" (*PA* 287), "matter as effectively occupying space, its resistance, its inertia, its mobility, as we experience these characters" (*PA* 15).

And so now he has his model complete, an abstract, geometric, material world, as designed by Minkowski, a behaviorist model arrived at by elaborating Watsonian behaviorism, together with the movements of activity and conduct designed to achieve contact experience on the part of the individual. A good place to start, assuming that the next step would be the interpretation of the concrete world with its living human individuals in terms of the model. But this is not only where Mead started, it is also where he stopped. And so he missed the possibilities of translating his model into the terms of experience which make it possible to interpret activity as a source of reliable knowledge. The champion, who would raise his candidate for priority of dependence in the method of inquiry – "contact experience" – to a place of eminence on a par with the 'reason' of the Continental rationalists and the 'sense experience' of the British empiricists, failed at the very last. He did not fail, however, without indicating a direction in which success could be achieved.

VI. DEWEY

Dewey was a pragmatist: that is to say, he sought an instrumental method for testing the meaning of ideas in the light of their consequences. His emphasis, however, was practical rather than theoretical. What he advocated was a way of testing meaning by means of the practical approach through broad and immediate social consequences. The direction of conduct by beliefs was to be decided in this way.

Dewey was very anxious to bring together again what the Greeks had sundered: pure knowledge and practical activity. For the Greeks, he observed, Doing was not intellectually respectable in the way that Knowing and Being was.[16] But in this effort Dewey managed somehow to reduce knowledge to the status of an instrument for accomplishing the practical without raising practice to the level of a source for reliable knowledge. His aim was practical rather than knowledgeable, but being a philosopher rather than a man of affairs the result was an instrumental theory of meaning. "The existentialist basis of a universal proposition is a mode of action" (*L* 271). Dewey was thus the last of the philosophers who endeavored to settle technical matters at the common sense level by "formulating a theory of knowledge and of mind in relation to nature" (*QC* 86).

Dewey noted that "action is at the heart of ideas" (*QC* 167). Hypotheses are always intended to be "tried in action" (*QC* 194). But he confused ideas with action by his insistence that "knowing is a form of doing" (*QC* 205). And he let the emphasis of the "theory in which knowing and doing are intimately connected" (*QC* 214) become shifted so that "the final import of the conclusions as to knowledge resides in the changed idea it enforces as to action" (*QC* 245). "Thought ... is a mode of directed overt action" (*QC* 166), and "a question is a demand for action on someone's part" (*L* 169). Like James, Dewey was concerned with the influence of thought over action, as well as with the

---

16 John Dewey, *The Quest for Certainty* (New York, 1929, Milton Balch), pp. 16–18. Hereinafter referred to as *QC*. *Logic* (New York, 1938, Holt), pp. 57, 73. Hereinafter referred to as *L*.

verification of thought by action. He thought of ideas as the instruments of action. If "reflective knowledge as such is instrumental" (*QC* 218) and "the only means of regulation" (*QC* 219), it was because they were both incomplete parts of the same enterprise, the solving of a problem in which the object is as much involved as the subject (*QC* 233f).

There is some reason to suspect that Dewey thought of the scientific method as a practical tool rather than as a method for seeking the knowledge of abstract laws capable of application. Science has a method in which activity is central, the experimental method in which controlled observations by means of instruments furnishes the leading edge, but with thought and feeling involved: thought involved in calculations and feelings involved intuitively in the choosing of hypotheses – all very far from Dewey's conception. With small changes, he might have discovered the usefulness of activity as a source of reliable knowledge, but as matters stood, like his predecessors in pragmatism, he missed. His accomplishments were of course considerable, but not in this direction.

VII. CONCLUSION

The American pragmatists more than most philosophers were concerned with practice. But they thought of it in some tangential way. Either it was concerned with meaning as a matter of clarification and limitation, or it was a practical effort to hold down speculation to what was considered feasible, or it was a model for constructing a theory of activity which was never completed, or it was a plain man's rule of thumb for getting on with the job. It is possible to look on activity as an elucidation of meaning in a perfectly legitimate fashion, but that is not a philosophical endeavor in any way comparable to the scientific method. The experimental method in philosophy would have to consider activity as a way of verifying or falsifying any hypothesis, which is an altogether different consideration from the theory of meaning. Moreover, it has little or nothing to do directly with practice. The scientific method is not concerned with improving practice, it is concerned with discovering the laws of nature; and if its results can be employed in practice with astonishing success, that is still only a byproduct of the method and not its principal aim. The pragmatists walked all round the problem of how to develop a philosophical correlate of the experimental method of the physical sciences but they never did turn to approach it directly.

A hidden assumption may have vitiated all the attempts of the American pragmatists to found activity on reliable knowledge. The hidden assumption underlying most fundamental inquiry of a philosophical nature is the rationalist assumption: that reason by itself is competent adequately to represent reality. This was Hegel's assumption, and it can be made legitimately if and only if reality itself is altogether rational. Only Bergson among the philosophers has openly challenged it. Thanks to Bergson we know of an alternative. One can take the intellectualist point of view from which it appears necessary to tame activity by reducing it to a formula suitable for inclusion in a conceptual scheme (the pragmatists). Or one can take the action point of view according to which philosophy has the task of deriving its valid statements by making them strictly in accordance with concrete events (the scientists). James did undertake the latter attempt for philosophy even though on the whole he was unsuccessful. That is why Whitehead said that he was anxious to rescue the thought of Bergson, James and Dewey from "the charge of anti-intellectualism, which rightly or wrongly [sic] has been associated with it."[17]

I have tried to show in this chapter that thanks to the pragmatists we now know there is such a problem as the hidden assumption. And in philosophy it often happens that a problem fully recognized is a problem well on its way to solution. In philosophy, it has been further argued, progress consists not in answering a question in any final way but only in refining the question. Thanks to the pragmatists, then, we have begun the process of refining the question of how activity can be a source of reliable knowledge.

---

[17] Alfred North Whitehead, *Process and Reality* (New York 1941, Macmillan), p. vii.

CHAPTER XI

ON BELIEFS AND BELIEVING

Everyone has beliefs, with some of which, at least, he is familiar; but few understand the nature of belief. In this chapter therefore I propose to examine belief as such. My approach will not be to present its analysis from the first steps onward and in full view, but to offer the conclusions arrived at from a searching analysis which has accumulated over the years until now it seems that something like a general picture is possible.

I shall not here examine the question of the truth of beliefs nor will I be concerned with their verification or falsification. Those issues belong to the thorny problems of induction and its justification or to the analysis of the abstract deductive structure of logic and mathematics. My concern here will be with the phenomenon of belief itself.

The presentation will be made in six separate parts. These are: (I) the causes of belief, (II) the initiation of believing, (III) the compulsion to belief, (IV) degrees of believing, (V) the structure of belief, and (VI) the condition of believing.

I. THE CAUSES OF BELIEF

It will be best to begin with definitions of belief and believing as the terms are to be understood here. Believing may be defined as emotionally accepting a proposition, and a belief as a proposition that is held to be true. Hume distinguished between a belief and a recognized fiction by noting that the former has a feeling attached to it while the latter has not.[1] Believing according to this definition is a particular subjective state, and beliefs are inherently subjective. We must be careful to remember, however, that there is a distinction between believing considered as a subjective state on the one hand, and the *contents* of the belief, considered as objective on the other. Propositions after all do

---

[1] *Inquiry*, V, II.

have reference as well as sense, and belief has to do as well with their correspondence. It would be fair to ask whether there would be any beliefs if there were no world beyond the person, since even subjective states are dispositional. At the same time, apparently there is some kind of need to believe – a "will to believe", James called it – even though what the belief is belief *in* may depend upon the evidence which is presented. A belief is a faith in a condition or an occurrence in nature. It could be objective or subjective; that is to say, it could refer to something in the external world or to a state of the believer. There is nothing inconsistent in holding that the causes of belief are twofold: (1) some sort of external compulsion, and (2) some kind of subjective need.

(1) First, then, let us consider external compulsion as the cause of belief.

Beliefs first occur as propositions whose truth we are compelled to acknowledge because the evidence seems to demand it. Of course the propositions involved do not have to be true; it is only necessary that the evidence seem to be of a sufficiently strong nature to make the acceptance of the propositions unavoidable. They are accepted at the time as though they were true, and subsequently they are held in the same way.

The initiation of a belief, then, is the surrender of the individual to a compulsion. Given the fact of his attention, he is not free not to believe should the evidence present itself as sufficient to support the truth of the proposition. Thus propositions have built into them, so to speak, a certain force, and it is the insistence of this force which constitutes the belief, which is for the individual a passive affair.

Beliefs, then, are responses to stimuli. Something impinges upon the human individual and occasions him to respond in this way. The sources of belief, the stimuli, may be external or internal, they may come from events in the external world or they may come from changes in bodily states. In all such cases, however, the stimuli are objective to awareness. It is clear that they are not arbitrary, not the result of some act of the will, not a mere impulse or whim. We are not free to believe whatever we wish to believe but whatever appeals to us for good reasons to be true. What has been called an instance of 'wishful thinking' is a proposition we would like to have accepted by belief and for the moment may persuade ourselves has been accepted. Thus delusion or self-deception may be a source of belief, but not for long. In the end the individual must have reasons for his beliefs other than merely the desire to believe in them. The 'will to believe', however strong it may be, is in the end impotent.

Beliefs are always held for what, to the believer at least, appear to be good reasons. That the reasons may be poor ones judged by objective standards, and may indeed be false propositions, is irrelevant to their status as beliefs. False propositions when presented as such have never been accepted by belief. This shows both that the will is not a free agent so far as belief is concerned and that beliefs which carry reason with them exercise a certain force on the individual believer. One reason for a belief is that it is about something which it has never occurred to the individual to doubt. Just as in many instances the question of belief was never entertained by him, so doubt was not, either. Many beliefs came naturally to him and he never went through the formal process of accepting them. Such for example are the beliefs which the anatomical structures and physiological functions occasion. Would it mean anything to say that the individual 'believes' he must keep on breathing in order to continue living? Breathing assumes that air containing a sufficient amount of oxygen to sustain life and to carry away the exhaled carbon dioxide will continue to be available in the immediately surrounding environment, that the oxygen inhaled will be extracted by the lungs, and so on. But the individual does not know that by breathing he involves himself in a host of beliefs of this sort. Usually he does not know what he believes about this or most things because he has never thought about it. But make him think about something, raise it to the level of his consciousness, and he will recognize that he does believe it.

The belief in the stability of the environment, that for instance the ground will be there offering the same degree of resistance when we take the next step, that the horizon will decline tomorrow morning disclosing the presence of the sun, that the stars will be in their accustomed places, are all so fundamental that we do not associate them with belief at all. But the point is that we are not free to *dis*believe in them; we are passive patients of the effects they exert on our belief.

(2) So much for external compulsion as a source of beliefs. Now we shall have to consider the second source, that of physiological need.

Beliefs persist because they are needed. The needs are organ-specific. This means that for an individual to reduce his most pressing needs, such as those for food and sex, or even his less exigent ones, such as the needs for activity and security, he must first have beliefs respecting the possibility of obtaining reductions. He would not search for food in a certain place or in a certain way if he did not believe it was to be found there in that fashion.

But in a certain sense believing does double duty. For there is not only the need for belief in connection with the possible reduction of the organ-specific needs, but in the case of one of them this becomes the need for belief itself. The particular organ associated with beliefs is the brain. That man has a need to know is shown by the fact that the brain is unable to develop unless a language is introduced at an early age. Man, as Waddington has wisely observed, is an "authority acceptor."[2] He actually needs to have a certain amount of beliefs, and these are furnished to him by his culture; in his early years he functions as a "receiver of culturally-transmitted information"[3] when in fact he is too young to test the truth of what he learns.[4]

A particular set of beliefs is not necessary, but beliefs of some sort are necessary, and the necessity can easily become transferred from the general to the particular because of the resemblance between them. If a smoker asks for a cigarette, it is the general he refers to: any member of the class will satisfy his request, and even though he cannot smoke a general cigarette, only a particular one, it is not a particular one that he requests but only *any* particular, and this involves the general. What is true of the cigarette in this case is true of his beliefs. He has needs, and he has beliefs with respect to their reduction. He believes that he needs a cigarette, even though it has been established that in many cases another belief will cut across it and cause him to abandon the belief, such as the belief that cigarettes cause lung cancer.

Beliefs of a fundamental nature become necessary to the individual because they furnish the ground of his integrity. They are the source not only of the consistency requisite for his actions if these are not to be self-defeating but also of the reasons why there are any actions at all. Beliefs are the motives for actions, interposed between the needs and their reductions. Thus for instance if a thirsty man picks up a glass and goes to the tap with it, he does so on the basis of the belief that there is water to be had. Any need-reduction involving activity presupposes beliefs with respect to the ends of the activity.

Belief, then can be conceived as a steady state. A certain number of beliefs are requisite to the normal functioning of the individual. Some can be exchanged for others, but there are always beliefs. From the

[2] C. H. Waddington, *The Ethical Animal* (London, 1960, Allen and Unwin, p. 29.
[3] *Ibid.*, p. 175.
[4] *Ibid.*, p. 151.

question of the truth or falsity of beliefs nothing can be ascertained with respect to their existence as beliefs. Beliefs may or may not be true, in the sense that it is true (or false) that they *are* beliefs (as for instance when an individual supposes that he holds a certain belief when in fact he does not but only wishes that he did and so pretends to himself that he does). But with respect to their reference beliefs may be true or false. However, whether they are true or false they have a tendency to persist. It is easier to continue to hold a belief than to give one up or to substitute some other belief. Believing is such a deep necessity that beliefs are sometimes held despite the evidence to the contrary.

To call them beliefs, then, means that the believer holds them true, and whether or not they are in fact true does not matter for this purpose. An individual without beliefs would be paralyzed; he could not act at all. He would be in the position of the catatonic schizophrenic who has a belief that the external world is his own creation (solipsism) and that therefore action with regard to it is unnecessary and even superfluous.

The individual with settled beliefs experiences an equilibrium which offers relief from tension. The equilibrium is provided by a consistency among beliefs. Beliefs tend to be reinforced by other beliefs held by the same individual, with which they are consistent, and by the similar beliefs of other individuals in the same society. The consequent harmony furnishes the feeling of comfort. There is a pervasive sense of well-being to be obtained from the settlement of beliefs and the absence of any challenge to them.

It is satisfying in its own way for the individual to know what it is that he thinks he should do and to feel the integrity which is the result of the consistency of his beliefs. Beliefs are usually held for reasons, but when they are held without reasons they are called collectively 'faith'. It is well known that faith is comforting. What is not as well known is that faiths are very common; there is no shortage of faiths. It is a curious fact, and not so familiar to the faithful, that *all* faiths are comforting, the degree of the comfort being measured only by the strength of the faith. But this is only another version of the necessity for belief and for the way in which that necessity is felt. Between surrender to the insistence of a belief and that acceptance of authority we have already discussed, is a very short distance.

II. THE INITIATION OF BELIEVING

It is now our task to discuss the capacities for believing which are parts of the structure of the individual. The individual has been traditionally understood to have three capacities. These are: for thought, for feeling, and for action.

The lines of deviation are by no means clear, and, as we shall presently note, the sources of belief do not always lend themselves to separation in this way. An induction, for instance, is clearly an intuition, which is a kind of feeling; but it moves across deductive structures to choose their premises, and so is involved with thought. The encounter with authority often results in the estoppal of action but it arouses feelings. In general, however, the three capacities hold as legitimate categories.

We shall be concerned in this section with the way in which beliefs *arise from* thoughts, feelings and actions as active psychological functions. But the individual may be passive in his confrontation with the evidence for beliefs, and in this way, beliefs are *needed for* thoughts, feelings and actions. We shall show the relation of the psychological capacities to beliefs, actively here and passively in the next section.

First, then, with respect to the way in which beliefs arise from thoughts, from feelings and from actions.

It is not difficult to see how beliefs could arise from thoughts. Opinions can be settled by reasoning from propositions already held, using ordinary rules of deduction. Reason has earned a bad name and misled many people by its willingness to operate validly from premises which are factually false or if true then too limited. Generally speaking, the criterion of consistency has been put forward in logic at the expense of the criterion of completeness, with the result that either limited or false premises seem adequate for deductive purposes. Intuitively-minded people in this way come to distrust reason because they have seen the absurdities to which it has sometimes led.

But the method of self-persuasion by rational means can start from any one of a number of places. For instance, an individual could argue that since he is a reasonable being, what appeals to his emotions or intuitions must also be reasonable. He could, in short, begin with faith in the logic of his feelings, and in this way thought could produce convictions concerning the truth of propositions which were then accepted as beliefs.

Thought can be a source of beliefs as a result of reasoning, but also as we have just seen, by endorsing the feelings as reasonable. Much the same can be said for the ability of thought to endorse actions in a similar fashion. What a man does again and again, if accompanied by some measure of success, will always strike him as being eminently reasonable. The pragmatic justification of beliefs is the most popular way in which thought can be employed to render actions secure.

We have been speaking of deliberate methods of accepting beliefs, methods consequent upon thought operating as reason or endorsing by rational means beliefs which arise from the feelings or actions. But beliefs may arise without self-conscious and deliberate thought directly from the feelings and actions, and we have next to examine these.

First, then, the beliefs which arise directly from the feelings. Let us go back at this point to the generic definition of belief. We found it to be the emotional acceptance of a proposition, the feeling that a proposition is true. It might now be asserted that the primitive form of the acceptance of beliefs is through immediate feeling. A proposition may appeal to the individual as true without his recognizing that any distinction exists between the proposition and his feelings about it: the feeling, so far as he is concerned, *is* the proposition.

Belief here arises simply because it is natural to the individual to trust his own intuitions. As he feels, so he is safe in believing. Since rational systems are all limited systems and start from axioms which cannot be proved (except in some anterior system), it is conventional to say that all starting points for systems of beliefs are intuitive. All sets of beliefs sufficient to the individual are mixtures of elements, but those which contain a greater proportion of intuitive elements are apt to be either irrational or anti-rational.

The preferable situation is one involving a minimum number of intuitive elements and a maxium amount of reason; in short, a system which is founded on the least number of unprovable assumptions and the greatest number of theorems which can be reached through reason and illustrated by fact. This, as Peirce was at pains to show, is apt to be a system where the unprovable assumptions consist solely in the methods of reason and fact themselves.

We have finally to consider beliefs arising directly from actions without being worked over by thought or even intuited through feeling. What we do often enough convinces us of its rightness. In short, it is what we do, if we do it over and over, that conveys to us without benefit of either reason or feeling a belief in what we do. Belief itself is a habit engendered by the habit of doing. Peirce made much of the connection between belief and habit. "The feeling of believing is a more or less sure indication of there being established in our nature some habit which will determine our actions."[5] In some places he even speaks of the "belief-habit."[6] Every act is the dramatized equivalent of a concrete proposition, a proposition on the move, which in itself constitutes a belief; and the oftener the act is repeated the stronger the belief becomes. Religious leaders are aware of this connection and so counsel a rigid adherence to ritual, for they know that ritual reinforces beliefs. To do something is already to be committed to an act of belief, because it anticipates a certain effective result; and to do it again and again as a matter of habit carries with it a powerful belief in the resultant efficacy.

Belief arises from all three of the capacities in a formal way through deliberate inquiry. The scientific method is a highly structured pattern of behavior intended to settle belief. It is an activity, of course; but both thoughts and feelings are intimately involved, the former as mathematical calculations primarily, and the latter as intuitive insights such as the choice of hypotheses to be investigated or the selection or the invention of the instruments to be employed. Activity is merely the leading edge of the process, which engages all three of the human capacities to the fullest.

Thus it seems clear that beliefs can arise from thought, from feeling, from action, or from a combination of these. More often than not the separate strands of human behavior are difficult to isolate, and beliefs seem to be the result of the posture of the whole personality of the individual in his ordinary as well as in his exceptional contexts. But the psychological initiation of believing is very far from being the whole story of the origins of beliefs. We have been looking at the way in which beliefs arise inside the human individual. But compulsions from the outside, often usually in the form of evidence for truth, which comes also from the outside, always seem to be involved in the beliefs which exist, so to speak, on the inside. Our private beliefs are often dictated externally. We have to look next, then, at the ways in which beliefs come to us from the world.

III. THE COMPULSION TO BELIEVE

In the previous section it was shown how beliefs arise from thoughts,

---

[5] *Collected Papers of Charles Sanders Peirce*, C. Hartshorne and P. Weiss, ed., 6 vols. (Cambridge, Mass., 1931–35, Harvard University Press), 5.371. See also 5.398, 2.435.
[6] *Ibid.*, e.g., 5.510, 5.516, 5.523, *et passim*.

feelings and actions. We shall need to make here the more important point that beliefs which are needed for thoughts, feelings and actions do in fact function as compulsions exercised upon the psychological individual.

That they do so is attested by the fact that the individual does not take his stand on himself, not even when considered as the subject, but on the object with which because of some need he is driven to be preoccupied. He is not concerned with himself in relation to the object because his concern with the object preempts the field of his attention. Thus his beliefs tend to be not about himself but about the world.

Since the individual is many-sided and flexible, his beliefs may come from any one of a number of sources, and it is often difficult to say in any given instance which one of these has been mainly responsible. Among the sources of belief are: action, analogy, authority, common sense, custom, deduction, dreams, the ego, emotion, experience, forced conviction, habit, intuition, pathological conditions, physical resistance, revelation, social pressure, thought, tradition.

It is usually possible to show that each of the sources of belief exercises its compulsion primarily upon some one of the three capacities.

As the next table indicates, there are many ways in which the beliefs which are needed for thoughts, feelings and actions can exercise compulsion. Beliefs arise from many external sources in each of the capacities. The sorting is only a rough approximation to what actually occurs, and there is much overlapping. I have listed only the chief items, but no doubt there are others.

THOUGHT	FEELING	ACTION
	belief	
analogy	dreams	previous action
argument	ego	authority
common sense	emotion	ordinary experience
conviction	intuition	custom
deduction	pathological conditions	habit
	revelation	resistance
		social pressure
		tradition

Beliefs are needed for thought. It would not be possible to think except on the basis of a belief in the relations between propositions. There are assumptions underlying ratiocination on the basis of which it becomes possible, and assumptions are nothing more than beliefs of which we are usually unaware. In logical and mathematical systems they are made explicit as axioms, but even in casual, informal thought they exist. Thus for thought to be possible there must be some kind of surrender to the compulsion of starting beliefs.

Beliefs are needed for feelings. They are in fact the contents of feelings and therefore come before, for otherwise what would there be to feel? No one *just* feels in a belief, he feels that something is *true*; and so the belief is anterior to the feeling. A belief is a feeling fixed upon a topic, and for there to be such a feeling there must be a topic, and a fixation. Thus for feeling to be possible there must be some kind of surrender to the compulsion of a belief.

Finally, beliefs are needed for action. No one merely acts but actions are taken in view of some prior belief, some assurance that the action is called for. No one acts impulsively and when he does so it is in view of previously channeled behavior. Habits are formed by the repeated carrying out in action of what was previously accepted by belief. Thus habits have strong effects upon action; we tend to do again what we have done many times before. But we would not form such patterns of behavior were it not for the beliefs already held. Thus for action to be possible there must be first some kind of surrender to the compulsion of belief.

IV. DEGREES OF BELIEVING

Belief as such is neither a thought nor an action but a feeling. It will be remembered that in the definition set forth at the outset of this study believing was described as emotionally accepting a proposition, and a belief as a proposition that is held to be true. The feeling of belief occurs in various degrees of intensity, and we shall want to make note of them here.

A qualitative list of the gradations, reading down from weak beliefs to strong ones, runs somewhat as follows.

Hearsay
Possibility
Probability
Credence
Certainty
Dogma

A 'hearsay' is a report, a rumor, something one admits may be true but to which for the time being one accords very little belief. A hearsay does not have much force about it, and is backed up by few if any facts. It is received as a matter of gossip and entertained lightly in the foreground of awareness. One attends to it briefly and allows it to pass without serious examination. Consider the following examples: 'Is it true that his business is being sold?', 'They say that Tom and Mary are secretly engaged'.

A 'possibility' has slightly greater strength than a hearsay. It is something with a small degree of intrinsic appeal. Without supporting evidence it nevertheless appears under the guise of truth. It occurs as a suggested explanation or even by itself as a proposal, but one is slightly inclined to hope that it is true without at the same time either knowing that it is or being willing to investigate. It is entertained longer than a hearsay but also may be allowed to pass without further inquiry. For instance, 'Perhaps he meant to suggest that he would go to her assistance if she needed him'.

A 'probability' is a proposition which seems to have slightly better than half a chance of being true. While not appealing in any absolute way, one is more inclined to accept than to reject it. One is likely to retain it for considerably longer than a hearsay or a possibility, and to grant it belief until something with more plausibility appears to take its place. It is the last stage before the degrees of knowing, and may slip forward into knowing or backward into disbelief. Thus it is retained but without any strong degree of surrender to it. Example: 'One-third of all American marriages end in divorce'.

A 'credence' is a proposition under the first degree of knowing. It is something we know is true, on the basis of a high probability in its favor. There is solid evidence to support it even though such evidence may not be altogether conclusive. It is trustworthy and usually reinforced through its acceptance by others. One feels justified in placing some reliance on it, while not counting on it completely. It comes under the rubric of tentative knowledge, and on the basis of it some things might be done. Example: 'Adding fluorine to drinking water strengthens teeth and prevents their decay'.

A 'certainty' is a piece of knowledge. It is something one feels is true, for it comes equipped with sufficient evidence. This is what is usually meant when one says that one 'knows'. There is little room left for reasonable doubt, and any evidence to the contrary would be met at first with surprise and scepticism. It is that state of conviction on the basis of which one is prepared to act. Most conduct has a similar degree of support by feeling. Example: 'The earth is kept in orbit around the sun by gravitational attraction'.

A 'dogma' is an absolute belief. It is a proposition which occurs as definite knowledge on the basis of which one is prepared to die if necessary because of the impossibility of disbelief. Thus it is the basis of the sanity of the individual. He could not live without it. A religious creed is an example, but there are other sorts of dogma which have never been officially proclaimed as such. Examples: 'Thou shalt not kill', 'All men are mortal'.

If the above analysis of the degrees of believing is correct, certain inferences would follow from it.

The first of these, and the most obvious, is that belief is not an all-or-nothing affair, as some authorities have sought to claim,[7] but does admit of degrees. I have mentioned only a few; no doubt many more could be discovered. At the lower and weaker end, belief is only a trace, the faintest of impressions left by an idea and apt to fade entirely. At the upper and stronger end, belief is so irrefrangible that nothing short of death could terminate it.

The qualitative continuity of shadings admits of shifts in beliefs; they can grow or decline, become permanently fixed or disappear. A belief is a feeling, its acceptance is emotional. The brain stem reticular formation and most likely the entire nervous system is eventually involved in any such general disturbance as acceptance would entail. Hence belief is a function of the whole individual, of entire man.

The existence of gradations of believing in a strict continuity from weak to strong is not to be taken as indicating a lack of structure. In the next section, then, something of this structure must be shown.

THE STRUCTURE OF BELIEF

Most of the beliefs of the individual are unconscious ones, beliefs that he holds and from which he acts without knowing that he holds them. Beliefs may be covered over by more recent learning or concealed by internal inhibitions. The necessity for the maintenance of the integrity of the person operates to exclude anything which may destructively threaten it, and the recognition by the individual of what he is really like may function as such a threat.

But hidden as they may be, the beliefs are still there, susceptible to revival upon the presentation of an appropriate stimulus. This could be any occasion, say, which resembles the occasion upon which the belief was originally acquired. Some beliefs are stubborn affairs, and it

---

[7] Brand Blanchard, *The Nature of Thought*, 2 vols. (London, 1950, Allen and Unwin), Vol. I, p. 117.

has simply never occurred to the individual to recognize them. These are the beliefs which are the strongest and they are not confined to physiology. Many of the religious and political beliefs of the individual which were present in his society from his birth and which he accepted because those around him did so, too, are of this nature.

There is a limit to the number of beliefs of which the individual may be aware at any given time. He is capable of holding in the foreground of his consciousness very little indeed. Most of his beliefs are stored in his unconscious mind, what has been more traditionally called 'memory'. Memory is the record of beliefs, and recall is the process of raising a belief from memory (or the unconscious) to conscious awareness. 'Mind' is the name traditionally given to the sum of the individual's beliefs, conscious and unconscious, and of his psychological attitudes toward them.

An inventory of the contents of the mind, then, will tell us much about the structure of belief. We find in it (1) a 'public retention schema', (2) a 'private retention schema', (3) a morality, and (4) a technology. I have already discussed the first two in an earlier chapter but here they are being developed more fully for another context. Accordingly, we will need definitions and explanations, and so it will be well to devote a few words to each of the four.

(1) By 'public retention schema' is meant a system of social beliefs interpreted as rules of procedure whereby cognition is enabled on the one hand to apply its fundamental categories to sort out the data subsequently disclosed to sense experience and on the other to guide behavior. The public retention schema represents as closely as possible in the individual mind what in the society is disclosed as the set of assumptions as to what of primary importance its particular institutions have in common. In this latter sense I have named it the 'implicit dominant ontology'.

Kant talked about a structure for beliefs. In the same spirit it should be possible to speak of the contents of universal beliefs, in some such fashion, for instance, as Frazer has found for primitive societies in *The Golden Bough*. Similar sets of assumptions for civilizations have not yet been adequately formulated. Perhaps the underlying beliefs contain some which could be sorted out interculturally. But in any case more exist intraculturally. Communication between individuals in a given society depends upon the common assumption of the same set of fundamental beliefs.

(2) By 'private retention schema' is meant an unconscious set of

experientially acquired and emotionally accepted and endorsed dispositional states.

The elements of the two schemata are rarely sorted by the individual holding them. The private schema is peculiar to him; the public schema is common to all members of a given culture. The two schemata together constitute the beliefs of the individual.

(3) The set of guidelines as to how the individual may and how he may not conduct himself towards his fellows within his particular society is contained in the public retention schema as a special part of it. The good and the right are codified by the society in its laws, and the individual is constrained to follow them, which is to say, to behave within the limits of what is allowed by them.

He may have a private morality of his own, and this will be either consistent with the public morality or at variance with it. Accordingly, his behavior will benefit society or bring him into conflict with it.

(4) Less well known is the technology, which is a definite part of the structure of individual belief. There is no profession or informal activity within a society which does not call for the use of material tools. Some knowledge of the proper uses in such cases is contained both in the knowledge of formulas and in the familiarity with actual procedures. A violinist, for example, is not only one who has some knowledge of music but also one who believes, if you like, that when the violin is operated in such and such a way, music will result. Such technological beliefs are rarely recognized as beliefs, and yet they constitute a large part of the daily recall of the individual. The formulation of a set of assumptions for civilizations, referred to in (1) above, depends upon the degree of development of their technologies. The more complex the technology the more abstract the implicit dominant ontology and its role in the public retention schema.

The vast structure of belief which I have here been describing can exist only at the level of the unconscious. The human capacity for awareness may be highly concentrated, but in terms of its contents at any given instant it is a very thin affair indeed.

From the point of view of awareness, then, it is correct to assert that the individual has two sets of beliefs: those of which he is aware and those of which he is not. And the unconscious beliefs are in turn divided into two subsets: those of which he has at one time or another been aware but of which he is not aware now, and those of which he is not now and never has been aware.

The two divisions are the occasion of some confusion. For instance, there are those beliefs that we profess to hold and those we do in fact hold. The precipitation of action, and especially of critical action, separates what the individual believes from what he pretends to himself that he believes, for he acts usually on the basis of his genuine beliefs. The genuine beliefs which the individual holds without knowing about them may be brought to the surface and recognized. They may be invoked by relevant thoughts, feelings and actions.

The propositions which are the contents of belief are either true or false (or indeterminate) dependent upon their consistency if they are logical propositions or upon their correspondence if they are factual propositions. Given that the individual's professed beliefs may or may not be his genuine beliefs, and that he acts from beliefs whether conscious or unconscious, it follows that he is ignorant of the source of many of his actions, that he makes mistakes, and that his actions may conflict. His actions indeed must conflict as often as do the beliefs from which he acts. It is not too uncommon to hold conflicting beliefs, since two beliefs which do conflict may have come to the individual from different sources and upon different occasions, and their opposition may never have been recognized, not, anyhow, until they issue in self-defeating actions.

To the extent to which beliefs are settled, harmonious, and held in common with others, it is legitimate to call them rational. And since the greater part of beliefs are held unconsciously, either after having once been known consciously, in which case they are collectively called memories, or having never been known consciously, in which case they are called unacknowledged assumptions, a proper name for the sum of them would be 'the rational unconscious'.

This does not exhaust the whole area of unconsciously-held beliefs, however. There are also the irrational beliefs which are held in the same way; and they may be called irrational because they conflict either with each other or with the beliefs held by others in the same society. They are irrational not in the sense that they are in no wise amenable to reason but only in the sense that it is inconsistent to hold them in that society and at that time and place. Although irrational beliefs fall into well-recognized categories, they are peculiar to given individuals the details of whose particularization of the irrational beliefs are their own. This is the part of the unconscious which interested Freud.

It is legitimate to call beliefs knowledge only when they have been verified by some reliable process; which means either established correspondence with fact or valid deduction from other propositions

already known to be true. Beliefs considered knowledge are not war-
ranted thereby as absolutely true but only as probably true. Even in the
latter case it is always possible we might discover that the propositions
which we hold to be true and from which we deduce others by valid
logical steps are not true at all, or at least not true to the extent to
which we thought them to be. Thus beliefs when held properly are not
held absolutely. That there are no known absolutes may itself be the
only known absolute; and even this proposition may have to be
handled gingerly to provide for the arrival or discovery of exceptions.

VI. THE CONDITION OF BELIEVING

We have now to consider what it means to be in a state or condition of
belief, how it feels to be inclined toward a given set of thoughts, feelings
and actions whether these are ever actualized or not.

The world is for the individual a major opportunity. It is the vari-
colored scene of his most basic need-reductions, the means of his
immediate and even of his longer-range survival, and it is the container of those ingredients which enable him to become more intensely
himself. He is a whole to his parts and this counts upon many occasions;
but there are more, far more, occasions on which it matters only that he
is part of a larger whole. Self-concern from this point of view is a
waste of time: he can help himself only by being concerned with the
object. Thus his natural posture is to take his stand on the object,
because that is where not only the challenge but also the advantage
lies. To take his stand on the subject, on himself, as he sometimes does,
is secondary, artificial and contrived. He does not feel happy with it
and he does not do it with ease.

So far as his attention is concerned, he is usually away from home.
To himself he is for the most part a stranger who is busily engaged in
acting somewhere out in the world. He is too directly concerned with
that world to be very much concerned with himself except indirectly.
The result is that he comes to know himself slowly and imperfectly, and
only as an outsider. He may take his stand on the subject in order to
reason and to plan actions, but he does so in great ignorance. Knowledge comes to him from the self and from the external world, in both cases
with surprises and often with the disclosure of undesirable properties.
The process of coming to the full stage of maturity is attended by the
acquisition of beliefs, beliefs about the external world chiefly but also
about himself and the problem of his place in that world.

There is no more comforting state for the individual than the possession of a sufficiently wide body of settled beliefs. To serve adequately the feeling of security the beliefs must be sufficiently wide to confer the direction of behavior on any situation which might conceivably arise. Systems of philosophy which become incorporated in dominant institutions are of this character: the Thomistic philosophy, or Marxism, for example. Of course it is wise to remember at this point that the depth and range of beliefs is no guarantee of their truth. Philosophers from Xenophanes to Hobbes have warned that even if the existence of God be assumed to have been demonstrated, on the grounds that the universe must have had a cause, this is no warrant to justify claims to a more intimate knowledge of His nature and preferences. Yet men continue to operate religious institutions on the basis of such claims. Many religions have achieved great eminence and yet are in serious conflict; Hinduism and Christianity, for instance. Astrology has represented the largest body of accepted beliefs for the greatest number of people over the longest run of time, and indeed is still accepted by some; yet it is patently false.

Settled beliefs lead to habits of action, for actions tend to follow from beliefs in so far as they are not initiated impulsively, and even then when the impulses follow well-established patterns of behavior and are merely a matter of timing they may do so still. The formal examination of beliefs, the one recommended by Descartes and immediately repudiated, or better still the ones submitted to the scientific method for corroboration, gives the individual greater control over his behavior even though it may be the source of the temporary discomfort of doubt.

CHAPTER XII

ADAPTIVE RESPONSES AND THE ECOSYSTEM

I. THE TWO KINDS OF EMPIRICISM

There does not exist at the present time any comprehensive and consistent theory of knowledge which has been generally accepted. This is
particularly regrettable in view of the fact that the area of reference is
an empirical one. Perhaps the reason for the lack is twofold. The
philosophers for the most part pursue their investigations into the
topic in some disregard of what the scientists are doing. As for the
scientists themselves, so many specialties are involved that no professional effort is made to put the results together. The findings are
perhaps changing too much for anyone to undertake the framing of a
single hypothesis which could account not only for all of the significant
data but also for many of the lesser theories.

Philosophical epistemology has looked in to the question of how knowledge is acquired in accordance with one set of assumptions, scientific
psychology has examined the same subject matter from the perspective
afforded by quite another set. What lies behind the distinction is a sharp
divergence which must be brought out into the open and examined if we
are to bring the two streams together in any productive fashion.

Recently epistemologists were in the habit of analyzing their subject
matter introspectively and in terms of the knowing process. The corresponding period in scientific psychology was the period when classic
and operant conditioning were developed by the reflexologists and
behaviorists, from Pavlov to Skinner respectively. But the philosophers
have not to this day given these developments sufficient consideration.
Since then, a great deal of information has been supplied by the
various sciences, by the neurophysiologists and ethologists, for instance. Although no one is able yet to comprehend the processes of
acquiring knowledge, thanks to the various specialists we are beginning
to understand something of the complexity involved.

How then did it happen that the philosophers went their own way unmindful of the investigations conducted by the scientists? Perhaps it was a matter of fear of encroachment upon a professional preserve, or perhaps it was a genuine misunderstanding. In either case it does not matter. The best course is to be concerned with the truth, not with who discovered it. What does matter now is that we see that it was a blind alley into which the divergence led the philosophers. This becomes clear when we take a close look at the philosophers' methods and findings.

Philosophy has accepted its private role too docilely. It is time to ask whether metaphysics has to be Berkeleyan and epistemology Kantian. Berkeley's position looks weak from this distance. Even though solipsism cannot be refuted, it has been noted that it can be useful without the subject provided we remember that it is the unification of the perspective from a subject and not the subject himself that is wanted; and if we remember further that the proposition, 'to be is to be perceived' calls for some stretch of the imagination respecting the being which was not perceived yesterday but is today.

As for the Kantian tradition, three errors stand out; these are: that all learning is deliberate, that the individual is limited in his learning to that of which he is aware, and that he understands the full implications of what he has learned. Back of both Berkeley's and Kant's positions is the one problem that epistemological analysis by itself cannot explain: that awareness is always one abstract level higher than its contents. That this remains true even when the contents is the problem of awareness itself produces the paradox of knowing.

There was an attempt on the part of one movement in epistemology to get away from all subjective assumptions, and it gave rise to the work of Peirce and Whitehead. Their findings have not gained any very general acceptance. Earlier workers like Meinong had little more success.

The modern tradition of revolt against the subject as the basis for knowledge took its start with Thomas Reid. G. E. Moore began by endeavoring to prove, after Reid, the independence of knowledge from the knower, but he ended by showing the fascination and self-sufficiency of the subject. Moore taught us how to talk exhaustively about our ordinary private experiences, and Wittgenstein taught us how to learn more about such experiences by examining the ordinary language we use when we do. The theories of both men were based on an arbitrary abstraction which was, in the opinion of some, unwarranted.

Private experience is qualitative and therefore indescribable. And the analysis of the language we use will not help because it means more than we intend due to its incurably universal nature.

There is a tacit agreement in all this that nothing beyond the unaided sense plus the dictates of simple reasoning will be used to illuminate the observations of the subject with respect to his own experiences. No instruments to extend the sense organs, no mathematics to extend the reasoning. The observations, the argument and the conclusions must be such as an individual unused to philosophical analysis could undertake were he to learn how to concentrate upon his own mental processes.

But why such limitations? And what could anyone hope to discover from this approach? The theory that the best way to learn about the workings of ordinary experience is to confine the examination to that experience itself is surely unsound. The understanding of anything is difficult enough when we use all of the tools at our disposal. How much worse then to suppose that a problem will have a simple answer provided only that we approach it in a simple way and confine the investigation to the most rudimentary of levels.

The difficulty can be traced back to Kant, who began by assuming that the world as such and our essential selves in the bargain are inherently unknowable, both the thing-in-itself and the noumenon being forever beyond the bounds of possible investigation. The conditions under which experience could take place were given in the experience, that is to say, assembled arbitrarily by Kant from the metaphysical debris left to him by all of his predecessors. With the broken and fractioned categories used as roughly catalogued sets of classes of phenomena which could be selected and arranged in space and time by the mind, he provided a mechanism which took the inquiry away from the external world which the mind sought to know and directed it toward the way in which the unknowable external world is 'known' as a set of appearances.

After that, not only for those who accepted Kant and followed him but also for those who rejected him with such fascination that they never dreamed of being able to avoid his formulations altogether, it became easy to simplify the process of knowing still further, until simplicity itself became the watchword and the subject was examined for such traces of knowledge as might have clung to him through no fault of his own. For despite his limitations – despite, that is to say, his epistemological isolation from the real world – some knowing still does occur. One might in fact conveniently have asked Kant how it happens that the conditions under which experience is possible make that experience possible if there is no correspondence between what is experienced and the external world.

In the account which has been conventional since Kant, that part which is known of the world goes along with the knower and does not remain independent of him. Thus subjectivity is inescapable in relativism. In the writings of the later Kantians, as in Kant's own work, what "judgments" refer to is contained in the judgments, values for example are properties of value judgments, and if of objects then only of their potentialities for subjective experiences. C. I. Lewis for instance could think of nothing further removed from the subject than subjective relativism.

Kant has made such inroads into everyone's unconscious presuppositions that to this day it requires almost a deliberate act of will to make the induction necessary to rise to a quite different point of view, one in which the observer is free to see the object without the interference of the spectacle of his own vision obtruding itself in the foreground.

The simplicity of the account is quite enough to make us view it with suspicion. *A fortiori* we know how very complex the situation of knowing a sense experience is. Effects are always simple because they are always qualitative, and qualities are always simple. But we are in search of causes. It is necessary to go outside a field in order to find the necessary equipment and the requisite detachment with which to examine it. The equipment might be instrumental and the detachment a matter of perspective. For there are levels of analysis below the ordinary level: the empirical sublevels where as a matter of fact we are apt to find the causal mechanisms of the events which take place at ordinary levels.

But even at ordinary levels evidence can be found which conflicts with the Kantian interpretation. For instance, environing factors are responsible for awakening and arousal. The high degree of alertness called consciousness is a very tenuous affair. It is entirely dependent upon novelty of input, in particular upon the ascending reticular activating system.[1] Monotony of input will incline a subject to sleep.[2] Thus consciousness is dependent upon the external world, and no less so because it is a state of the subject, for it is a function of a certain

[1] Herbert H. Jasper, *et al.*, eds., *Reticular Formation of the Brain* (Boston, 1958, Little Brown).
[2] H. W. Magoun, *The Waking Brain* (Springfield, Ill., 1960, Charles C. Thomas).

selection of stimuli. Since internal states are by no means self-contained, the isolated analysis of consciousness is unwarranted by the facts.

Organisms are open systems whose existence is made possible by continual interchange with the environment. All animals are conditioned by those material objects present in their environment which are needed for nutrition. Unfavorable local conditions often compel the human animal to range farther out than his sense organs will make possible. Hence the use of abstract thought, which functions like a distal receptor for logical elements. Human animals, then, are in addition conditioned by their knowledge of absent objects. This they do in terms of the universals of language; that is to say, they recognize the class membership of present objects, and classes imply the membership also of absent objects, many of them in fact, very many more than present objects.

Man then is in some important way a product of his entire environment and helplessly dependent upon it. It is a large world and he is a small organism. The key perhaps is contained in the fact that knowledge is a variety of nutrient.[3] Without a certain amount of it early in the development of the child, the brain would not come to full maturity. The world containing the information the child needs exists temporally on both sides of him and so is independent of him. He has little effect upon more than very small portions of it. The human individual can alter material things in his available environment in the present and some things in the future, and he can know through his knowledge of them about similar objects at a farther remove in space and time.

It happens then as we have already noted in an earlier chapter, that activity is just as much a source of reliable knowledge as sensing and thinking. The limitation of the traditional epistemology is that it did not take this fact into account. The additional limitation and perhaps the more crippling one is that the observer tried to be both observer and object observed. He observed the object but talked as though he had also observed himself observing the object. In this way he managed to turn the investigation round so that he learned about himself and not about the object.

We shall revert to this point again. Meanwhile it may be more instructive to look at the reason why this shift in interest managed to come about. The key to the explanation is in the ambiguous use of the concept of empiricism.

[3] Joseph Altman, *Organic Foundations of Animal Behavior* (New York, 1966, Holt, Rinehart and Winston).

Both philosophers and scientists describe their inquiry in terms of empiricism – the appeal to experience in general and to sense experience in particular. The common use of the term has served to conceal a profound difference in their assumptions and procedures. If we examine its meanings in order to define the differences we might make possible a future collaboration.

We shall refer, then, to philosophical empiricism as 'empiricism I' and to scientific empiricism as 'empiricism II'. In the two kinds of empiricism it is possible to discern two sorts of relationships. Philosophical empiricism (or empiricism I) is concerned with the relation between the subject and the object which the subject treats as though he were observing himself observing. Scientific empiricism (or empiricism II) is concerned with the relations between two or more objects which the subject can observe and, if possible, verify.

Let us suppose that an observer is present when a car hits a tree. We may understand the event to be at right angles to the observer, thus

$$\text{observer} \rightarrow \left\{ \begin{array}{c} \text{car} \\ \downarrow \\ \text{tree} \end{array} \right.$$

Now the difference between philosophical and scientific empiricism can be defined more sharply. In empiricism I – philosophical empiricism – the interest of the observer is centered on the effects on himself of his observations of the car hitting the tree; more specifically, on the extent to which his observations enter into and distort what is observed. In empiricism II – scientific empiricism – the interest of the observer is centered on the effects which the car hitting the tree has upon the car and the tree.

It follows that in empiricism I the philosopher will learn something about the limitations of human knowing and in empiricism II the scientist will learn something about the world. The philosopher is preoccupied with the extent to which his senses distort reality, but the scientist is eager to know whatever can be known even though it be within limits. In information theory language, the philosopher will study only the extent to which he has to operate by means of noisy channels, but the scientist will receive the signals and store the message.

There is another important distinction between empiricism I and empiricism II at which we have already hinted. The philosopher has insisted on relying for knowledge upon the unaided senses, while the scientist has employed both instruments and mathematics. The difference in results has been enormous. By the method of empiricism I there have been no gains in knowledge, whereas by the method of empiricism II the gains have been dramatic. For the scientist (though not for the philosopher) empiricism has presented a special problem ever since it was learned that there do exist material objects which cannot be observed by means of the unaided senses. The scientist accordingly has had to extend empiricism to include those material objects which are not immediately available to the unaided senses but only to instruments; such objects as the elementary physical particles, the radio stars and the quasars, for instance. Then, too, there are intermediate types of objects which can be seen *through* instruments: macromolecules and cells through microscopes, and planets and interstellar gasses through telescopes.

There is then a shortcoming to philosophical empiricism from which the scientific variety does not suffer. For all events stand in the same relation to the observer so far as considerations of knowledge are concerned, but they do not stand in the same relation to each other. The philosophical empiricist is caught up in the sterile repetition of similarities of experience; while the scientific empiricist benefits from the richness of differences. There is a complexity in the findings of the experimental sciences which is not to be had in knowledge theory.

Against those who contend that some of the statements made about the external world are true in a sense which makes them independent of the knower, the charge is made that there can be no such independence, But this cannot be successfully claimed, for those who make the charge are in the same case. If, in other words, Bill asserts that all the statements made by Tom about the moon are conditioned by the fact that it is Tom who makes them, then the same charge can be made against Bill's contention; for both Tom and the moon are parts of Bill's external world, and therefore any statement made by Bill denying the unconditioned nature of Tom's assertions can be made also about Bill's. The denial that a criticism is true does not make what is criticized true, but it doe leave open the possibility ol its being true. The accusation of subjectivity involves an infinite regress of accusations and is therefore not worth pursuing.

Experience can be analyzed from two points of view as determined by different types of interest: for what it will disclose about the subject and what it will disclose about the world. Admittedly, both are always involved, but the dependencies are not equal. For surely there would be a world if there were no subject (though there might be no knowledge), this much must be assumed from their relative differences in endurance; but there would be no subject if there were no world. Thus the subject depends upon the world for its being and the world depends upon the subject only for there to be knowledge of the world. The varieties of experience disclose various features of the world, but the subject is somewhat more limited. What is known is always known in the same way, but it is not always the same things that are known. In terms of variety of interest, therefore, the subject cannot compete with the world.

There is a possible resolution of the problem by means of which philosophical empiricism can justify its inquiry. Suppose that we assume it to be an undertaking that somehow got stuck half way; for once the extent of the noise in the channel is identified it can be discounted and the components of the signal, which consists in legitimate and accurate information, can be utilized. In other words, when philosophical empiricism completes its inquiry, the findings of scientific empiricism can be rendered more precise and reliable. We do need to separate out in what we hear the sounds issuing from our own organism, for then we shall be more certain that those which remain are signals which reach us from the external world.

The mistake the philosophers have made is that when faced with the doctrine of empiricism they have tried to be empiricists themselves instead of building a framework for empiricism. For empiricism as a doctrine cannot be empirically demonstrated, and this is what has occasioned all the difficulties for the philosophical empiricist. Kant did indeed build such a framework but only by excluding the reality of the external world. What is needed is a framework which will include it.

II. THE WORLD AND ITS EMERGENT ORGANISM

Before it is possible to discover an acceptable theory of knowledge, we shall have to learn more about the structures with which we shall be dealing. Accordingly, we can no longer talk about 'subject' and 'object' as though there were nothing more to them than can be accounted for in the consciousness of the subject. The 'subject' – of knowledge, that is – is a complex animal organism belonging to the human species. The 'object' of knowledge is anything in the complex and highly structured material world. Our problem, then, will have to be phrased differently.

What is the relation of the organism to its environment at the point where the kind of interaction between them which we wish to examine takes place?

A word first in this connection about the environment: first its function and then its structure.

Functionally, it is a shifting one if we consider the cycles at short range, and not only diurnal cycles but annual cycles and beyond. For everything in the material universe is engaged in a continual process of motion and change; and the changes consist in exchanges of forms, there being, so far as we can ascertain, no formless matter.

Structurally, the material universe consists in a hierarchy of energy-levels of organization: physical, chemical, biological, psychological and anthropological, at all of which levels there are characteristic material objects. These objects are not usually encountered in the order in which their positions in the levels of organization would indicate but in considerable disarray. The world is a mixed-up place, consisting of the elements of order but containing both order and disorder and more often out of order.

Now a word about the organism. It is a changing material organization made up of elements of the various levels which lie below it in the hierarchy, and it too contains sublevels each with characteristic material entities which interact when disturbed. As usual we are confronted with complex mechanisms which rise at higher levels to simple effects. Many integrative levels are involved, beginning perhaps as low as the level at which the movement of ions is measured in microns and milliseconds, and proceeding through the levels of neuron firing and sensory coding to the level of the gross behavior of human individuals.

As we have noted, the organism is an open system, but with this difference from other species that the greater the number of individual members the greater the range of the material environment with which its interchange must be effected. As it alters an increasing portion of the environment, it is in turn altered.

Our account cannot possibly be complete if we do not say a word about the evolutionary process by which the organism emerged from the world. As we know by now, phylogenetically it developed the organization which it has through its capacity for making adaptive responses to selective pressures from its immediate environment. The key to the understanding of the organism and all of its substructures and processes is its relation with the environment from which it emerged and upon which it depends for vital interchanges.

Knowledge and its acquisition, which it is our aim to account for in this chapter, takes place within the human organism but cannot be understood without a prior understanding that it comes from the external world and goes back into it; comes from it in the shape of information and goes back into it in the shape of action.

Like all animals, man has emerged from a background to which he has had to adapt in order to survive. But his struggle with his environment has kept him unstable, and his effort to survive has committed him to a process of development. Evolution is the story of the compromises necessary to insure survival. In the course of large numbers of generations, he has learned to alter his environment, and to the extent to which he has done so he has himself been altered. Lately he has been compelled to adapt to an artificial environment which in time will no doubt exert new selection pressures of an unpredictable force which are sure to change him radically.

It is still puzzling why the complexity of a large brain and elaborate nervous system was the price exacted for survival in his case and not in the case of the very much older cockroach and horseshoe crab. Science notoriously is concerned with *how* rather than with *why*, but here the *why* holds the key to the *how*. We are still engrossed in the mechanism at this point, and have no choice but to ride out our interest in it. We can find some hints of the form the solution to the puzzle may take in a study of human evolution, and perhaps other hints from an examination of the current stage of progress.

We are faced at this point with two evolutionary developments which have deposited residuary elements: learning and instinct. We have already noted that the human individual has a large, early and eager capacity for learning. The small child is a bundle of curiosity and the aware individual continues the process even though in somewhat reduced measure. Like all events, a man learning can be examined from the developmental or the morphological perspective. For a long time the genetic level of analysis was examined historically in the theory of evolution, now the emphasis has shifted to the structural studies of genetic coding.

The conception of man as an individual with a capacity for learning but with no particular built-in direction has been a recurrent one. The mind, the Stoics insisted, is at birth an unmarked wax tablet upon which experience writes, and for Locke it was still a *tabula rasa*, a blank page. The behaviorists assumed the truth of this conception and accordingly sought to explore only what experience was writing. Their investigations have been very successful but they have not uncovered the whole picture. The point is that epistemology is no longer without technical resources. Knowing may be considered a kind of information processing which will best be explained through a study of the neurophysiological structures and functions.

Although instinct went out as a scientific theory when no evidence could be found for it, thanks to the European ethologists it is coming back stronger than ever, for now there is some evidence, at least among lower animals. We are discovering that perhaps there is an inheritance of behavior. There evidently do exist goal-directed action patterns which are passed on to the members of successive generations, particularly those patterns having to do with feeding and breeding and related needs. This has been shown to be true of some of the higher animals by the recent ethologists, notably by Konrad Lorenz, N. Tinbergen and others. Perhaps it also exists in the human animal, though the evidence for this is at present wanting. The contents of the instinct consist in deposits of capacities passed down to successive generations through the genes. Thus when we talk about instinct and learning we are talking about the older learning and the newer learning, and not about anything else.

Instinct in its modern version may consist in two related conceptions, the conception of organ-specific needs and the mutual ordering of their corresponding drives at need-reduction. It is possible usually to reduce only one need at a time, although there are exceptions. The instincts, in the contemporary version, are nonspecific. The brain at birth in all probability does not contain ideas but only tendencies toward structured behavior.

The tendency to extend drives beyond need-reduction is certainly present, and this leads to the storage of the materials requisite for future need-reductions. In the case of striated muscles it leads to the construction of artifacts, but, unfortunately for fast need-reduction, it leads also to destructive behavior. The former is manifested in the accumulation and organization of material cultures, the latter is manifested in wars. We shall return to this theme at the end of our study where all of the various threads of the argument are brought together.

III. ADAPTIVE RESPONSES AND THE INTERACTION CYCLE

The human individual may be regarded as a self-regulating mechanism which is responsive to external and internal messages. The problem of the resultant activity may be formulated somewhat as follows. Given the order of past learning and the storage arrangement together with the evaluation of information, to predict the behavior. Stated in this way it is obvious that the large number of variables involved renders analysis with our present equipment difficult if not impossible. Perception, cognition, learning, all of these terms describe what we would now call the receiving and storing of information. But we do not know what constitutes effective encoding or how information is sorted.

Somehow, a fresh start has to be made. In place of the now antiquated 'subject' and 'object' of knowledge, it would be more helpful if we talked in terms of adaptive responses and the interaction cycle. But just where should the investigation begin? Before this study is completed, we shall see that any division is arbitrary because it has to be made in what is essentially an integrated ecological system which has neither a beginning nor an end.

Before we are in a position to discuss either adaptive responses or the interaction cycle it will be necessary to understand what is involved. Traditionally, it has been a simple matter, for conventional epistemology has assumed on the one side a subject which is entirely defined by conscious awareness, and on the other a material object no more complex than its most superficial appearance to the unaided senses.

No doubt the ancestry of these conceptions can be traced back to the mythical *"res cogitans"* and its companion-piece, the less mythical *"res extensa,"* of Descartes, the forebears of the mental and the physical which bear an illegitimately equal responsibility for ontological reality. However, it is their limitations in epistemology with which I am chiefly concerned here. The mental and the physical are both oversimplified descriptions of what are actually multi-level structures in a continuous series. And the distinction unfortunately has been preserved even by those who prefer to start with other assumptions. The "phenomenalistic" and "physicalistic" distinctions of Goodman for instance are no different.[4]

As we saw at the outset of this study, the whole enterprise was an artificial abstraction, for it depended upon an analysis made from the point of view of the subject, a point of view, incidentally, which no subject ordinarily takes. In perception, for example, the subject sees a yellow patch. This is what occurs, but it is not what traditional epistemology claims. It claims that he sees (or knows or understands or is aware of) himself seeing the yellow patch, when in fact no such event

[4] Nelson Goodman, *The Structure of Apperarance* (Cambridge, 1951, Harvard University Press).

occurs. The analysis of sense experience which we have come to take for granted is actually a highly sophisticated affair constructed on suppositions unverified and probably unverifiable because untrue.

But the interaction cycle in this conception is not based on the subject but on the object. In any realistic conception, the organism which emerged from the world is continually influenced by that world through its impinging elements. From a broad point of view it becomes apparent that the subject functions to transform objects. Because a melon on the vine smells good, a man eats it, and this is the way in which the melon gets broken down by enzymes in order to fuel a more complex organism. In the same case, it is because a builder sees the potentialities in the tree that its wood is first transformed into timber and next into lumber from which he then constructs a house. True, he had to have the requisite knowledge and he it was who initiated the process if we count only the active steps. And the subjectivist in epistemology has been in the habit of doing just this. Yet the stimulus lay in the existence and potentialitites of the tree, without which the whole procedure would have been impossible. Passive objects may function instigatively; that is to say, they may trigger behavior, as for instance the female does through her attractiveness. Instigative behavior in the human individual is not a mere analogy with control mechanisms. It is a description of the automatic responses which may occur, as indeed they do so often in critical situations.

Suppose a man were to stumble over a stone and then kick it in anger. In such an instance the stone has acted as a stimulus merely by being where it was when the man walked into it. It resisted his incursion into its integrity more than the bone in his leg was able to correct for, and so he was hurt. He responded in a way that might have injured another organism but not a stone. Thus the stimulus had a physiological effect; but the man made a psychologically-prompted response which had very little effect.

Now let us suppose another event. One man punches another. He did so, let us say, for psychological reasons. The first response is a physical pain, the second a chemical production of adrenalin, the third a psychological evocation from memory of a similar fight, the fourth a higher psychological feeling of anger and humiliation. And this is, all told, only the reception of the stimulus. The integrated response may be a counterpunch or a movement away from the offender, etc. The situation could of course be still more complicated. There could be a much-delayed response consisting in all of the steps I have recounted except the last. And the last could occur but only many years after it has been stored when it is recalled in connection with the occurrence of a similar experience.

What I am suggesting is the inadequacy of any account of sense experience made before the discovery of the integrative levels. The integrated responses to immediate stimuli are qualitative and therefore unitary, just as the stimuli themselves may be. But the appearance of unity is deceptive, as the existence of integrative levels and their interactions discloses. Because our knowledge of the central nervous system is inadequate we are in no position at the present time to understand all that happens. Suffice to say that at the lowest of the physiological levels the stimuli have their effects, and these are well below attention. They range upward from the vaguest feelings of discomfort to the level of intense conscious concentration, with many intervening levels awaiting full analysis and description.

The subject is both an active observer and a passive recipient of impressions. It would perhaps be better to say that the subject is a physiological subject (discounting for the moment the levels lower than the physiological) which interacts with relevant proximate portions of the environment. The study of interactions therefore would have to be a cross-field undertaking, including a considerable knowledge of findings drawn from a number of experimental sciences. There are levels of complexity in the human organism hitherto unsuspected, and these now range from the internal chemistry of the cell to the outer influence of the ecosystem. Each probably plays its unique role in the acquisition of knowledge. This makes it necessary to include in the consideration every relevant interaction between the organism and its environment. We shall henceforth have to consider knowledge as the lodged elements of the external world which have been properly processed by mechanisms in the inner world as a result of interaction taking place at the highest levels.

The observer is stimulated qualitatively, and it is the track of this stimulation and its outcome that we have to examine in its proper sequence of steps. When perception occurs, there is first a determination respecting exposure: he can turn his head to look in a different direction and so lay himself open to what is there, including its surprises. But then he must take an active part in the reception of the consequent sense impressions; he can receive them only as conditioned by what he has previously experienced. Here classification lends a primitive hand. If they are novel impressions and so do not lend themselves to classification, then the incoming signals are degraded and he sees them as lower in form, if necessary only as colored shapes. When he says, 'I see that tree' what he is saying is that he has received and at once classified a colored shape because it was immediately recognizable as a member of a class which has been made familiar to him through his previous experience of other members.

If no class is readily available in this fashion, the colored shape is left at that, pending further classification. But then there would be little or no gain in knowledge, for classification as an initial stage is necessary. The result of the interpolation of the abstract component is that relatively exact reproduction is made possible. For complex patterns have to be extracted from the received material if the knowledge obtained by the subject is to be in good correspondence with the segment of the environment from which it was derived.

Of course we should examine a more sophisticated situation using two or more senses, a situation in which for instance the observer turned his head to look in the direction from which a sound was coming, or toward a sound and a touch, as when someone takes him by the arm and says 'Hello' while he is looking in a different direction. But in these instances, also, a kind of dynamic response takes place. He must actively make the effort to receive the impressions and to interpret them as signals, otherwise he is not experiencing. Having a sense experience is to be compelled to make an active response, which sounds paradoxical but actually is not. There is no confusion in saying that his senses in so far as he is awake and alert are on hair trigger controls and can be fired by sounds, tactile sensations, colored shapes, and the like. They are inactive but their activity can be set off by elements in the environment.

It is legitimate to look at sense experience from another perspective, and if the one I have been describing is legitimate at all, then we can say in extension that receiving a sense experience in so far as the observer is active means making an adaptive response. The process is automatic. For to the extent to which elements in the environment have made their impression upon him, and to the extent to which he has endeavored to call up the requisite knowledge which makes it possible to receive them adequately, he is altered by them but they are not altered by him. In short, the world as experienced remains relatively unchanged, while the subject experiencing is relatively changed. The knower adapts to the world and not the world to the knower. I am referring of course to mere sense experience and not to the actions on the part of the observer which may follow from it. H e may as a result of the information he has gained wish to make over a segment of the world, but the world is not made over in the meantime by his mere reception of the information.

First, then we should undertake to establish the existence of an interaction cycle of a broad nature, upon which all of the subsidiary functions can be plotted. The interaction will take place between events in the material world (which of course include organisms) and one quasi-segregated part of it (in this case a particular human organism). The external world from this point of view is a world of ongoing material existence consisting of an array of variously organized interacting materials in some degree of order and disorder at various integrative and energy levels.

The organism is an energy-producing open system whose activities are directed toward the reduction of organ-specific needs requiring continual interchange with its external environment.

Let us begin, then, by supposing some material thing or event as a stimulus. That it is received by an organism is due to the special irritability of living tissue. What happens within the organism can best be described as an arrangement of physiological and anatomical processes, starting with sensory afferents and ending with motor efferents. The receptor organ through a process of specialization sorts out some of the specific properties of the stimulus which permit peripheral coding. This is how it gathers information concerning the external and internal environments which transducer mechanisms then convert into the impulse coding of neural signals.

Neural conducting and relaying mechanisms are responsible for summatory synaptic transmission and the propagation of the signals from peripheral end organs to the central nervous system, indicated by spike potentials and partly influenced by centrifugal control. The signals are received when the sensations they arouse are conducted across synapses and through the spinal cord and the brain stem, to terminate in either the medulla or the thalamus as direct relays of afferents (the lemniscal system). In addition there is an extralemniscal system in the brain stem and thalamus which is slower and more diffuse and which accounts for vigilance and attention.

One function of the central mechanism is to preserve and prolong the effects of external stimuli. The neencephalon with its highly evolved cognitive and volitional activities mediates between afferent sensory input and efferent motor output and is capable of programming behavior. The control of neuromuscular activity is initiated by motor neurons in the ventral horn of spinal grey matter and in the motor nuclei of cranial nerves. The motor path begins with the spinal and cranial nerves and divides into the pyramidal and the extrapyramidal systems, consisting in direct and diffuse descending efferent pathways to the end plate and muscle spindle where isotonic contraction and hence overt activity takes place. Some of these pathways are inborn stereotyped processes, the ones for instance which control such internal functions as alimentation and respiration; others control the processes which provide the reduction of the primary organ-specific needs, such as the need for sex, for aggression, and for sleep.

The entire process thus far could be considered a first stage response to the original stimulus. But there is a second stage response, and it is one which as we have noted may well be delayed. The immediate response is postponed, and this allows for a scanning of alternatives since there is usually more than one possible response. The alternatives are tried internally by means of images before the one selected can be acted on. The delay may be a matter of seconds; more likely it is one involving days, months and even years and decades. For it requires a second stimulus, and one of a different sort. There must be something in the external world which leads the belief to become an occasion for action. The subject behaves in accordance with his most fundamental beliefs even when he does not understand the source of his motives.

There is thus an original stimulus which occasions a covert subjective response, and later a second stimulus which occasions an overt objective response. This occurs in the form of feedback loops, interoceptive as well as exteroceptive, and particularly for the present context proprioceptive, all components of the mechanisms regulating goal-directed activities. In the larger sense in which experience ranges over intervals of time, it is fair to describe the alteration of the information-storage-activation process as an adaptive one.

The higher regulatory system finally makes possible the gathering of detailed information concerning the environment by means of complex signals, the planning and execution of skilled manipulatory acts. The psychological level of awareness of sensory reception and of gross muscular exertion, involves abstract symbols and intricate material tools. Through the use of elaborate cognitive processes the subject tries to understand his environment, and through his ability to execute immensely complex activities he tries to control it. The two aims involve both continual interaction with the environment and repeated application of the suppositions which in this way are tested and revised.

Together they make possible the development of those adaptive patterns of behavior which are necessary to deal with novel material things and events in a specific environment.[5]

This is the view of the situation when the observer takes his stand on the object. It discloses the nature of the knowledge process looked at from outside the organism in such a way that both the structure and the activity of the organism can be plotted against the background from which it emerged and with which it must continue to interact if it is to survive as an organism. But now what is the perspective when the observer takes his stand on the subject? Note that it must not be identical with the subject, for this would provide him with no perspective, since the subject does not contain a perspective on itself.

The object as seen from the subject may be any one of four kinds. It may be a material thing or some part, for any part of a material thing is itself a material thing; it may be a property of a material thing; it may be a class of material things; or finally, it may be a class of classes of material things. Material things present themselves as wholes, usually in terms of some quality. For the quality always appears first to the sensing observer. He is perforce aware of the insistence of its vividity and only afterwards perceives the class to which it belongs; later still he is mindful of its relations, internal and external. Thus the role of the material thing or event as present to the observer is qualitative and this is the nature of it as stimulus. Evidently there is an intermediate domain which is qualitative between the subject of knowledge and the objects which are known, and to it we will next have to direct our attention.

IV. THE SITUATION AT THE INTERFACE

What we have been trying to establish is that knowing is an adaptive response. We cannot distinguish between learning and knowing except to say that learning is how knowledge is acquired. Learning is learning to know, knowledge is an abstraction of what is learned. This is the last stage at which the knowledge will remain in isolation. For as soon as the knower detaches the knowledge from the learning process, he immediately hooks it up with what he knew already and so it becomes system-dependent, incorporated as an ingredient in the sum of knowledge by means of which he lives, in which connection it is called beliefs.

---

[5] Altman, *op. cit.*

But now we have a recognizably different situation. Starting with an instance of empiricism I, we have found ourselves in the different situation of empiricism II, only with this variation, that where empiricism II discovered linkages between elements in the external world, now we find the same linkages between elements in the internal world as though the former had been mapped onto the latter. The observer believes that what he 'knows' corresponds more or less accurately with what is 'out there', and he confirms this by acting accordingly, that is to say, by moving among the material objects in predictable ways to exercise predictable effects. And to the extent to which he finds what he has come to expect, then he knows that he has been correct in his estimations of the meanings of his impressions. Of course there are always elements and even whole situations the observer did not expect, and to the extent to which he comes upon these, he is compelled to revise his beliefs. The adjustment is usually made in him. He is successful in effecting changes in the external world only to the extent that he has learned to fit himself into it.

The ecological interface of sensory confrontation is qualitative and therefore can never be adequately known. Yet it exercises the utmost influence over knowledge. The selection of differences among stimuli insures a continuance of arousal. That consciousness itself depends upon novelty of input surely has a meaning for the participation of the observer in his choice of exposure to a diversity of materials in his immediate environment. This perhaps is the point at which the helplessness and passivity of the sensory equipment, particularly the peripheral end organs, are congruent with the active role of the centrally located cortical functions in sensory reception, and especially the role of the reticular formation of the brain stem in providing a sufficient degree of awareness.

The new element in the present explanation is the large degree of self-determination in perception, provided by the capacity to select the exposure to stimuli. There is no reason why self-determination cannot be reconciled with the realistic theory that learning is passive and experience immediate, that in other words, there is no reason why the kind of conceptual framework which Kant for example insisted on as a precondition of all experience cannot be combined with the degree of immediate knowledge which is usually excluded by reason of the very existence of such a framework.

The reconciliation works somewhat in the following way. The observer takes a hand so to speak in deciding just what in the immediate environment is to be grasped, and he does so without distorting the degree of truth involved. The doctrine of immediate perception is retained along with the conceptual elements which make it possible. What takes place in perception is that an internal model is made of the form of some segment of the material world. The connecting link is a train of waves, and in this form the pattern somehow makes its way from the sensory end organs to the brain, although we do not yet understand the process whereby it is reconstituted to produce a resemblance of the original stimuli in the external world. The resemblance is remarkable, in fact it is considered an identity, just as the doctrine of immediate perception requires.

The description applies primarily to naively sensed material, but some of the incoming sensory signals are interpreted symbolically (as indeed they are intended to be), and then we have language, which is to say, the construction of a useful and socially acceptable coded description of those facets of experience most likely to be repeated. Since such experiences in the future will not be limited to present objects, the language has perforce to be extended to include absent objects, some of which are sure to be engaged in future encounters. Language is a man-made device for furnishing an organism with the information concerning its encircling environment which will initiate the mechanical activity necessary to alter that environment. The analogy is between force, at the energy level of the physical and information at the much higher energy level of material culture (the anthropological).[6]

Among incoming stimuli, therefore, language will have to be included. Spoken or written language, considered as a set of stimuli conveyed by sound waves, constitutes a conventional signalling system. Coded messages suggest methods of decoding. The meanings communicated in this way are divided into two parts. Each meaning has: (1) a segment of common agreement, and (2) a segment of difference of meaning based on the peculiar angle of refraction of the receiving subject. Again qualities at the interface must be considered, this time the pitch and tone of the spoken word, or the cast of sentence of the written word.

What is stored in memory by means of feedback loops consists in images, and these are chiefly of two kinds: pictures of the concrete world and pictures of abstract symbols. The first is a kind of perceptual or qualitative representation, and it is immediate; the second is a kind of conceptual or relational representation and it is mediated. In either case

---

[6] J. R. Peirce, *Symbols, Signals and Noise* (New York, 1961, Harper and Bros).

language, which is always one degree removed from its reference, is in the end a kind of labelling. Not only do general classes function in cognition under these circumstances, representing as they do chiefly absent objects, but such classes can be related to other classes, which is a purer form of cognition, for now there can be an abstraction from particular instances in order to obtain results which can be applied to all.

It is at this point that we first encounter the fixed status of knowledge. The ready reference library of closed neural nets with their stored images and ideas, is a memory bank from which a selection and recall is always possible. The key to recall is what it was earlier recognized to be: some variety of association. Awareness is now a single process in which associations are fused, for now the stimuli may issue as they initially did from the external world or they may issue from the memory bank. What a man sees may invoke what he remembers about this class of objects, and so release an activity which has been learned. Both the behaviorists and the ethologists as a result of very precise experiments have a great deal to say about this process.

For the interaction of the known elements there is now an inner staging area in which models are made of the outer world and dealt with appropriately. The inner world at this point becomes so complex that its investigators have tended to forget or ignore as irrelevant the fact that all of its contents (though certainly not their distortions) have originated in the outer world. Husserl's theory of knowledge has been founded on the disregard of the importance of this fact, namely, that what issued from the outer world still belongs in meaning to that world and continues to refer to it. Husserl has been followed into the subjective corner because once there introspection seems capable of dealing with the essentials of reality safe from the incursions of experimental science.

The Husserlian inquiry is conducted by the knower having as his equipment only his consciousness and (unwarrantedly) its observer who is presumed not to be identical with his own self, a double subjectivity which is not in agreement with the facts. For it would seem that all of the idealists of this variety count one or more persons than empiricism certifies. There is not only a subject who is deemed to be the self and as a separate entity his consciousness, but there is also an unnamed observer who is distinct from the self though sometimes confused with it and who has the advantage of an intimate viewpoint which permits him to report on the goings-on which take place between the self and his consciousness.

Husserl guards the inner world of the subject as though it were a place apart in an absolute sense and the only real domain. But no man's consciousness is an island, either, and what preserves the inner world from any sort of serious isolation is the assistance of a second and later set of stimuli from the outer world and continuing trains of their successor stimuli. For the world impinges on the individual in a way which will not allow him to retreat into himself taking with him only those elements he has already received from the outside, as though at some point he were equipped to cry, 'Hold, enough!'

For the consciousness of the individual and its dual function with respect to the contents of the inner world and the continually incoming stimuli from the outer world, there is an analogy which is helpful. The central nervous system may be considered a servomechanism. It can act on the basis of information received to change the effect of the information which will be received on a later occasion in accordance with a present goal. And so the chains of interactions connecting the inner and outer worlds are seldom if ever entirely broken.

No matter how intense the degree of absorption of the self with the inner world, there is a continual hammering upon it of incoming stimuli, for these never stop. Thus deliberate awareness (awareness of awareness, which more often than not is what is meant by the "self") is compelled by the situation to face two ways: towards the contents of the inner world and toward the stimuli from the outer world, both of which present themselves as messages. Husserl's mighty effort to forget the external source of the contents of the inner world and to ignore its unendingness is no more than a misleading subterfuge for evading the other connections which that same contents possesses irrefrangibly. But broken connections still have the capacity to assert themselves as connections, and to jostle those other connections which the incoming messages from the outer world bring with them and insist on fitting into the integrated picture.

A belief, we have already noted, is a feeling that a proposition is true, and by 'true' here is meant having a one-to-one correspondence with things and events in the outer material world. It can be a weak feeling or a strong feeling. The strength of the feeling is a function of the way in which the conviction with respect to the truth of the proposition was formed. Beliefs, like habits, arise gradually or they occur because of the strength of previously accepted materials, which is to say because of connections with older beliefs. Habits may be regarded as the results of the accumulation of later and similar stimuli.

Thus images stored in the memory bank involve beliefs, and this is the aspect of knowledge from which actions are triggered. Men do not think before they act; the thinking has already been done in the making of the value judgment which decrees in advance what is to be done under such and such circumstances should they ever arise. Beliefs are acted upon when stimuli present themselves as occasions because of their reminiscent similarity to other occasions. Thus the way is prepared for an effect upon the material things in the same outer world from which the first stimuli arose. And now the interaction cycle is at last completed, showing events at the interface to be crucial.

It has been asserted that a machine is a man with a single purpose. The analogy between man and machine is often held to be unacceptable because it seems to imply that man is simple. But this is not an essential part of the analogy, for it would be preferable to assert also that a man is a multipurposed machine. In this day when we have developed machinery to the point where it can think fast and in terms of large strings of numbers and has before it the prospect of many choices, we shall have to learn to dislike the analogy less and less. For the machine is no longer limited to a single purpose, and a man may be considered a many-purposed machine without doing harm to the understanding of his subtle and intricate nature.

There is no question about the existence of an organized condition for the observer, and the analogy which has been pointed to so often recently between the organization of man and automata has many interesting implications. Every organization in so far as it functions may be regarded as a finite-state machine. Now every machine operates within an environment with which it interacts. Where the machine ends and the environment begins is a question of convention based on size of organization. For instance the cell is a machine in this sense and the heart an environment, or the heart is the machine and the body the environment, or the body is the machine and the neighborhood the environment. A finite-state machine is a black box when we consider only what goes in and what comes out and not what happens inside. In ecology we consider the available environment as inside the black box.

The organism is a flexible kind of organization, which means only that the individual is capable of making a variety of responses to the same stimulus, and when confronted with similar stimuli on different occasions may react quite differently. The important thing to remember is that even among the lowest of human intelligences there is some organized activity so that the total effort is constructed upon an analogy to ergodic ensembles of functions. Flexibility is in effect a many-one relation but that is only another way of viewing what we have come to call adaptive responses. At this point the cycle speeds up in its accumulated effects upon the environment and the result is the construction of a material culture.

Man in search of the supplies to reduce his needs is locked into a system from which the only missing element is the explanation of why his needs extend beyond those of all other animals. He cannot himself be at once an ingredient of an ecological system and an investigator of that system from the outside. But from the inside it is possible to develop an integral theory. What he controls presumably is not his needs but the order in which he seeks their reduction, the firing order of the drives. This requires of him a prior consideration of his whole situation, both with respect to the domain of his endeavors – in his case the available environment and more particularly the special areas in which he is likely to discover the materials for specific satisfaction. The difference between man and the other animals is that man has characteristically selected his stimuli in advance, and thus to some extent takes a hand in determining his responses.

It is generally agreed that a machine could be programmed for any number of operations, and this would be 'rational'; but it is further agreed that no unbroken machine (except man) is capable of making 'irrational' responses. We need to investigate whether 'irrational' responses are not after all responses whose rationality is not yet sufficiently understood. Variability has to be included with invariance in any system complete enough to account for all of the circumstances. That man is at the moment the only machine which is programmed to take account of accidental circumstances neither discounts his machine-like properties nor excludes the possibility of building a chance machine in the future.

Consider in this connection the analogy which could be made between infinite-state machines (Turing machines) and a man who had access to a library which was continually engaged in the process of making acquisitions to its collection.

The limiting case, as Potter suggests, would be "the control systems which began to ask embarrassing questions about why they do what they do."[7] This can be embarrassing even when the control system is a man, for we do not as yet know the nature of the human goal. It would include immediate survival surely, and ultimate survival too if the

[7] Van Rensselaer Potter, Review of John M. Reiner, *The Organism as an Adaptive Control System* (Englewood Cliffs, N. J., 1968, Prentice-Hall), in *Science*, 160 (1968), p. 652.

interest in religion is any index. The continuance of the species is a biological rather than a specifically human goal.

Otherwise, however, a direction can be discerned. Living organisms and their environment (which includes living as well as nonliving elements) are inextricably interrelated, and interact continually by means of an exchange of materials. The domain in which they do so is an ecological system (or ecosystem). The effect of the interchange sustains life in one generation of individual organisms and sustains the species through the dual processes of genetic and epigenetic inheritance. The genetic inheritance is transmitted through the genes. The epigenetic inheritance is transmitted by way of material culture.

The development of complexity among the elements of material culture not only sustains man but also enlarges his habitat, so that now the environment with which he effects an interchange through the alteration of materials extends not only downward into the depths of the sea and below the surface of the earth, but also outward into the solar system to include the moon and other planets. One direction of mankind is toward the extension of the amount of the environment over which he exercises control. Extrapolating from this it can be asserted that man's ultimate aim is to construct for himself an ecological niche out of the whole of the cosmic universe.

Life can be conducted on innumerable terms and under many limited conditions. Witness the new study of cabin ecology for application to life in underwater and space vehicles.[8] Information affecting behavior is conditioned by its status as knowledge. For just as the morality of a given act is a function of the established social morality,[9] or of what Hardin, following Fletcher,[10] calls "the state of the system at the time it is performed,"[11] so by analogy it is true that the relevance of knowledge is a function of the state of the ecosystem at the time it was learned. This on the intensive side; but there is also an extensive side. If for example an individual were to learn that life on many planets, in this galaxy and others, is a high probability, then he would tend to see himself as a mere sample of the human species and understand the meaning of the importance of the type, and this would give him a kind of secular security.

Yet he needs more even for his limited purposes, for ecology provides

---

[8] William B. Cassidy, "Bioengineering and Cabin Ecology," in *Science*, 162 (1968).

[9] James K. Feibleman, *Moral Strategy* (The Hague, 1967, Martinus Nijhoff).

[10] J. Fletcher, *Situation Ethics* (Philadelphia, 1966, Westminster).

[11] Garett Hardin, "The Tragedy of the Commons," in *Science*, 162 (1968), pp. 1243–48.

a valuable framework but only one within which to fit those interactions which sustain human life. However, there is considerable evidence that nothing less than the entire universe is required to reduce one of his needs, the need for an ultimate security which can only be satisfied by a kind of symbolic superidentification with that universe or its cause.[12]

There are fresh signs that man has been handed over to his own responsibility. Since he is an adaptive organism, much can be done by designing the kind of immediate environment to which he will be required to adapt. Material culture is largely a plastic affair and can be molded into any desired shape. By anticipating what would happen to him were he to adapt to a given environment and then by making over that environment into a new type of material culture, man could produce any desired type of human individual. This is on the external material side. On the internal genetic side it is already well understood that in the foreseeable future, through DNA and the genetic code, the desired type of individual could be designed.

Thus both material culture and genetic coding are the forms of self-conditioning which will be available to the species. But how to determine what should be done with them is another problem altogether, and one we are even further from solving. In which direction should evolution be encouraged to go? We do not know; but there is a hint that the extent to which we can control the processes is only a natural method for accelerating a predestined development, one in which our former ignorance is to be preserved.

V. MATERIAL CULTURE AS SELF-CONDITIONING

We have made in the present study little more than a survey of some recent discoveries in the sciences which could influence the turn in knowledge theory. It is time to bring some of these discoveries together in order to see whether we can reach any conclusions, however tentative.

We began by noting the divergence between philosophical and scientific empiricism. The former was impoverished by the isolation of the subject of knowledge; the latter, because of the many separate lines of investigation, was left without integration of any sort. We need to acknowledge the limitations of inquiry but without discouraging the search for new knowledge.

[12] Feibleman, *op. cit.*

By examining the process of evolution in which we can watch the emergence of the human species from a very much larger and more durable environment, it is possible to see how knowledge has been a tool of survival, although its function in the process of interplay between man and environment has not traditionally been taken into account. The effect on material objects of human action has not been judged relevant to the theory of knowledge even though it is an end product; and the only interest left has been the way in which knowledge is acquired. But such an account is incomplete and will serve only as the description of a single act of knowing.

The older knowledge theory has had therefore to be supplemented by the substitution for the classic subject and object of knowledge of adaptive responses and an interaction cycle. On both sides: that of the knowing subject and that of the known object, complex integrative levels are involved, requiring a much more elaborate theory of inter-action.

The problems of knowledge are eventually seen as the problems of the interface between subject and object where qualitative encounters are the rule. Human cognition is made possible by delayed response, for it provides the time during which stimuli from both the inner and outer worlds can be brought together. It not only allows for closed circuits to operate with the knowledge of general classes but also provide the arena in which stimuli from the inner and outer worlds can be properly integrated.

The passivity of the subject in the face of the insistence of the properties of elaborate material systems and the necessity for under-standing these by accounting for them in language, which includes the representation of absent objects, makes of the knowledge process a subordinate part of the ecological system in which both the organism, its species and the immediate environment with which it continually interacts, function together as organized parts.

The element in experience which must be retained at all costs is the search. As a factor in access to information, the search is conditioned by both facilities and constraints. The facilities are provided by sources of already coded information: files and memory banks, for instance, and the constraints are the inherent difficulties which inevitably stand in the way: noise, negative information, the inaccessibility of sources, etc. It is not too well known that laws – physical laws for example – are to be counted among the sets of constraints. Intelligent learning must provide in addition to information the amplification of facilities and whatever concessions to sets of constraints are found necessary; in terms of the older epistemology, a determination to concentrate not on what the limitations of knowing are but on what the facilities are, in a word, on what within those limits can be truly known.

CHAPTER XIII

THE REALITY GAME

In this study I propose to suggest the lines of investigation which ought to be taken by anyone wishing to determine whether some of the ideas discovered in the theory of games, supported by the philosophy of culture and the theory of finite automata, can be productively employed in epistemology.

I. ORIENTATIONS

Games are common social phenomena; games of all sorts exist in every society. And they are played for all sorts of reasons; for relaxation, for profit, or just for the satisfaction of winning (psychological enhancement). 'War games' played in peace time are practice sessions, but war itself is a game, as the application of the theory of games to offensive military strategy in world war II effectively demonstrated. The theory itself grew out of the mathematical interpretation of economic behavior in the well known work by von Neumann and Morgenstern,[1] but it has been developed since then by a host of others.

If epistemology is the theory of how knowledge is possible and ontology is the theory of what there is, then game theory is a suitable analogy to the philosophical predicament of the individual who is obliged to employ the perspective of his culture to play for his own continued existence by means of whatever strategy he can personally devise in order to conquer his opponents, which are the forces opposed to him in the world in which he lives.

In order to suggest the possibility of applying game theory to epistemology it will be necessary first to recognize that the conditions of knowledge under which the experience of the individual takes place

---

[1] John von Neumann and Oskar Morgenstern, *Theory of Games and Economic Behavior* (Princeton, 1947, University Press).

are always mediated by an ontology, that is to say, by a system of metaphysical ideas.

Classical epistemology suffered from a serious short-coming in this respect. For it has dealt for the most part with deliberate and conscious experience only, when the fact is that experience is a much wider category and embraces all sorts of impressions and sensations which occur subliminally and which can be coordinated only by means of a theory of being. Classical epistemology has not taken into account the degree to which it is involved with metaphysics. Every theory of knowledge assumes some theory of reality; every act of experience is conditioned by the anticipation of an encounter with something.

Few philosophers have attempted to make up for the shortcoming. Only Kant's *Critique of Pure Reason* suggested the framework of a theory of the beliefs about being in terms of which knowings could occur. Though his efforts were crude and inadequate, and in the end will not do, they do suggest the direction in which inquiry could proceed.

Every pioneer whose discoveries are of sufficient magnitude has to his credit two accomplishments. In making his own contribution he is often responsible for uncovering a field of investigation, so that even after his own work has been left behind his mark remains on the discovery of the field. Others who come later and whose own contributions show a radical departure from his own will still owe much to him.

That is the situation with respect to Kant's proposal. The subjective-relativistic character of his contribution leaves the investigator into the nature of reality no choice but to repudiate it. There is little comfort in a theory which tells us that, by definition, what we want to know that is nontrivial – about ourselves as well as about the world – is inherently unknowable. But at the same time all subsequent investigators must remain in his debt for pointing out that experience can take place only under the conditions which make experience itself possible even though he did not describe those conditions in terms of a system of metaphysics which transcends experience.

The reality game makes another such proposal concerning the nature of those conditions which are presupposed by experience. The following are its guidelines.

Knowing means playing the reality game. Participation in the reality game is usually involuntary and in any case always unavoidable. That is to say, it occurs as a natural phenomenon in any given society whose stability has enabled it to exist for a sufficient length of time to guarantee that its members will regard it as substantive. An individual plays the game in virtue of his membership in the society.

The game lends itself to being known but is seldom understood for what it is. A theory of reality is what all members of a given culture believe in but few recognize and by definition none question. It belongs to the class of fundamental theories which are displayed in the contrast between divergent cultures. The reality game is therefore a high abstraction and one noted by only a few specialists.

Despite its usual involuntary nature the reality game has in view the highest of stakes. It is played for immediate survival and for ultimate survival. Playing the game for immediate survival bears a striking resemblance to economic games, which indeed are a part of it. Playing for ultimate survival is less well known except under the name of religion. It is possible for the two to run together, as they do under another name in the Soviet Union and in Communist China.

For the individual at any given moment the reality game implies nothing so grandiose. His experience is more discrete, it occurs piecemeal and in little.

All actual confrontations between the individual and other material objects are one item wide: one artifact, one class of artifacts, one other person, one group of persons.

But such encounters are cumulative over time. The person interacts with the entire material universe but acts deliberately only in terms of the world that he knows. As he increases his knowledge his range of behavior gradually increases. For instance he is no longer confined to the surface of the earth but is able to range somewhat beyond it. He interacts, in other words, with his available environment, and thanks to recent advances in technology his available environment now includes the solar system. He always knew about sunlight and acted in terms of it, but not about cosmic rays and so these have not materially affected his behavior.

II. THE BACKGROUND ONTOLOGY

Experience is culturally conditioned. That is to say, for the individual it differs from culture to culture. Those who reject the theory of cultural conditioning, on the grounds that it cannot be shown from within a culture, are overlooking the fact that their objections are subject to the same criticism; so that if the justification for cultural conditioning cannot be demonstrated, neither can the evidence in favor of its rejection. And therefore we may if we wish take into the account a set of variables of cultural origin. The constants are the elements of the structure itself.

When we probe into the behavior of the individual what we find are elements of the cultured person, that part of the individual which is the result of modifications during his lifetime by the material culture in which he functions. The range of such modifications is enormous; it runs all the way from muscular habituation to the conscious holding of general beliefs. A convinced Christian differs widely in his religious beliefs from a convinced Hindu. But we do not need any evidence so lofty. At the other end of the spectrum of behavior we find that the Asian is trained from childhood to sit on the floor for hours without discomfort, a minor accomplishment which the European accustomed to chairs can not equal.

The cultured person is the individual who deliberately holds an ontology in terms of *knowing*. Holding an ontology in terms of *being* is the condition of any individual who is born into a culture; it is far commoner experience than knowing about the being in question. Institutions and authorities, customs and traditions, embody the knowledge. The approach to the consistency of such material lies through the existence of an ontology. The ontology so held is concrete, and should be distinguished from the abstract variety. An ontology is inherent in material cultures and accounts for their organization whether anybody happens to know about them or not. It appears there either concretely in the consistency rules between divergent sets of empirical data or abstractly in the deliberate application of formulations to the interpretations of cultures as the conceptual constructions projected by professional investigators who consider their work independent of any and all application.

Now an ontology is a systematic set of propositions concerning what is real. And by 'real' here is meant having the kind of being which is required by those other kinds of being which are strong enough to support transactions; the kind of being for instance which consists in actual material existence or the kind which consists in logical possibility.

The personal acceptance of an ontology is reinforced when it is found that most other persons in the same culture believe in the same ideas and have the same feelings. It is further reinforced when it develops that to a very large extent the courses of action of most persons in the culture are similar. Holding an ontology in terms of *doing* means behaving instinctively in ways which are consistent with the culture.

In sum, knowing, being and doing in terms of a background ontology is what, as a matter of fact, accounts initially for the existence of cultures. It consists in those ideas, and as a consequence, those actions which are both allowed and suggested by an ontology which lurks invisibly but pervasively in the background.

The concrete, or background, ontology provides the cultural matrix which makes possible the translation of ideas into feelings.

The intimate association between relations and qualities has never been adequately explored. I should add parenthetically that the term, qualities, as used here includes the higher and more pervasive qualities called values. The clue is contained in the distinction between discreta and continua, and, although it is too large a topic for discussion here, perhaps Gödel has shown the way in proving that a contradiction may be found without assuming the hypothesis of the continuum, so that discreta are independent.[2] If certain ideas are held, only certain feelings are possible. The ideas do not determine the feelings but they direct the feelings toward specific preferences by setting the range of values in which those feelings are allowed. For instance, the conviction that art should be representative, on the grounds that so much of the history of art has been of this character, inhibits the appreciation of abstract painting.

The concrete ontology is to be found in those very assumptions which a knower feels he does not need to discuss because they are so self-evident that no one would think to question them. That other observers have different sets of assumptions never occurs to him, but even if it did he would immediately proclaim the obvious superiority of his own set without feeling under the necessity to make any examination or comparison.

The way the background ontology functions is not to stimulate actions but to furnish the conditions for action. It is powerless by itself; it does not actually *do* anything. But it lends itself to the selection of acceptable preferences among those which are available. Because of the presence of the background ontology, a preference will have to satisfy certain conditions which characterize it as belonging to a particular order of things. What von Neumann and Morgenstern say about "standards of behavior" and their stability[3] applies equally here. To function as a background ontology means to have become so generally

---

[2] Kurt Gödel, *The Consistency of the Continuum Hypothesis* (Princeton, 1940, University Press).
[3] *Ibid.*, p. 42.

accepted that nothing incompatible with it can stand and nothing compatible with it can be overruled.

The background ontology is a transparent affair. It exists only in the elements of agreement between divergent sets of empirical data, in the congruence of sets of preferences, in the deducibility from chosen goals of admissible behavior. It is not material but logical; its only impact is when it is denied or crossed. Thus it functions quietly but no less efficiently for being invisible, for that is the nature of most though not all diffuse phenomena. It is not the nature of gasses for instance. But then the kind of diffusion under discussion here is pervasive and undetectable by ordinary methods.

There are many ontologies which could function as the background in a reality game. Familiar examples are furnished by Hegelian idealism, Marxist materialism, Aristotelian realism, and many variants of these and other types are of course possible. Ontologies to be employed successfully in the reality game are to be found in old societies (India for instance), in deliberately founded societies (the Soviet Union), or in originative philosophers who characteristically occupy themselves with such pursuits. In every case the situation holds only for those who are sufficiently convinced by a particular ontology to be able to hold it below the level of awareness, that is to say, to understand all other things in terms of it.

III. PLAYING THE REALITY GAME

Every one deals with the world – and with himself as a segment of the world – in terms of a fixed conception of reality. This will correspond to the chosen game. What game is played therefore depends upon the player. It is the player's conception of reality which prevails. No matter for this purpose that his conception may largely overlap with those of most others in his society; it will be his and his alone that we will be concerned with, for the overlap is not so complete as to constitute a congruence, and the difference is unique.

The player's conception of reality corresponds to the totality of the rules of the game. Every instance of knowing is a play. The selection of that which shall be known is a choice. The move is the occasion of a choice, and it may be by design or by chance. The reality game consists in a sequence of moves, and a move is one of a sequence of choices. The strategy of a player is his selection of the sequence of application of the rules governing his choices, which otherwise remain free. The reality game resembles backgammon more than it does chess, for in back-gammon, chance, in the throw of the dice, decides what moves the player will make; and in the reality game the energy exchanges within that portion of the world to be known is from the position of the player determined by chance.

The course of the reality game is determined by the sequence of choices made by the knower. What he learns is determined by the strategy planned for his experiences. The arrangement and number of plays is decided in advance by his previous knowledge, that is to say, by what he already believes. It is not possible to eliminate altogether the occurrence of surprises, but their frequency is an inverse function of the complexity of his state of information, i.e. of his already accepted system of ideas, that is, of his ontology. Put more simply, the greater his beliefs the less he is able to learn. For the tendency to suppose that experience fulfills expectation is very strong, and this tendency will ride over and conceal the occasions when experience does not fulfill expectation and even some when experience runs counter to it.

In the reality game there is no stop rule. The game continues indefinitely so long as there is a player. However, unlike other games, which terminate when there is a winner, the reality game produces fatigue in the player; the longer he plays, the less his interest in the game. Life begins the game, death puts an end to the sequences of plays which were producing less and less in the way of results. When the knowledge which has been acquired equals the ontology which made the inquiry possible, the inquiry ceases. Experience continues as an appearance, but its function in the acquisition of information has all but come to an end. There are no openings available, no more plays to be planned, no more moves to be made.

There are reasons why the reality game must remain for the moment nothing more than an analogy. A strict mathematical formulation of game theory is not possible for the reality game; not enough is known about the number and classes of counters which each player could have at his disposal. The mathematical requirement of an exact formulation of intuitively discovered ideas cannot be met, but the analogy may have a value all the same. It may serve to show the relations between ontology and epistemology in practice, which is what we set out to do.

In this presentation I intend to abstract away all of the ordinarily concrete details. The reality game is played without deliberation, without material counters, without its details in space and time, more as a sort of structure of a game. We shall be dealing, in short, with certain kinds of perspective relationships and with the bare possibilities of moves without making any actual motions or taking any particular readings.

Learning may be compared with the two-person game because given the knower and that part of the world which consist in his immediate environment, each seeks dominance over the other. That the knower tries to conquer the world through the acquisition of maximum knowledge about it is beyond question. That the world seeks dominance over the knower will call for an extended explanation. I am not here setting up any sort of anthropomorphic theory, only supposing that there are events in the world which can be construed in this manner. The world plays its hand by means of novelty and surprises, and every instance of resistance to the strategy of the knower is a move in the game.

The reality game is of the hybrid type. That is to say, the acquisition of knowledge resembles the zero-sum game which is played for amusement only. The use of the acquired knowledge resembles the non-zero-sum game where the sum of all payments is not zero and not a constant but depends upon the behavior of the knower. We shall confine our attention here to the zero-sum-two-person game, since all other types can be reduced to it.

Our two 'players' in the reality game will be a cultured person, the knower, and something beyond him that he knows. It changes in relation to his activities concerning it, and he alters his activities correspondingly. Thus the game analogy holds, though this time played by one knower and one subject which may just possibly not be a knower (though of course also which may, as when for instance that which he knows is another person or knower).

The counters differ from game to game. The situation in the reality game is more like chess than it is like checkers, for the counters are not all alike but are of many different kinds. The counters of the reality game are qualities, sets of preferences, or, in the common parlance, convictions, prejudices, strong feelings. These are flexible and so allowed for variations so long as they can be subsumed by some general principle. Behind them there is a deeper arrangement which for convenience can be described as a system of ideas, an order determined by imputation, that is to say, by the pure problem of distribution, providing a degree of balance and of quasi permanence. It is not well understood how the various counters and their separate moves are not independent pieces or actions but rather properties of the system as a whole.

The situation in game theory is that of the player and his cooperative opponent. It is obvious that two persons must agree about the game and accept the conditions imposed by its rules, which is nearly all that the game consists of. After that it is a question of moves. Each seeks to win over the other, and the game is designed to provide this for one and for the other, but which one is to be decided by the playing of the game itself. The player needs the aid of his opponent for otherwise there would be no game; and although the opponent, too, wants to win, his cooperation is required if anyone is to do so.

Now if we compare with this the situation in the reality game, we may perhaps see the illustrative value of the analogy. The cooperative opponent is in this case the partly changing world to be known. In the reality game the world presents itself to the knower, though, as we have seen already, not entirely in the terms he might have wished and only partly in the way he had anticipated. Conditions are not strictly determined and much remains for the knower to find out about the problems confronting him. In some encounters the opponent offers resistance and answers moves with moves of his own, in which case the player is obliged to shift to the defensive and make purely preventive plays; in other encounters the opponent gives ground, to the player's advantage.

For this purpose (even if for this purpose alone) we will have to consider the observer as a finite automaton which can be programmed to receive a certain range of input signals and as a result to change internal states leading to an output sequence consisting of overt actions.

The machine analogy which has come into such prominence lately has much to offer even though it cannot be pushed too far. Imagine a Turing machine with a finite number of internal states and an infinite tape, so constructed as to receive random inputs sufficiently numerous to contain both finite ordered sets of signals and indefinitely large disordered sets, including some it cannot read. We have then from its input-operation-output not only the sequence, experience-decision-action-experience-decision-action, but also insufficient information-poor judgment-precipitate action, alternating with either sufficient information or in any case with the actuality or the possibility of learning from poor experience and of good experience from learning. Freedom is a function of disorder and disorder is a function of chance; we would have to make sure that the machine did not operate too well.

Man himself is a machine we know how to reproduce but do not understand. In the case of both man and machine what we are looking for is the theory of a perfect machine which could be programmed by an ideal language. Thanks to recent discoveries in genetic coding and also to a growing understanding of the nature of the possible feedback from an almost completely artificial environment, the planning of human improvement is possible, and thanks to the development of more and more sophisticated automata abstract theory will soon be tackled by the machines themselves.

There is one crucial distinction. We have to be able to mark off the class of objects which are in the perspective O, say O_1, O_2, O_3, ... O_n, from the class of objects which make up the perspective, P (P_1, P_2, P_3 ... P_n). We can do this best perhaps by giving a recursive definition of P.

> BASE: Any part of the nervous system is an element of P.
> RECURSION: If a sight S and a touch T are in P, then ST is in P.
> RESTRICTION: No other material objects are in P.

If a train of light impulses from some external source is once encoded by a transducer (say the eye), and a similar chain from some contact with a physical object is encoded by muscle spindles, then their combination in the neencephalon is also in P. And if nothing else is in P, then the class of objects of O from which the trains of nervous impulses were first stimulated are not in P.

A properly programmed automaton will be equipped with names which it can match against the impulses and either store for further use or utilize in changes of state. Thus the question of names becomes paramount, for the names are names of classes of objects rather than names of the objects themselves, for we say 'I see a pink patch' rather than 'I see a pink patch named Sue that I saw once before'. Names are combined in languages.

At this point it is advisable to revert to a more general consideration. The language of philosophy is an intermediate connective between a person thinking about the composition of the world and the world. To use language properly in this way, it is necessary to understand by means of the language, and not to stop at the understanding of the language itself. To be arrested and captivated by the language is never to reach the reality to which the language was designed to refer. It is to become a philologist rather than a philosopher.

Now admittedly, there are faults in the language and its perfect reflection of the world is never completely attained. Despite the aforementioned discreteness of the individual encounters which take place at the gross macrocosmic level, there is at the finer microcosmic level a continuous streaming of similarities and differences analogous to ergodic ensembles of functions. Thus there is legitimate reason to pause and reflect upon the effectiveness of the language.

This reflection is what Wittgenstein recommended. But he meant us to do so only in order to clear up the difficulties and not to remain preoccupied with the language because of them. His procedure is therapeutic and the prolegomenon to more efficient understanding. To be stopped at this point and to remain transfixed by the problems is to be defeated by the procedure which had been adopted. A good analogy would be that of a patient who had given up being psychoanalyzed half way through the treatment and who therefore had become more preoccupied than ever with his own internal states and so unable to reach that stage in his analysis where he could be turned effectively back to the real world which his neurosis had occasioned him to leave in the first place.

Those who wish to play the reality game most successfully must learn how to think about the language by means of which philosophy reflects the real world without forgetting that this is only a preparation for the final stage which is to think in the language about the world.

It is well known that there is a gap between any language and the world which must of necessity remain because there are aspects of the world which can never be adequately described, and rather prominent elements at that, qualities for example. This feature is reflected in the language by means of what are called undecidable propositions. And if this is true for any language then it must be true for every ontology.

A concrete ontology does not include those propositions which are intuitively held to be undecidable. Among undecidable propositions are all those generally belonging to religions, those for instance concerning the existence or non-existence of God. Thus an adequate ontology would remain open-ended. A belief remember, is a feeling that a proposition is true, and truth is a matter of correspondence. Believing in a system of ideas means choosing in advance a certain set of courses of action. "Believing" in an ontology means deciding in advance on the limits of possible action. Now it is characteristic of ontologies that they cannot be "precisely described" in Turing's sense; for them there exist no effective algorithms. Convincing a person of the truth of an ontology is the same in effect as programming a machine. We can be sure that in a relevant context a certain procedure will be carried out, although we cannot predict the quality of the attitude which will accompany it.

A man may entertain an ontology, that is to say, he may consider it as a candidate for belief. Or he may believe it, in which case the roles are reversed and he is in the grip of it, powerless to disbelieve or to act in any fashion which contradicts it. The deeper he is penetrated by his culture, the less he can exercise the option not to play. All reality games are in the hands of desperate gamblers who would sacrifice anything within their power for success in the next move.

The object of the reality game is the same as it is for all other games: to win. Winning the reality game can be adequately described as reducing in some measure the need for ultimate survival. This can be accomplished through feeling in one of three ways: (1) by reducing the ego in order to gain a place at the center of the world (essential belonging), (2) by expanding the ego to encompass the world (megalomania), or (3) by superidentification with the world or its cause.

Next in order of course is the question of strategy. In terms of active moves, a player (1) supports his own culture by reinforcing its concrete ontology (conformity), (2) seeks to insert his own private beliefs at the center of the concrete ontology (ambition), or (3) makes up his own rules for the reality game. In the first case he will be in the position of many other players, in the second case he will be a member of a very small group of players, and in the third case he will play alone.

It is as though a mechanic were equipped with a repair kit and when confronted with a broken machine had to select the appropriate tool before going to work. Every action is undertaken in order to right a wrong, to restore a malfunctioning unit to proper functioning, or to introduce a missing element. The ambition of every player of the reality game is to bring the world into some correspondence with his conception of it. When he loses he knows that something was wrong with his strategy, and perhaps even with the restrictions of the game which did not allow him to play over a wide enough field. From time to time the game is revised, and when it is, he has to familiarize himself with the new rules and make the proper adjustments.

INDEX